'Ladies, Please Don't Smash
These Windows'

'Ladies, Please Don't Smash These Windows'

Women's Writing, Feminist Consciousness and Social Change 1918-38

Maroula Joannou

BERG
Oxford/Providence, USA

First published in 1995 by
Berg Publishers
Editorial offices:
150 Cowley Road, Oxford, OX4 1JJ, UK
221 Waterman Street, Providence, RI 02906, USA

© Maroula Joannou

Library of Congress Cataloging-in-Publication Data
A catalogue record for this book is available from the Library of Congress.

British Library Cataloguing in Publication Data
A catalogue record for this book is available from the British Library.

ISBN 0 85496 909 8 (Cloth)
       1 85973 022 1 (Paper)

Printed in the United Kingdom by WBC Bookbinder, Bridgend,
Mid Glamorgan.

For Gillian Beer

'We are not going to leave writing to be done for us by a small class of well-to-do young men who have only a pinch, a thimbleful of experience to give us.'

Virginia Woolf. From her address to the Workers' Educational Association, May 1940.

Contents

Acknowledgements

Sections of this book have appeared in *Literature and History*, vol. 2, no. 2, November 1993, Sybil Oldfield (ed.), *This Workingday World: Women's Lives and Culture in Britain 1914–1945* (Basingstoke: Falmer Press, 1994), Daphne Patai and Angela Ingram (eds), *Rediscovering Forgotten Radicals: British Women Writers 1889–1939* (Chapel Hill and London: University of North Carolina Press, 1993). I wish to thank the authorities of the Monks House Collection at Sussex University for access to Virginia Woolf's Reading Notebooks and Lesley Hall, Assistant Archivist at the Wellcome Institute, London for access to Marie Stopes's papers in the Institute. The cover illustration, Vanessa Bell, Interior with Housemaid, is reproduced by kind permission of the trustees of the Williamson Art Gallery and Museum, Birkenhead and I am indebted to the Women Artists' Slide Library, London, for their help in locating the owners of the painting. Carla Ball kindly compiled the index.

VOTES FOR WOMEN

Ladies, if we had the

power to grant, you should

have the Vote right away.

Please don't smash these

Windows, they are not Insured.

SIDNEY MARKS

The Jeweler.

THIS NOTICE APPEARED IN A SHOP WINDOW AT THE TIME OF THE
WINDOW-BREAKING BY SUFFRAGETTES. MARCH, 1912

Evelyn Sharp
From *Unfinished Adventure*, John Lane, 1933.

Preface

This book began its existence as my doctoral thesis. The four years I spent living in Cambridge and working on it were my first opportunity to read and think with relatively few distractions after many years as a full-time teacher. To my college, New Hall, I shall always owe much, not least for the legendary helpfulness of the portering staff and the company and stimulation which some of the younger feminists in the college provided. I am indebted to John Reynolds and the staff of the Cambridge University Library, particularly Janice Fairholme in the West Room, for their unfailing efficiency and courtesy, and to the administrators of the Cambridge University Le Bas Research Studentship in English, the Jebb Award, and the Edinburgh University Women's Fund for generous bursaries which I gratefully acknowledge.

The continued access to the university library and to the university computing services that was essential for the completion of my work when I was not resident in Cambridge was made possible through the hospitality of the many friends who were prepared to welcome me as a house-guest during holidays and week-ends. For their understanding and support which did much to help a tempest-tost project come safely to rest, I must thank Sana-al-Khayyat, Jean Beach, Eileen Gribbon, Maureen Hackett, Pam Hirsch, Felicity Hunt, Lee Jenkins, Margaretta Jolley, Sarah Patterson, Helen Phillips, Suzanne Raitt, Morag Shiach, Julia Swindells, Deborah Thom, Bobbie Wells, Mary Wilmer, Emma Wilson and other members of the feminist academy of the university library tea room whose help I regret that it is impossible for me to acknowledge individually.

I also thank Kate Pretty, Penny Wilson and Heather Glen, then Senior Tutor, Graduate Tutor, and Director of Studies in English at New Hall respectively, Lisa Jardine for her support during her time as Secretary of the English Faculty, and Jean Chothia and Kate Flint who acted as my internal and external examiners.

Although writing this book has occupied and extended my life for the best part of the last ten years its origins go back further. I have happy memories of the part-time classes I attended as a student at the London University Centre for Extra-Mural Studies (now part of Birkbeck College) in the late 1970s and early 1980s which laid an excellent foundation for later intellectual work. The ideas in this book have been explored in a number of WEA and University Extra-Mural classes which I have taught in London, Essex, Bedfordshire, Hertfordshire and Cambridgeshire. Like all teachers of adults I have learned much from my students. If they recognise in this book much that originated in our discussions together, then that is how it should be.

I am especially grateful to the many mature women students whose insistence on the importance of referentiality and on linking women's writing to the insights derived from their own lived experience as women, has usefully complemented my own interest in feminist theory. Much too is owed to all the friends in the adult education movement, the women's movement, and the Labour movement, with whom I have shared a common intellectual purpose, commitment, and endeavour, and whose thinking has informed and enriched my own. In particular, Andy Croft and David Margolies have always been solidly and reliably supportive, trusted unreservedly to dispense sensible advice at the end of long-distance phone calls at inconvenient times. I have learned much from conversations with both of them over the years and my writing has also benefited considerably from David's skills as an editor.

The deepest debts are the most difficult to acknowledge adequately. They include those to my sister, Androula, and to my father and mother, Christophis and Eugenia Joannou, whom I thank for their absolute determination that their daughters should have more opportunities than they had themselves.

The late Margot Heinemann was the most generous of mentors and the dearest of friends during all my time at New Hall, encouraging me to begin my research, and, despite her very poor state of health, insisting on reading it very carefully at the end. The good-humouredly expert answers which she patiently gave to the countless questions I asked her about the 1920s and 1930s were largely responsible for converting an underdeveloped sense of the period into a properly informed one. I am indebted to Margot not only for the generosity with which she shared her wealth of knowledge about the past, but also for many important insights which she gave me into the present, and for teaching me how and why the purpose of recovering the past is to change the future.

Finally, I was inestimably privileged to undertake my doctoral research with Professor Gillian Beer who agreed to supervise me at a point when both my morale and productivity were at a very low ebb and I had almost lost my belief in my own ability to express what I wanted to say. The many hours she unstintingly devoted to reading and commenting on my work, with tact, wisdom, acuity and kindness, restored my confidence in myself and helped me to express my ideas with far greater precision and clarity than before. This book would not exist without Gillian Beer to whom it is dedicated with affection and respect.

Introduction: Towards a 'Women's Agenda'

This book is concerned with writing by women but being a woman is no guarantee that one's writing will challenge patriarchal norms nor that it will reflect a specifically woman-centred discourse. As the experience of women in Western societies, as far back as we have documentation to show, has been within patriarchal societies, women's experience needs to be analysed not only within the context of specific patriarchal cultures but also as a consequence of them. As Elaine Showalter has put it, 'gender is not only a question of *difference* which assumes the sexes are separate and equal; but of *power* since in looking at the history of gender relations, we find sexual assymetry, inequality, and male dominance in every known society.'[1]

Ladies Please Don't Smash These Windows has several key objectives. Much of my investigation is historical and I am concerned with recovering representations and meanings which the author and the first readers of many of my chosen texts would probably have recognised as feminist at the time. Here feminist consciousness lies in the textual traces of a process of questioning and self-awareness; a process which may never have been fully completed or which may sometimes prompt insights retrospectively in the reader or writer. I do not imply that a fully thought-out programme or an assumed political position ever existed on the part of the woman writer. Neither do I imply that feminist consciousness takes the form of a set of beliefs and values which exist prior to the act of writing and which the act of writing then reveals to the reader. When a text is later re-read for the discursive construction of the meaning of gender such a reading will relate to both the meaning prevalent at the historical moment of production and to present-day understandings of gendered experience. I therefore attempt to offer feminist readings of texts from the vantage point of the early 1990s in order to release the feminist potential within texts written in the past.

The two halves of this project cohere to form what I have defined as a 'women's agenda' for the analysis of the writing of the inter-war period. The recent expression, a 'women's agenda', denotes the determined, if not

---

1. Elaine Showalter, 'Introduction: The Rise of Gender', in Elaine Showalter (ed.) *Speaking of Gender* (London: Routledge, 1989), p.4.

concerted, efforts made by women to express their own concerns as women, to question the legitimacy of practices that exclude or marginalise such concerns and to resist the interests of women being subsumed under other categories or being lost from sight.

The point that literary criteria have traditionally had a bias against women is hardly new. But it is one that needs to be re-iterated in the context of writing in the inter-war period as the existence of a 'women's agenda' at that time has yet to be properly recognised. The agenda that is visible to the historian and the literary critic from a distance of half a century is largely a function of our own desire to uncover hidden or potential meanings. A 'women's agenda' was not necessarily visible to women at the time. Such a joint venture had not yet been thoroughly established and would not have been considered feasible. But that does not mean that the agenda was altogether absent.

My attempt to establish a 'women's agenda' begins from the premise that women's life experiences have been enabling as well as restrictive. Men may have much to answer for, but they have not expunged women's subjectivity from literature nor women's agency from history. The struggle against women's oppression has to date determined much, one might wish to argue too much, of the feminist theoretical agenda. However, a woman's definition of self that is premised upon her sense of victimisation may itself be disempowering. If, as Janice Raymond warns, the kind of relating that women primarily engage in is that of narrating pain, then women who bond in victimisation 'are, in real ways, encouraging women to remain victims in order to sustain the bonds'.[2]

Feminists cannot be satisfied with a notion of women as helpless victims of circumstances nor with a notion of literature as merely a locus of patriarchal representations. It is essential, therefore, to move beyond the analysis of works which portray women in the role of victim, best illustrated in *The Well of Loneliness* and *Swastika Night*, to examine patterns of resistance in women writers who attempted to find new idioms and strategies for expressing women's experience in texts such as *Three Guineas* and *Orlando*. In order to establish such patterns of resistance I have made no distinction between major and minor, or between lesser and better-known, writers but have chosen instead to concentrate on the thematics they share: 'The extraordinary woman', as Virginia Woolf succinctly remarked in 1929, 'depends on the ordinary woman.'[3] To put her, as I do, in the company of Katharine Burdekin and Radclyffe Hall is

---

2. Janice Raymond, *A Passion for Friends: Towards a Philosophy of Female Affection* (London: Women's Press, 1986), p.183.
3. Virginia Woolf, 'Women and Fiction', in Leonard Woolf (ed.), *The Collected Essays*, 4 vols (London: Hogarth, 1966–7), vol. 2, p.142.

to deepen and enrich the connections that Virginia Woolf wished us to make; it is to take her at her word.

The wider enquiry of this book is located within socialist-feminism. The magnetic attraction Marxism has sometimes exercised over the feminist imagination has been primarily due to its theory of equality which has been responsible for inspiring political action and changing political practice all over the world. However, Marxism's claim to a unique vision of universal justice and human liberation has suffered irrevocable damage as a result of the dramatic collapse of the regimes in Eastern Europe and the disintegration of the former Soviet Union. Marxism is not, of course, a monolith, and cannot legitimately be held to be synonymous with any of the uses and abuses of power which have been carried out in its name. As Tony Bennett has pointed out, 'what is invested in the currency of Marxism – and consequently, the practical issues at stake in either preserving or jettisoning it – varies from one institutional site of its discursive application to another.'[4] But it is, nonetheless, true that regimes whose institutions were in theory underpinned by Marxist ideas had in practice come to be equated largely with the evils of inefficient command economies, poverty, environmental disaster, and continuing gender inequality. The end of 'the short century' – beginning with the ideal of socialist revolution in 1917, finishing with its wholesale rejection in 1989 – calls into question the adequacy of Marxism's explanatory powers.

Since the late 1960s socialist-feminist criticism in Britain has developed in a critical relationship with socialist criticism and has produced its own critique of Marxist theory. In contesting Marxism's ordering of political priorities it has also questioned its theoretical priorities. Socialist-feminism has questioned the usual dichotomy between the public and private spheres of human activity and broadened our understanding of power to include its more subtle and evasive operations. Socialist-feminist critique clearly acquires new significance as Marxism is forced to re-assess its own history. Although the great strength of the Marxist critical tradition has been its opposition to all forms of exploitation, Marxist theory has not, until relatively recently, addressed itself directly to gendered identity, nor has it given serious attention to the ways in which women have experienced oppression informally in personal and family relationships. The specific forms that the socialist-feminist critique of Marxism has taken have been diverse, but there is also some degree of consensus. Very broadly, socialist-feminists, while accepting certain tenets of Marxist thought (including the necessity to engage with questions of class and to relate literature to its social conditions of production and existence) have attempted to redress the neglect within the Marxist tradition of the personal, the domestic and

4. Tony Bennett, *Outside Literature* (London: Routledge, 1990), p.30.

the sexual. It is these areas that I examine in *The Rector's Daughter, The Death of the Heart, The Thinking Reed*, and *The Weather in the Streets*.

In the 1930s Marxist critics such as Christopher Cauldwell and Alick West tended to pay insufficient attention to the complex mediation of social reality in literary texts and to see the relationship between literary works and society in ways which now appear highly simplistic. Unless a work had some obvious connection to immediate political concerns it ran the risk of being labelled irrelevant or of attracting that most damning of epithets, 'bourgeois'. The response to Richardson, Lehmann, Bowen, West and Woolf in the 1930s and later has been dogged by criticisms of what Marxists and socialists have wrongly imagined to be a fundamental lack of seriousness about public issues in their writings. In so far as I insist on re-assessing women who have been dismissed or undervalued because their textual politics have been perceived to lack social relevance, I am in debate with other cultural critics on the left.

That which is self-evident or which has already been culturally conceded need not be stridently claimed. The 'desire and the right of women to help in the world's housekeeping',[5] as women's aspirations to full and equal citizenship are characterised in *Pilgrimage*, was not generally acknowledged in the inter-war period. The principal objective of the women's suffrage movement – votes for women on the same basis as men – was finally achieved in 1928, but the notion that man was innately superior to woman was not banished, even among the liberal intelligentsia, until long after the 1914–18 war. In October 1920, for example, Virginia Woolf wrote to *The New Statesman* to object to a reviewer's endorsement of views attributed to Arnold Bennett amounting to the fact that intellectually and creatively man was superior to woman and 'no amount of education and liberty of action will sensibly alter' that situation.[6]

> Woman is undeveloped man . . . if one could die of the loathsome visions . . . I *must* die. I can't go on living it . . . the whole world full of *creatures*; half human. And I am one of the half-human ones, or shall be, if I don't stop now.[7]

These utterances occur in *The Tunnel*. The sense of shock felt by Dorothy Richardson's young heroine on discovering the definition of woman as 'undeveloped man' in an encyclopaedia closely resembles, and anticipates by ten years, the dumbfounded reaction of the narrator of *A Room of One's Own* to the discovery in the British Museum of books on

---

5. Dorothy Richardson, *Pilgrimage*, 4 vols (London: Dent, 1938), vol. 4, *Clear Horizons*, p.351.
6. Virginia Woolf, 'The Intellectual Status of Women', *New Statesman*, 9 October, 1920, p.15.
7. Dorothy Richardson, *Pilgrimage*, vol. 2, *The Tunnel*, p.220.

Introduction

women written by 'men who had no qualification save that they were not
women', and to the learned treatise on the 'mental, moral and physical
inferiority of women' patronisingly contemplated by the eminent Professor
von X.[8] We may fail to fully appreciate the radical dimensions of women
writers' attempts to insist on the value of woman-centred perspectives if
we forget that prejudice of this kind was general in the inter-war years.

To understand the feminist ideas underpinning much women's writing
it is necessary to refer, briefly, to debates between women after 1914. At
the risk of simplification, two major strands within feminist thinking may
be identified; 'new' feminism, with an emphasis on how women differ
from men, and 'old' feminism, with an emphasis on the equal status of
men and women.[9] The 'new' feminist's espousal of difference was opposed
by 'old' feminists like Winifred Holtby and Vera Brittain who feared that
such an emphasis would jeopardise women's claim to equal treatment with
men. The bold experimentation with narrative of Virginia Woolf and
Dorothy Richardson may be seen to reflect the feminism of their sisters
in the social and political sphere. And, despite the different forms in which
they are articulated, their concerns are broadly the same. How could
difference be expressed so that it was neither oppressive to women nor
politically counter-productive?

A number of recent feminist works have greatly helped our
understanding of women and the literary modernist movement. Shari
Benstock, Rachel Blau DuPlessis, Gillian Hanscombe and Virginia S.
Smyers, Susan Gubar and Sandra M. Gilbert have all thrown light upon
the connections between modernism and gender.[10] Rachel Blau DuPlessis
has defined as 'writing beyond the ending' the 'invention of strategies that
sever the narrative from formerly conventional structures of fiction and
consciousness about women'.[11] Gillian Hanscombe and Virginia Smyers
have emphasised how women modernists violated both social and literary
conventions, arguing that the woman modernist, unlike her male
counterpart, is 'not unconventional; she is anti-conventional'.[12] Shari

8. Virginia Woolf, *A Room of One's Own* (London: Hogarth, 1929), pp.43, 48.
9. Feminist historians have called for an end to the framing of women's history in this
way. See Joan W. Scott, 'Deconstructing Equality – Versus-Difference: or, the Uses of
Poststructuralist Theory for Feminism', *Feminist Studies*, vol. 14, 1, Spring 1988, pp.49–
50.
10. Shari Benstock, *Women of the Left Bank: Paris 1900–1940* (Austin: University of
Texas Press, 1986); Rachel Blau DuPlessis, *Writing Beyond the Ending: Narrative Strategies
of Twentieth-Century Women Writers* (Bloomington: Indiana University Press, 1975);
Gillian E. Hanscombe and Virginia L. S. Smyers, *Writing for their Lives: The Modernist
Women 1910–1940* (London: Women's Press, 1987); Sandra M. Gilbert and Susan Gubar,
No Man's Land: The Place of the Woman Writer in the Twentieth Century, vol. 1, *The War
of the Words* (New Haven and London: Yale University Press, 1988).
11. Blau DuPlessis, *Writing Beyond the Ending*, p.x.
12. Hanscombe and Smyers, *Writing For Their Lives*, p.11.

– 5 –

Benstock has made the general point that, 'once women Modernists are placed beside their male colleagues, the hegemony of masculine heterosexual values that have for so long underwritten our definitions of Modernism is put into question'.[13]

What has emerged from recent studies is a clearer understanding of how the history of women's modernist practice is the history of hitherto unheard voices being made audible. The woman in rebellion against all forms of fixity and decorum was greatly assisted by new insights into the fluid nature of psycho-sexual identity after the translation into English of Freud. She made use of new modes of writing to explore previously subterranean aspects of women's lives. Breaking the sentence and the sequence of plot the woman modernist found new opportunities to speak her own sense of self and to express her marginality.

The premise that there is a stable correlation between experiment in language and radical structures of feeling has strongly influenced feminist critical attitudes to the writing of the 1920s and 1930s. Experimental modes of writing are clearly of crucial interest to feminists. They had revolutionary significance and not just for the women to whom they gave a voice. As Virginia Woolf observed, in making the woman's voice heard one might 'destroy the very foundations and rules of literary society'.[14]

But modernists sometimes asssume the unified self to be merely a fiction, the effect of language, and that it is *only* by breaking down the old 'stable egos' of character and the traditional aesthetic assumptions that new forms of communality may be achieved. This must be open to question. Whatever the attractions of the decentred self for the avant-garde writer – and they were considerable – it is easy to forget that many feminists of the 1920s and 1930s did not subscribe to them. Traditional modes of writing are resilient. Many women writers did not doubt their usefulness and saw nothing strange about expressing radical subject matter in old forms. The decentred self, it may be argued, is a concept of strictly limited relevance to women, gays, blacks and members of other disadvantaged groups struggling to assert the identity as full human subjects which has traditionally been denied them. In so far as realist modes were, and still often are, the first or the favoured recourse of oppressed groups, they must remain a potentially productive quarry of feminist investigation.

There is ample space within feminist critical theory to accommodate different modes of writing. To systematise a demarcation between traditional and experimental modes of writing is to perpetuate an artificial division more rigidly than many women of the 1920s and 1930s believed

13. Benstock, *Women of the Left Bank*, p.6.
14. Virginia Woolf,'Mr. Bennett and Mrs. Brown', in Leonard Woolf (ed.), *The Collected Essays*, vol. 1, p.334.

to be necessary. In practice, women writers often crossed the hypothesised demarcation line. And they criss-crossed it. For example, a traditional work, Flora Mayor's *The Rector's Daughter*, was enthusiastically published by Leonard and Virginia Woolf at the Hogarth Press. Winifred Holtby, whose fiction could not have differed more greatly from Virginia Woolf's, was her first biographer and remains among her most perceptive. Radclyffe Hall wrote the formally conservative *The Well of Loneliness* surrounded and supported by avant-garde women in the cradle of literary modernism, the left bank of Paris.

I believe that it is necessary to explore the uses and potential uses of both realist and anti-realist modes of writing, devising strategies to distance ourselves critically from any closure of the options available to women that may ensue from realist modes of writing, and from the danger of solipsism in anti-realist ones. The coupling of works contrasting markedly in form but having other affinities is sometimes useful as is shown by my analysis of *Orlando* and *The Well of Loneliness*. No useful purpose is served by re-running within feminism the aesthetic debate between realism and modernism that took place within Marxism between Brecht and Lukács.[15] Rather, Eagleton's comments on Brecht should be kept in mind when thinking about women's writing, 'the dismantling of our given identities through art is inseparable from the practice of producing a new kind of human subject altogether, which would need to know not only internal fragmentation but social solidarity'.[16]

The texts I have chosen are weighted towards realist modes in order to complement the growing number of works on modernism and to avoid treading ground already covered in *Women of the Left Bank*, *Writing for their Lives* and *Writing Beyond the Ending*. Although there has been a welcome revival of interest in individual women writers of the 1920s and 1930s inter-textual studies are still few and the area as a whole is still lamentably under-examined. Margaret Lawrence's *We Write as Women*, remains a useful, if now very dated, introduction to women writers of her day. Nicola Beauman's *A Very Great Profession*, is largely a descriptive rather than an analytical work documenting the 'woman's novel' (domestic fiction which was read by middle-class women). Alison Light combines new insights into conservative modernity and the links between national and feminine identity with a refreshing interest in popular fiction in *Forever England*. The most important contribution to this field is Claire Tylee's illuminating and scholarly study of the effects of the 1914–18 war

15. See Bertolt Brecht, 'Against Georg Lukács', (trans.) Stuart Hood; Georg Lukács, 'Realism in the Balance', (trans) Rodney Livingstone; reprinted in Perry Anderson et al. (eds), *Aesthetics and Politics* (London: New Left Books, 1977), pp.68–86, pp.28–59.

16. Terry Eagleton, *Literary Theory* (Oxford: Blackwell, 1983), p.191.

on women's imaginations, *The Great War and Women's Consciousness*.[17]

Valentine Cunningham has drawn attention to the absence of women writers in many literary histories of the inter-war period in *British Writers of the Thirties*. He argues that women writers 'cannot be simply left, as most books about the 1930s leave them, out of the account'.[18] As Cunningham has pointed out, Storm Jameson, Stevie Smith, Sylvia Townsend Warner, Rosamond Lehmann, Naomi Mitchison, Antonia White, F. Tennyson Jesse, Winifred Holtby and other 'resuscitated names from the Virago Modern Classics List are all most competent novelists, and some of them are much more than that'.[19]

Feminist research has shown the literary achievement of many of Cunningham's 'competent' and 'more than' competent women novelists to be inseparable from their sense of themselves as women, from their questioning and radical outloook on society, or from their critical engagement with the key issues of their day. We must, therefore, not only insist upon the full restitution of women writers to accounts of the 1920s and the 1930s but also specify precisely on what grounds we believe that re-instatement should take place. My contention is that if the women writers discussed here have been omitted from literary histories it is not just because their competence has been questioned. It is because those histories themselves have often been framed in terms which have marginalised, disadvantaged or disqualified the woman writer. For example, two widely-respected works on the 1930s, Bernard Bergonzi's *Reading the Thirties* and Samuel Hynes's *The Auden Generation*[20] both approach the literature of the decade with an emphasis on poetry and, on the Auden–Isherwood circle, thus excluding analysis of important women novelists.

The literary texts of the past are a key site for the construction of gendered experience but only as part of a wider social totality. Literary texts are not only constituted by society; they in their turn help to constitute the social formation in their day. Inscribed with their own ideological meanings, works of literature have the potential to transmit representations

17. Margaret Lawrence, *We Write as Women* (London: Joseph, 1937); Nicola Beauman, *A Very Great Profession: The Woman's Novel 1914–1939* (London: Virago, 1983); Alison Light, *Forever England: Femininity, Literature and Conservatism Between the Wars* (London: Routledge, 1991); Claire M. Tylee, *The Great War and Women's Consciousness: Images of Militarism and Womanhood in Women's Writing, 1914–1964* (Basingstoke: Macmillan, 1990).
18. Valentine Cunningham, *British Writers of the Thirties* (Oxford: Oxford University Press, 1988), p.26.
19. Ibid.
20. Bernard Bergonzi, *Reading the Thirties: Texts and Contexts* (London: Macmillan, 1978); *The Auden Generation: Literature and Coterie Politics in the 1930s* (London: Bodley Head, 1976).

and values discursively; to question, dislodge, perpetuate, or to leave intact contemporary assumptions. They also have an important *interpretive* function in relation to our understanding of gendered historical and social relationships. As Alan Sinfield has argued, texts are 'constructions of conceivable lives ... interpretations and evaluations of perceived possiblities in the real world'.[21]

Specific difficulties and contradictions beset the representation of feminist consciousness in modes of writing as diverse as autobiography (*Testament of Youth*), the modernist experimental novel (*Orlando*), speculative fiction (*Swastika Night*), the political tract (*Three Guineas*) and the short story ('The Daughters of the Late Colonel'). How does one begin to re-assess woman-centred texts written at a specific historical conjuncture, the 1920s and 1930s, in order to better our understanding of the vexed relationship between politics and aesthetics?

Through detailed analysis of *The Weather in the Streets*, *The Death of the Heart*, and *The Thinking Reed*, I shall develop the argument that men and women may be situated differently as readers of texts that focus on romantic love. The high value that women have learned to place on love conflicts with the male pursuit of status and wealth. Each of these novels makes fine distinctions between different strata of the English middle-class and the relationship of each of the central women characters to the English class system is a deeply troubled one. These novels of sensibility inscribe the traditional relationship of women to men, and of women to the class system, but the relationships inscribed are in many senses deeply ambivalent ones which resist while they acquiesce. My reading of these texts unearths radical discontents expressed at the level of women's private structures of feeling and I suggest that these texts create as much anxiety in the reader as they may dispel.

Women writers have been disadvantaged because radical and socialist critics with a special interest in the writing of the 1920s and 1930s have been generally far more adept at recognising men's aspirations than women's. To borrow Judith Fetterley's helpful phrase, men have proved themselves 'resisting readers' of women's texts, a resistance that has been deeply lodged within literary criticism. For the male reader to read attentively such woman-centred texts as *The Weather in the Streets* or *Three Guineas* is to risk seeing his reflection in a distorting mirror, to find himself the 'other' and to submit to the kind of experience that in a patriarchal society has too often been the woman reader's. Whatever the reasons for the structuring absences of women in many accounts of the 1930s the effect is the same. If the desires and determinations of both sexes are not defined and analysed, then the desires and determinations of one sex will be read

21. Alan Sinfield, *Society and Literature 1945–1970* (London: Methuen, 1983), p.1.

as being the same as, or allowed to stand in for, the desires and determinations of the other. As the authors of a recent study of gender and reading have put it, with 'textuality firmly in male hands, men never have to face the risks inherent in genuine reciprocity'.[22]

The awkward critical response that originally greeted the women whose work I analyse reflects men's inability to comprehend women's unorthodoxy. As attention to the critical reception of these texts will illustrate, the male critic has often seen 'not merely a difference of view, but a view that is weak, or trivial, or sentimental, because it differs from his own'.[23] The critical response to Dorothy Richardson provides many pointed examples of male prejudice. Thus in reviews of *Pilgrimage* one frequently finds disadvantageous comparisons between Dorothy Richardson and James Joyce or Marcel Proust on the grounds that the substance of Richardson's life, or that of her central character, Miriam, was too slight to make her eccentricities of style palatable.

If we compare their circumstances objectively, Miriam Henderson hardly appears to have *less* experience of the world than Joyce's characters, but a devotee of *Ulysses*, Conrad Aiken, argues that 'if one takes one's seat in the balcony, say of such a mind as that of Stephen Dedalus, or even Leopold Blum [sic], it is obvious enough to any merely *male* reader that the variety of entertainment is going to be strikingly greater and richer and deeper'.[24] Apparently unaware of Richardson's marriage to Alan Odle, he observed that the author's 'feminist attitude' appeared to reflect 'the natural withering of the spinster'.[25] Leon Edel candidly described his initial resistance to being asked 'to enter the mind of a young adolescent – a female adolescent'. He writes: 'I could not adopt the one "point of view" she offered me, an angle of vision that required more identification than I – as indeed many of her male readers – could achieve. It is doubtless much easier for a man to enter into the mind of Daniel Prince going to a rendezvous with an actress than the mind of a moody young English girl in a German girls' school.'[26] A third critic of Dorothy Richardson's, John Rosenburg, complained of a 'girl's rebellion against a man's world – a rebellion that, because it was a youthful one, sometimes excessively

22. Patrocinio P. Schweickart, introduction to Elizabeth A. Flynn and Patrocinio P. Schweickart (eds), *Gender and Reading: Essays on Readers, Texts, and Contexts* (Baltimore: Johns Hopkins University Press, 1986), p.xix.

23. Virginia Woolf, 'Women and Fiction', p.146.

24. Conrad Aiken, *A Reviewer's ABC: Collected Criticism of Conrad Aiken from 1916 to the Present* (New York: Meridian, 1958), p.330.

25. Ibid.

26. Leon Edel, *The Modern Psychological Novel 1900–1950* (New York: Hart-Davis, 1955), pp.70–1.

belittled men's capabilities and faculties'.[27]

As Stephen Heath has observed, 'men have been trained simply to read, they have the acquired neutrality of domination, theirs is the security of indifference'.[28] But domination, as Heath is, of course, himself aware, is far from neutral. Inscribed within the terms in which the literature of the inter-war period is sometimes discussed, introspection *versus* social engagement, sensibility *versus* commitment are the values and polarities men have seen as important. If the woman writer who is the object of the male critics' scrutiny wishes to signify her dissent and attempts 'to alter the established values – to make serious what appears insignificant to a man and trivial what is to him important',[29] the resulting entanglements, the dissonances and disagreements, are complex to unravel and demand careful recovery and analysis.

Whether or not feminist writings, and works of fiction in particular, are tendentious, solipsistic, clichéd or self-indulgent, they will tend to be read as such whenever the tide of critical opinion turns against feminism. The texts analysed in this book are radical in so far as their authors did not relinquish their desire to speak in the name of woman, to speak of women's experience, aspirations, subjectivity and sexuality. Indeed, the tenacity with which individual women affirmed their own political and aesthetic priorities is remarkable in view of the powerful pressures, self-set and external, on women to desist from so doing in the 1920s and 1930s when anti-feminism was ubiquitous among intellectuals.

Thus Vera Brittain gives prominence to a woman's perspective on the 1914 war, Virginia Woolf a consciously feminist slant to the critique of Fascism. Flora Mayor offers a spinster's view of spinsterhood, Leonora Eyles provides a woman's experience of the London slum, and Rosamond Lehmann, a woman's view of romantic love. Bestowing her highest compliment upon Emily Brontë and Jane Austen ('They wrote as women write, not as men write'),[30] Virginia Woolf expressed her own unqualified admiration for their courage: 'But how impossible it must have been for them not to budge either to the right or to the left. What genius, what integrity it must have required in face of all that criticism, in the midst of that purely patriarchal society, to hold fast to the thing as they saw it without shrinking.'[31] Much the same might be said of Virginia Woolf herself and of her many contemporaries whose work I discuss. Each writer questioned

27. *Dorothy Richardson: The Genius They Forgot – A Critical Biography* (London: Duckworth, 1973), pp.56–7.
28. Stephen Heath, 'Male Feminism', in Alice Jardine and Paul Smith (eds), *Men in Feminism* (London: Methuen, 1987), p.27.
29. Virginia Woolf, 'Women and Fiction', p.146.
30. Virginia Woolf, *A Room of One's Own*, p.112.
31. Ibid.

in her own way the prevalent assumption that what was serious, what was important, and what was worth writing about was the world of men. This commitment to the authority of a woman's perspective is the common thread that runs through otherwise disparate works and reflects and mediates the different positions on the spectrum of feminist awareness from which the woman writer speaks.

Critical Theory and Methodology

What we see through our feminist spectacles will of course inform what we choose to analyse, and perhaps also to some extent how we choose to analyse it. Feminist theory involves taking up a distinct stance or position in relation to its object, therefore, and thus in this sense cannot be regarded as politically neutral.

Annette Kuhn, *Women's Pictures*[32]

This book is feminist in its scope of enquiry, though feminism does not inevitably suggest its own methodologies; rather feminists are involved in 'the appropriation of existing methodologies for a newly-constituted project'.[33] There is general assent among feminist scholars to the proposition that such a project must be politically opposed to patriarchal practices. As Diana A. Fuss has pointed out, even feminist theorists who appear willing to displace notions of identity, self, experience and virtually every other self-evident category, are prepared to make an exception in the case of politics: 'To the extent that it is difficult to imagine a *non-political* feminism, politics emerges as feminism's essence.'[34] But as to the interventions that should be made, the nature of what needs to be analysed, as well as to the tools of analysis, there are major disagreements. Before setting out more specifically the particular view of feminist literary criticism which has informed this book, I wish to refer briefly to some influential tendencies within feminist literary criticism and to explain the particular problems I believe each approach presents.

The first observation that must be made is that feminist critical positions cannot easily be pigeonholed into national and geographical resting places. The dangers of labelling theoretical positions by literal or metaphorical nationality have been clearly stated by Elaine Showalter, who has emphasised that feminist activity is global, and its best-known exponents too internationally mobile, and too theoretically complex, to fit

32. Annette Kuhn, *Women's Pictures: Feminism and Cinema* (London: Routledge and Kegan Paul, 1982), p.70.
33. Ibid., p.71.
34. Diana A. Fuss, *Essentially Speaking: Feminism, Nature and Difference* (London: Routledge, 1989), p.37.

comfortably into any national niche.[35] One major body of feminist criticism, sometimes referred to as French feminism because it has been closely associated with France's three most influential feminists, Julia Kristeva, Hélène Cixous and Luce Irigaray, has argued that women cannot be heard at all in fictional representations, or can only be heard in a highly negotiated way, because the subject position from which the command of language comes is a patriarchal construct. There are, of course, substantial differences of opinion between French feminists to which Nicole Ward Jouve has drawn attention, pointing out what has been lost, unavailable or misrepresented in translation – of Cixous in particular.[36]

However, Cixous, Kristeva, Irigaray, and feminists with similar approaches, have all perceived woman as the subject of an ideology which denies the exploration of identity on the same terms as men. As all connections with 'essentialist' or 'empirical' definitions of woman must be severed, the opposition to patriarchal oppression effectively amounts to contestation of patriarchal aesthetic and metaphysical systems. Struggle is located *only* at the level of discourse and is purely verbal and linguistic. In such interpretations the role of patriarchal authority is always consistent, always militating to dispossess woman of her identity, always characterised by restrictive practices of one sort or another. Once woman is construed as a signifier in patriarchal discourse, any process of realistic representation in literary works becomes ideologically complicit. The 'feminine' is therefore identified in silence, absence, and incoherence. In other words, the outward signs of women's oppression become innate female virtues. Such work is often based on theories of psychoanalysis, or derived from linguistic theory which separates sign and signifier. It rejects linear narrative, the 'unified subject position', and the mimetic depiction of experience, and argues in favour of a 'natural' alliance between feminist theory and avant-garde forms of expression.

A major drawback of this kind of criticism is that it easily divorces literature from history. It often bludgeons literature out of its specificity and materiality and may easily lose sight of how the representation of women is linked to historical facts and to historically contextualised situations. Because women and their writings are always defined by absences and silences, these absences and silences may obliterate meanings which are actually present in women's writing. This may also happen if a hypothesised deep structure is privileged at the expense of the historical surface. One critic has specified the problems of such approaches: 'Stated

35. Elaine Showalter, 'Feminism and Literature', in Peter Collier and Helga Geyer-Ryan (eds), *Literary Theory Today* (Cambridge: Polity, 1990), p.181.
36. Nicole Ward Jouve, *White Woman Speaks with Forked Tongue: Criticism as Autobiography* (London: Routledge, 1991), pp.48–50.

in these ways, woman's plight seems overdetermined, the plot of her story too predictable, the modes of her actions and writing reductive. The authority of her experience rests in its sameness, its inability ever radically to alter its bases in fact or to transform that circumstance in fiction'.[37]

A second influential tendency within feminist literary criticism is sometimes designated Anglo-American criticism, a term accommodating critical writings with a Marxist or materialist orientation at one end of the spectrum and radical feminist separatism at the other. Such writing, while centrally concerned with the experience of women, is highly disparate in other respects. Individual critics have placed very different emphases upon the role played by historical, ideological, textual, material and psychic factors in shaping gender ideology. It is clear, for example, that the intellectual allegiances of two distinguished American feminist literary historians, Elaine Showalter and Jane Marcus, have been determined not only by their participation in the radical politics of the academic world but also by their participation in the radical politics of the world outside it. But others, such as Sandra M. Gilbert and Susan Gubar, appear to have less obvious social and political commitments and have been criticised for failing to address questions of class, religion and politics in their work.[38]

If women's experiences are different from men's, it is important to understand why. As feminist post-structuralists have argued, gynocritical approaches often fail to pay sufficient attention to the social construction of gendered difference, to acknowledge the importance of linguistic debate within feminism, and the crucial role language plays in constructing the meaning of experience. In such approaches women's experience is frequently assumed to pre-exist the discursive processes that give it its meaning.[39] Critical approaches of this kind, to which feminist poststructuralists object, may find difficulty in explaining how narrative structures operate at a textual level to naturalise relationships which are exploitative and distorted through ideology. Gynocriticism is often unable to deal adequately with women's writing which does not display anger at patriarchal oppression or which may even be hostile to women or to feminism.

While exhibiting the classic liberal virtues of tolerance and empathy there is always a danger that gynocritical approaches may take us no further than an all-embracing pluralism in which the biological signature of the author is sufficient guarantee of the interest and authenticity of a literary work. But formalist critical methodology, and the questions that formalist

37. Benstock, *Women of the Left Bank*, p.8
38. See Marilyn Butler, new introduction to *Jane Austen and the War of Ideas*, 1975; re-issued (Oxford: Clarenden, 1987), p.xxiv.
39. See Chris Weedon, *Feminist Practice and Post-Structuralist Theory* (Oxford: Blackwell, 1987), for the development of these arguments.

critics have highlighted, have an important part to play in feminist reading. Gender has symbolic meanings in addition to its historical and material ones. It is only by paying rigorous attention to practices of writing, to conventions of genre, to inter-textual relationships between literary texts and other forms of writing, theoretical and polemical, that we can arrive at properly informed judgements about literary works.

The study of women writers as a distinct and separate group, which is now a widely accepted practice, dates from the development of gynocriticism in the mid-seventies with a spate of studies on women's writing including Ellen Moers's *Literary Women* (1976), Patricia Meyer Spacks's *The Female Imagination* (1976), and Elaine Showalter's *A Literature of Their Own* (1978).[40] In her pioneering work *A Literature of Their Own* Showalter attempted to 'describe the female literary tradition in the English novel from the generation of the Brontës to the present day, and to show how the development of this tradition is similar to the development of any literary subculture'.[41] But such a project clearly has its own limitations. Inevitably, the history of cohabitation with men is to be found in the literary landscape that lies between Jane Austen, Emily and Charlotte Brontë, George Eliot and Virginia Woolf. The indirect reference to the power of men in two of the three stages that Showalter defines as essential to the historical development of a women's literary subculture (imitation, internalisation, and self-discovery) delineates the extent to which the lives of men and women have always been historically intertwined. Furthermore, many women will testify that their lives have been more closely intricated with the lives of men, as fathers, brothers and sons than with women of other races, that they have felt closer bonds to husbands and lovers than to women of other classes.

Women's life experiences have been different from men's and shared experiences clearly have important bearings on women's writing. But a feminist project should not attempt to make a permanent subtitution of one set of loyalties for another, 'woman-centred' for 'man-centred', although, as Sandra Harding has observed, 'it is true that first we often have to formulate a 'woman-centred' hypothesis in order even to comprehend a gender-free one'.[42] Gynocritical approaches are not the only possible feminist aproaches to women writers' texts. As many women writers have shown – Tony Morrison, Alice Walker and June Jordan are excellent

---

40. Ellen Moers, *Literary Women* (London: Women's Press, 1976); Patricia Meyer Spacks, *The Female Imagination: A Literary and Psychological Investigation of Women's Writing* (London: Macmillan, 1976); Elaine Showalter, *A Literature of Their Own: British Women Writers from Brontë to Lessing* (London: Virago, 1978).

41. Showalter, *A Literature of Their Own*, p.11.

42. Sandra Harding, *The Science Question in Feminism* (Milton Keynes: Open University Press, 1986), p.138.

examples – it is possible to write about women sensitively and in ways which validate the specificity of women's experience without postulating woman as a radically separate order of being.

The proposition that gender alone explains differences and variations in literary practices is one that threatens to divorce women's writing from other writing. Rigid separation is often unnecessary and unhelpful. Black women, for example, have frequently asserted that they have felt more in common with black men who have shared their political concerns and their painful experiences of racism than with white women in a hostile white society. The writing of black women is the product of a specific history of black people in which women, men and children have had to depend on one another 'because they had nothing and no one else'.[43] To read black women's writing is to realise that what the black writer – not just the black woman – inherited was a rich sense of belonging to a community and of sustaining love. In Alice Walker's words, black writers in a large measure 'owe their clarity of vision to parents who refused to diminish themselves as human beings by succumbing to racism'.[44] The writing of black women, therefore, demands to be read alongside the writing of black men. It is, after all, not history that is gendered but its telling.

To argue that there is no sphere of intellectual life which cannot be entered by women, but that there is such a sphere forever closed to men, is to confirm women yet again as the handmaidens of the irrational, the incoherent and the illogical. However, the rational, the logical and the ideational have never been the exclusive property of men. On the contrary, it is the possession of these very qualities which has empowered women to understand and to change their situations. Women should, therefore, strenuously resist male attempts to appropriate that to which they have no exclusive entitlement. The dangers of intellectual separatism are clear in the history of the word *lebensraum* (living room or space to live in) which was used by sections of the women's rights movement in the late Weimar Republic to designate the notion of a separate 'women's space' – nurturing, creative and wholly removed from the world of men.[45] The term was later appropriated by the Nazis and came to be associated with their eastward territorial expansion. It then became the responsibility of women to protect this space on behalf of the Nazis who claimed to be improving the position of women by creating further opportunities for them to gain respect as wives and mothers within the *lebensraum*. Stephen Heath has identified the potential dangers to feminism of emphasising sexual difference: 'a

43. Alice Walker, 'The Black Writer and the Southern Experience', in *In Search of Our Mother's Gardens: Womanist Prose* (London: Women's Press, 1984), p.16.
44. Ibid., p.19.
45. See Linda Gordon, 'Review Essay: Nazi Feminists'?, *Feminist Review*, 27, Autumn 1978, pp.101–2.

tourniquet operates in which the real necessity to claim difference binds back, and precisely from the difference claimed, into the renewal of the same, a reflection of the place assigned, assigned as difference. Patriarchy, men in its order, has never said anything but that women are – the woman is – different: they are *not* men.'[46]

If feminist criticism is not to concern itself simply with the criticism of texts written by women, nor with the exposure of patriarchy as a monolith, nor just with the retrieval of lost works, what is its role and purpose? I wish to argue that feminist criticism as a discursive practice within the academy must always be tied to feminism as the collective aspiration of women to understand the patriarchal organisation of society and to the collective desire of women to re-order existing social and political relationships. The purpose of feminist criticism is to help create a cultural, social and aesthetic climate that is receptive to such change. As Judith Fetterley has defined it: 'At its best, feminist criticism is a political act whose aim is not simply to interpret the world but to change it by changing the consciousness of those who read and their relation to what they read.'[47] Viewed in this light, retrieving lost works is one essential facet – but one only – of the wider enterprise of feminist literary criticism. I believe that feminist criticism should take proper account of the differences between women attributable to class, race, nation, age and sexual orientation. But it should also retain a loyalty to a definition of women as an identifiable group with interests in common and in whose interests social, cultural and political change must take place. This is irrespective of the differences between women we have identified, of the impossibility of speaking for all women that we have acknowledged, or even the problems that beset attempts to specify precisely what it is that women have in common, given the variable circumstances of women's social reality.

The real test of feminist criticism must be whether or not it is able to produce new understandings that bring about an enlargement and transformation of existing paradigms and frameworks. As Wolfgang Iser puts it, a 'response that depends upon the reader finding a reflection of himself [sic] could scarcely bring the reader anything new . . . (and literature would be barren indeed if it led only to a recognition of the already familiar)'.[48] Although it would be wrong to overstate the extent to which feminist understandings have penetrated beyond the feminist circles in which they originate, the fact that literary modernism cannot now be understood without reference to gender represents a significant

46. Stephen Heath, 'Difference', *Screen*, vol. 19, 3, Autumn 1978, pp.77–8.

47. Judith Fetterley, *The Resisting Reader: A Feminist Approach to American Fiction* (Bloomington: Indiana University Press, 1978), p.viii.

48. Wolfgang Iser, *The Act of Reading: A Theory of Aesthetic Response* (Baltimore: Johns Hopkins University Press, 1978), pp.42–3.

re-drawing of the twentieth-century literary map. Before the advent of feminist literary criticism Virginia Woolf was often an unread, if not unreadable, exponent of art for art's sake. The literary modernist movement was usually discussed without reference to gender as a crucial organising principle and frequently without reference to Virginia Woolf, Dorothy Richardson or H.D. The restoration and restitution of the reputation of Woolf and to a lesser extent that of other women modernists including Katherine Mansfield, Dorothy Richardson, and H.D. have been largely due to the patient efforts of feminist critics.

I have concentrated on the ideological and material determinants of writing and attempts to situate literary production in its historical context. The emphasis on the importance of context reflects more general trends in Marxist literary studies. The rejection of determinism, was, of course, a central tenet of the New Criticism. It came to be challenged by Marxist critics and others who argued that texts should not be severed from their histories. As a consequence, there is now widespread cognition, or more properly re-cognition, of the value of contextually-based approaches to literature. This renewed interest in context has not, however, meant a return to purely objective criticism or to the earlier notion of the text as an icon or oracle with one message to convey. Raman Selden, for example, called for a 'critical labour whose task is to produce the knowledge of a text's conditions of production' and to distinguish the historical, biographical, inter-textual, socio-economic, ideological and aesthetic materials that a literary text reworks.[49]

The intellectual labour Seldon advocates cannot, of course, be expected to make the meaning(s) of a text available for all time. But the knowledge of the structure of its determinants clearly helps to establish the limiting conditions of a text's production and thus the ways in which it is possible to understand that text. This, broadly, has been my own enterprise in relation to the literary representation of the lesbian, the spinster, Fascism and the First World War. The emphasis on context is not an abdication of responsibility for critical analysis of such works as *Orlando, The Rector's Daughter, Testament of Youth* or *Three Guineas*. It is, rather, the basis upon which a fully-informed reading of such texts becomes possible.

A text may, of course, signify something more, something less, or something other than its author intended and may sometimes signify all three. But unless we know what the author's intention was in the first place it is difficult to specify what that corresponding more, less or other may be. To say that a literary text cannot be reduced to the author's intention is not to say that what we know of the latter should play no part in our response to the work. A writer can never be completely unconscious of

49. Ramon Selden, *Criticism and Objectivity* (London: Allen and Unwin, 1984), p.114.

the external world nor wholly conscious of all the contexts; material, ideological, aesthetic, political, institutional, ideational, cultural, social, to which the text may at any time be related. Authorial awareness varies and for this reason the helpfulness of biographical information varies too. What the author wished to communicate and what the text signifies are in some instances effectively the same. In others – *Testament of Youth* is a clear example – there is little equivalence between extra-textual pronouncements about a work and the actual work itself.

Texts do not come into existence by accident. They are the products of intentional acts. However, it is mistaken to assume that all texts have the same intentional standing. The relationship between an author's biography and her work may be of crucial importance. Alternatively, it may be of little importance. This will depend largely upon the circumstances in which a work comes to be produced and read. The context – interpreted in the widest possible sense – allows us to decide which is the case. Katharine Burdekin, for example, is a writer about whom very little is known. *Swastika Night* has, therefore, been analysed in the absence of biographical information. But Burdekin is exceptional. Elsewhere, the usefulness of known biographical information varies considerably. I have, therefore, taken the view that it is proper to make different assessments of its importance in relation to texts by different authors, or even to different texts by the same author, for example, *Orlando* and *Three Guineas* or *The Well of Loneliness* and *The Unlit Lamp*. Wherever possible, biographical information has been used to supplement other contextual information and the biographical and social have been linked. The writer has been placed at the centre of enquiry in order that the intersections of her life and work may be explored. By placing emphasis neither on the text to the exclusion of the author, nor on the author to the exclusion of the text, I have attempted to provide new insights into the interaction between the two.

This book also concerns itself with the relationship between reader and text. In attempting to formulate my own position I have found the position that David Lodge offers in *After Bakhtin* helpful:

> It is of the nature of texts, especially fictional ones, that they have gaps and indeterminacies which may be filled in by different readers in different ways, and it is of the nature of codes that, once brought into play, they may generate patterns of significance which were not consciously intended by the author who activated them, and which do not require his [sic] 'authorization' to be accepted as valid interpretations of the text.[50]

50. David Lodge, *After Bakhtin: Essays on Fiction and Criticism* (London: Routledge, 1990), p.159.

To re-locate meaning in the reader, in the classed, gendered and racially-related knowledge that the reader brings to the text at a specific historical moment is to counter objections that reader-relations theory has taken insufficient account of the historical conditions of reading.

I have said that the focus of my method is largely historical; to re-locate ideological contestations and meanings, some of which were labelled feminist at the time of writing. I now wish to borrow from reader-relations theory a useful term, the 'horizon of expectations' to explain how such meanings and contestations relate to the present. The 'horizon of expectations' refers to the expectations that readers hold at a specific historical moment. Susan Suleiman in her introduction to *The Reader in the Text* has explained the positions of critics like Hans-Robert Jauss who have elaborated this concept.[51] According to Suleiman, Hans-Robert Jauss and others have seen their role as critics to be to find the questions which a text originally answered and thereby to bring out the hermeneutic difference between past and present ways of understanding a text.[52] They have argued that the writer's knowledge of what he or she believed to be the expectations of the reading public at the time is an inescapable aspect of the composition of the text, even if that text appears to criticise or to set itself against the grain of those expectations.[53] In my own analysis of texts I have applied the notion of the 'horizon of expectations' to explain Virginia Woolf's self-censorship in *Orlando* as a function of her awareness of her readers' attitudes to lesbian representation and I show how *Orlando* goes against the grain of such expectations in its narrative strategies.

A modern understanding of an earlier literary text will necessarily differ from the first because today's 'horizon of expectations' is different. This difference is the result of changes in the cultural, political, and social conditions and norms within the social formation which must influence later readings. In 1938 the analogies between the patriarchal organisation of the family and the state that Virginia Woolf attempted to draw in *Three Guineas* were too radical to be widely understood. The distance between *Three Guineas* and the 'horizon of expectations' at that time was simply so great that its pioneering intellectual qualities could often not be fully appreciated. This is no longer the case: the connections Virginia Woolf made have been theorised, widely discussed and popularised within the women's movement and elsewhere. Thus read from the vantage point of the 1990s *Three Guineas* may sometimes appear to speak more clearly to our times than it did to hers.

51. Susan R. Suleiman, 'Introduction: Varieties of Audience-Oriented Criticism', in Susan R. Suleiman and Inge Crosman (eds), *The Reader in the Text: Essays on Audience and Interpretation* (Princeton, New Jersey: Princeton University Press, 1980), pp.35–7.
52. Ibid., p.36.
53. Ibid.

As Jane Tompkins has pointed out, the term 'community of interpreters' has been widely used by reader-relations theorists as 'shorthand for the notion that . . . an individual's perceptions and judgments are a function of the assumptions shared by the groups he [sic] belongs to'.[54] The assumption here (unfortunately, Tompkins shares it with Lodge) is that the author and the reader is a man. But the sex of the reader or the interpreter engaged in attributing significance to formal signifiers is clearly of importance. For if the life experiences of men and women are different it is crucial to know whose perceptions and judgements prevail. As Jonathan Culler has put it, 'if the experience of literature depends upon the qualities of a reading self, one can ask what difference it would make . . . if the reader is a woman'?[55]

In my reading of *Orlando* I use the 'hypothesis of a woman reader', originally Elaine Showalter's,[56] to pinpoint the limitations of well-known readings of that text offered by a succession of male critics. While the 'hypothesis of a woman reader' has been criticised by Tania Modleski because it allows Culler and other male critics to arrogate to themselves the ability to '"comprehend" women, just as the generic term "man" in language is said to do'[57] and thus again to achieve universality at the expense of women, the 'sensible', visible, actual female reader that Modleski prefers to put in its place[58] invites the question which woman reader? As we have seen, issues of class, race, national identity and sexual orientation all potentially affect the ways in which women may be positioned in relation to texts. In my criticism of *Orlando* the 'hypothesis' of a woman reader is used purely to distinguish between the reader who has a politicised understanding of womanhood and one who does not and to unlock *Orlando*'s hidden sexual codes.

The final question I wish to address is one to which it is impossible to do full justice. What makes it impossible for some authors to break out of ideological and class positions that they have internalised while allowing others to transcend and negotiate them? And what, moreover, lies behind their choice of form, their mode of writing? I have argued so far that the preoccupations of each generation, race, sex and class, will find hermeneutic expression in the questions that its members ask. As Marx puts it, that being determines consciousness. I now wish to argue,

54. Jane P. Tompkins, Introduction to Jane P. Tompkins (ed.), *Reader-Response Criticism: From Formalism to Post-Structuralism* (Baltimore: Johns Hopkins University Press, 1980), p.xxi.
55. Jonathan Culler, *On Deconstruction: Theory and Criticism After Structuralism* (Ithaca: Cornell University Press, 1982), p.42.
56. Elaine Showalter, 'Towards a Feminist Poetics', in Mary Jacobus (ed.), *Women Writing and Writing about Women* (London: Croom Helm, 1979), p.25.
57. Fetterley, *The Resisting Reader*, p.viii.
58. Ibid., p.133.

unfashionably, that the concept of subjectivity has always had, and continues to have, a useful, indeed central, place within both feminist and socialist-humanist analysis.

To cut short a highly complicated and contentious set of arguments, what matters about the much-derided unitary subject (the idea of a coherent self with its analogue in the representation of individuated characters within fiction) is that it credits the individual, man and woman, reader and writer, with the potential for moral choices, growth and change. This potential may be illustrated through Wayne Booth's brilliant engagement with Rabelais.[59] In the course of this essay Booth accomplished several challenging tasks. He carefully interrogated the hitherto unrecognised sexism of his own critical practice, recognised the justice of feminist arguments, and called upon other men to join women in re-educating the imagination. It is impossible to explain a *volte-face* of this kind *except* as a deliberate and conscious political act that dazzlingly exemplifies the radical potential for growth and change that lies within all human beings. The diversity of writings discussed in this book from the tragi-elegaic tone of *Testament of Youth* to the tragi-prophetic tone of *Three Guineas* reflects the multi-faceted subjectivities of their authors as valuing, loving, feeling and rational human beings. But a shifting, complex, contradictory subject is still a unitary one. It is this complex sense of identity that enters all forms of self-knowledge and helps to account for aesthetic responses which defy prediction and escape narrow definitions of determination.

Just as solipsism is the Scylla which may befall explanation placing an exclusive emphasis on artistic freedom, so determinism is the Charybdis which may await explanation taking no account whatsoever of individual creativity. Women are neither wholly determined by circumstances external to themselves nor are they wholly free agents with unfettered control over their lives. The truth lies somewhere in between. As Kate Fullbrook has put it, 'women are born into social structures which they did not make, but from which they nevertheless benefit or suffer, and which place boundaries around them making it hard to alter who or what they are, what they can say, what it is possible to think and do.'[60]

A historically-based study of women's writing must reveal how a woman's own expectation of her role, her function and her purpose, is tied to values and to conventions of the kind in which characters in her fiction are also enmeshed. Such ties are not, however, inescapable and women's attitudes often reflect the influence of oppositional, emergent or alternative

59. Wayne Booth, 'Freedom of Interpretation: Bakhtin and the Challenge of Feminist Criticism', in W.J.T. Mitchell (ed.), *The Politics of Interpretation* (Chicago: University of Chicago Press, 1982), pp.51–83.

60. *Free Women: Ethics and Aesthetics in Twentieth-Century Women's Fiction* (Hemel Hempstead: Harvester Wheatsheaf, 1990), p.6.

value systems and often express resistance (which may be personal or collective) to the restrictive expectations and ideologies of their day. Examples of such dissident attitudes are Lolly Willowes's decision to opt for rural freedom rather than urban conformity and the defiance of rigid sexual stratification expressed by Virginia Woolf through Orlando's evanescent and changing sexual identity.

The fiction of the woman writer (Sylvia Townsend Warner, Flora Mayor, Radclyffe Hall, Winifred Holtby, May Sinclair) is an index to her own sense of personal growth. As Katherine Mansfield observed, 'art is absolutely self-development'.[61] But it is also an index to the hard-won freedoms of women in the public sphere. My investigation of literary spinsterhood reveals many instances of the woman writer's protracted struggle for self-realisation and of the empathy between the writer who had largely broken free from convention and her character whose life was still hemmed in by it. Joan Ogden, the frustrated medical student in *The Unlit Lamp*, is not a self-portrait of Radclyffe Hall. Mary Jocelyn, the self-sacrificing daughter in *The Rector's Daughter*, is similarly not a self-portrait of Flora Mayor. However, they owe much to the insights and contrasts produced by the authors' very distance from their heroines' predicaments.

To argue that struggle is a constant in many women's lives is not to argue that all women are constantly engaged in struggle or that the actual form that any woman's struggle might take will always be one that other women can condone. But it *is* to point out that in practice most women are hardly ever simply downtrodden, are very rarely simply acquiescent, and are almost never simply subordinated, and that women's writing is often richly illuminating in relation to the desires of women to improve their own situations and to take control of their own lives. This process is often characterised by a mixture of set-backs and gains; for example, what may be lost in struggle against economic oppression may be gained in emotional strength and vice versa. Feminist critical practice insists that the acts of writing and reading fiction must always reflect more than an individual's quest for self-knowledge or personal liberation. To know oneself is not only an end in itself but also a means through which one becomes better able to know the world. To understand the complex and contradictory interplay between women's struggles in life and in art we need to remember that the representation of women, while it may be inscribed in ideology, has also always been closely tied to real, historically-constituted, social situations, to the specificity of real women's lives. As Virginia Woolf observed in 1928, literary works 'are not single and solitary births; they

61. John Middleton Murry (ed.), *The Journal of Katherine Mansfield* (London: Constable, 1954), p.37.

are the outcome of many years of thinking in common, of thinking by the body of the people, so that the experience of the mass is behind the single voice'.[62]

Feminist criticism, then, needs to work at the level of the textual and the contextual *and* to illuminate the relationships between the two. The job of feminist scholarship must be to negotiate between textual representations of women and women in 'the real world'. Though I have moved away from women in 'the real world' to engage with the specificity of the literary text, I have consistently returned to 'the real world' to provide an analysis that I hope may be of use to women now.

62. Virginia Woolf, *A Room of One's Own*, p.98.

–1–

Vera Brittain's *Testament of Youth* Revisited: Women's Autobiography, Gender, Nation and Class

I belong to the few who believe in all sincerity that their own lives provide the
answers to some of the many problems which puzzle humanity.

Vera Brittain, *Chronicle of Youth*[1]

When is a feminist text not a feminist text? I wish to question the status of
Testament of Youth, the autobiography of the pioneering feminist, Vera
Brittain.[2] *Testament of Youth* is the best-known account of the 1914 war
by a woman. Yet we should be clear from the beginning that *Testament of
Youth* is not simply about the First World War. On the contrary, the early
and middle sections of the work dramatise Brittain's childhood in
Derbyshire and her education at Oxford University, which she interrupted
to join in the war effort, working as a nurse in Malta, London and France.
The later sections of the book detail her friendship with Winifred Holtby
to the year 1925. The war years actually occupy approximately one-third
of the autobiography. Yet references to *Testament of Youth* are almost
invariably concerned with Brittain's account of her part in the 1914 war.
Indeed, the poignancy of the text owes much to the vivid contrast between
the youth and naïvety of Brittain and the extremities of suffering to which
she was subjected when hardly more than a girl. The length of *Testament
of Youth* is formidable, some six hundred pages. However, the
autobiography's accessible style and engaging subject-matter have helped
to explain its abiding popularity.

Testament of Youth remains the only account of a woman's experience
in wartime which is widely known and read today. The book was
introduced to readers with no memory of the events it depicted after the
feminist publishing house, Virago, re-issued it in 1978. It was reprinted

1. Vera Brittain, *Chronicle of Youth: War Diary 1913–1917*, (ed.) Alan Bishop with
Terry Smart (London: Gollancz, 1981), pp.13–14.
2. Vera Brittain, *Testament of Youth* (London: Gollancz, 1933). All subsequent
quotations are taken from this edition. Page numbers will follow in brackets.

that year, and again in 1979 and in 1981, and has stayed in print for most of the time since. A five-part serial of *Testament of Youth*, adapted for BBC television by Elaine Morgan, and starring the actress Cheryl Campbell as the young Vera Brittain, followed closely in 1979, and was repeated in 1980. The third screening of *Testament of Youth*, shown again as part of a television season on war and peace on BBC2, was in October 1992.

Much of the interest in the book has rested in its self-consciously woman-centred point of view:[3] 'I see things other than they have seen, and some of the things they [men – my insertion] perceive I see differently.'[4] Vera Brittain attributed the immediate success of *Testament of Youth* to 'the elementary but hitherto ignored circumstances' that 'women as well as men had endured war experiences, which had led them to certain common conclusions about the state of the world'.[5] Among the accolades that have been conferred upon *Testament of Youth* is 'the war book of the Women of England'.[6] This tribute would seem to suggest that we should read *Testament of Youth* not simply as one woman's account of the war but as the authoritative and representative, if not definitive, study of women's war experience. At various times in her career Vera Brittain herself has claimed representative status for her work, and has said that she believed her autobiography to speak for the desires, experiences and aspirations of her sex and generation. A re-evaluation of *Testament of Youth* is overdue.

On the surface, the reputation as a feminist text enjoyed by *Testament of Youth* for over half a century seems unassailable. On what basis should its monumental stature be questioned? The challenge to the authority of the autobiography must begin by establishing its own discursive authority, by tracing its own discursive history. To do that we must establish how the movement that speaks for women is not what it was, why the author of this book is not the woman she was. To do that we must visit, briefly, the debates within feminism of the last decade.

The women's liberation movement in the 1960s and 1970s was predicated on the notion that shared experience acted as the basis of communality of feeling between women. Let Rosalind Delmar tell the story: 'The unity of the movement was assumed to derive from a potential

3. For Brittain's feminism see Muriel Mellown, 'Vera Brittain: Feminist in a New Age 1896–1970', in D. Spender (ed.), *Feminist Theorists: Three Centuries of Women's Intellectual Traditions* (London: Women's Press, 1983), pp.314–34. I am specifically concerned with *Testament of Youth*. My argument is that *Testament of Youth* must be viewed problematically as a feminist text. I do not dispute that Vera Brittain was a feminist.
4. Vera Brittain, *Testament of Experience* (London: Gollancz, 1957), p.77.
5. Vera Brittain, *On Being an Author* (London: Macmillan, 1948), p.165. *Testament of Youth*, according to Brittain, had sold 127,000 copies by 1946.
6. See Vera Brittain, 'War Service in Perspective', in George A. Panichas (ed.) *Promise of Greatness: The War of 1914–1918* (London: Cassell, 1968), p.367.

identity between women. This concept of identity rested on the idea that women share the same experiences: an external situation in which they find themselves – economic oppression, commercial exploitation, legal discrimination are examples; and an internal response – the feeling of inadequacy, a sense of narrow horizons.'[7] In the 1970s little if any importance was generally attached to the ways in which the constellations of gender, race, nation, class, age, and sexual orientation made women's experiences diverge. However, throughout the last decade or so many black, Jewish, working-class, lesbian and disabled women have posed painful yet urgent questions to the ways in which women's oppression had originally been conceptualised. The theoretical dimensions of these social and political questions are, I think, best and most succinctly explained by Michèle Barrett as 'politically salient forms of experiential diversity'.[8] As it is from *within* feminism that this book is written, it is from *within* the broad consensus on the crucial importance of 'difference' that the critique of *Testament of Youth* must come. Indeed, it is that concensus which makes such a critique not only legitimate but also imperative.

There is general agreement among feminists that relationships of class and race, in their historically specific forms, have resembled relationships of gender in so far as they have conferred radically unequal opportunities for the development and satisfaction of human needs. Indeed, the contributors to a theoretical work on autobiography, *Life/Lines*, make it clear that gender is no longer the only situating category of interest to them as feminists.[9] Indifference to the problematics of genre as inflected by class, nation, gender or race in autobiographical criticism is no more tenable than the indifference to the problematics of genre as inflected by gender, of which well-known theorists of the autobiographical genre from James Olney to Georges Gusdorf have been indicted by feminist critics.[10] The importance now attached to experiential diversity within feminist thinking must surely challenge the very idea of a feminist text able to address concerns shared by all feminists. It also means that a text cannot be considered a fully feminist text if its treatment of any of the key factors of gender, nation, sexuality, sexual orientation, race and class, is seriously open to question. My critique will illuminate how *Testament of Youth* is coloured by the specific anxieties and concerns of Brittain's social class

7. 'What is Feminism?', in Juliet Mitchell and Ann Oakley (eds), *What is Feminism?* (Oxford: Blackwell, 1986), p.10.

8. 'The Concept of "Difference"', *Feminist Review*, 26, Summer 1987, pp.29–41, p.10.

9. See Bella Brodzki and Céleste Schenck (eds), *Life/Lines: Theorizing Women's Autobiography* (Ithaca: Cornell University Press, 1988).

10. For a feminist critique of Gusdorf's seminal work see Susan Stanford Friedman, 'Women's Autobiographical Selves', in Shari Benstock (ed.), *The Private Self: Theory and Practice of Women's Autobiographical Writings* (London: Routledge, 1988), pp.34–62.

to the detriment of women of other classes. I shall also argue that *Testament of Youth* effaces other versions of war experience which may contest its own representations. I believe that feminist criticism has a responsibility to assess texts as and when doubts arise in relation to their ideological projects. By illustrating how fundamentally flawed *Testament of Youth* is, in all the respects I have outlined, I shall argue that it can no longer be accepted as a feminist text.

Janet Varner Gunn has stressed the importance of two moments of reading. The moments specified are 'by the autobiographer who, in effect, is "reading" his or her life; and by the reader of the autobiographical text' who is also in encounter with the text, re-reading his or her own life by association.[11] Reading a text in diverse historical periods may result in reading out diverse ideological meanings and for this reason we should perhaps start with the moment of reception. Specifically, the reviews of 1933 show us that feminists contemporary with Brittain do not appear to have been overly troubled by the issues I have raised in relation to *Testament of Youth*. On the contrary, they appear to have accepted the professed feminism of the author and her text at face value. Brittain's attempts to break free from home, to be allowed to leave Buxton and to escape the living death of provincial young-ladyhood, clearly strike a sympathetic chord. The veteran suffragist, Evelyn Sharp, whose own account of childhood was evoked in the same year in *Unfinished Adventure*,[12] warms to Brittain's personal struggles which happened 'contemporaneously with the more dramatic struggle elsewhere for women's freedom'.[13] Another vindicator of women's freedoms, Rebecca West, ponders upon 'an interesting piece of social history, in its picture of the peculiarly unsatisfying position of women in England before the war'.[14]

Reading the numerous reviews of August and September 1933[15] one

11. Sidonie Smith, *Autobiography: Towards a Poetics of Experience* (Philadelphia: University of Philadelphia Press, 1982), p.8.

12. *Unfinished Adventure: Selected Reminiscenses from an Englishwoman's Life* (London: Lane, 1933).

13. Evelyn Sharp, *Manchester Guardian*, 29 August, 1933, p.5.

14. 'The Agony of the Human Soul in War', *Daily Telegraph*, 15 September, 1933, p.10.

15. These include (all 1933) Naomi Mitchison, *Week-End Review*, 26 August, p.212; Storm Jameson, *Yorkshire Post*, 28 August, p.6; Evelyn Sharp, *Manchester Guardian*, 29 August, p.5; anon., *Morning Post*, 29 August, p.6; anon., *Queen*, 30 August, p.16; anon., *The Times Literary Supplement*, 31 August, p.571; Compton McKenzie, *Daily Mail*, 31 August, p.4; Roger Pippel, *Daily Herald*, 31 August, p.13; Pamela Hinkson, *Time and Tide*, 2 September, pp.1038–9; Storm Jameson, *The Sunday Times*, 3 September, p.8; anon., *Punch*, 6 September, pp.278–9; anon., *Listener*, 6 September, p.366; anon., *Church Times*, 8 September, p.272; Rebecca West, *Daily Telegraph*, 15 September, p.10; *New Statesman & Nation*, 16 September, p.332. A diary entry for 19 September states that 15,000 copies had been sold. See Alan Bishop (ed.), *Chronicle of Friendship: Diary of the Thirties 1932–1939* (London: Gollancz, 1986).

becomes aware how many critics were unable to challenge Brittain's positions because they were caught in the same historical moment and the same class structure. Indeed, a fresh significance becomes attached to the fact that a reviewer (Storm Jameson, Pamela Hinkson, Rebecca West, Naomi Mitchison) was born in the 1890s as was Vera Brittain.[16] 'It is the story of a generation – of mine and it may be yours. It recalls that moment of time in which we grew up – near enough the Victorian confidence, security, and self-discipline, to feel ourselves confident, and sharply enough aware of its cruelties to execrate them,' writes Storm Jameson in *The Sunday Times*.[17] References to the double significance of *Testament of Youth* as memory and as warning ('plenty of warning now for the young, if they will hear it')[18] are to be found in profusion. Pamela Hinkson 'can think of no book more likely to help to avert such another calamity than this, if everyone were to be obliged to read it'.[19]

Scrutinising these reviews one becomes more and more aware of how much power is exercised by the determinants of class and of age. It begins to seem that they overwhelm judgement even, that they *cannot* be challenged. One hopes that somewhere there will be an exceptional review, an exceptional reviewer. And at last comes Naomi Mitchison. Mitchison's path had crossed with Vera Brittain as an undergraduate at Oxford University. She too had served as a VAD nurse during the 1914 war. Her review of *Testament of Youth* asks us to see in the autobiography a naïvety which the reviewer herself can understand but not exonerate. It is authoritative precisely because Mitchison is able to write from the perspective of a participant in the war; able to speak with disarming authority and to make strange much (such as the connection between war and patriotism) that had hitherto seemed entirely natural. For Naomi Mitchison sees Vera Brittain not as the autobiographer sees herself, nor as Brittain would wish others to regard her. She perceives her not as prescient nor discerning but as the very opposite. To Mitchison, Brittain was not 'one of the rare adults who saw through what was being done to them; she did not realise that she and her generation were being smashed up and killed, not for honour and love of a dear community, but to uphold a system which they had scarcely thought about, but would have known as evil if they had.'[20]

Vera Brittain provides diverse and contradictory accounts of the genesis

16. Vera Brittain (b.1893); Storm Jameson (b.1891); Pamela Hinkson (b. 1900); Rebecca West (b.1892); Naomi Mitchison (b.1897).
17. Storm Jameson, 'Miss Vera Brittain's Poignant Book'.
18. Naomi Mitchison, 'This is What Happened', op. cit., p.212.
19. Pamela Hinkson, 'A Legacy', p.1039.
20. Naomi Mitchison, op. cit.

of *Testament of Youth* and I have selected some of the key points she makes in order that her own claims in relation to the text may be evaluated.

(1) What mattered was not that, at long last, this autobiography brought 'success', but that it created spiritual reassurance.

(2) After reading these books, I began to ask: 'Why should these young men have the war to themselves? Didn't women have their war as well? They weren't, as these men make them, only suffering wives and mothers, or callous parasites, or mercenary prostitutes. Does no one remember the women who began their war work with such high ideals, or how grimly they carried on when that flaming faith had crumbled into the grey ashes of disillusion? Who will write the epic of the women who went to the war?'

(3) With scientific precision, I studied the memoirs of Blunden, Sassoon and Graves. Surely, I thought, my story is as interesting as theirs? Besides, I see things other than they have seen, and some of the things they perceive I see differently.

(4) I meant to make my story as truthful as history but as readable as fiction, and in it I intended to speak, not for those in high places, but for my own generation of obscure young women.[21]

In descriptions of her project, Vera Brittain reveals tensions which are replicated in the text, tensions between the personal and the public, the subjective and the objective, and the unique and the representative voices. The autobiographical mode of writing dramatises the subject of the autobiography and makes the 1914 war knowable to the reader only in specific terms. Historical interpretations of the war are suspect in certain particulars, such as their exclusive focus on men. Literary interpretations are suspect in other particulars, their reductive representations of women. Both are refuted. Veering between the first and the third person ('my story', 'women have their war'), Brittain constructs a specific picture of the war. In her picture the unsung contribution of women (active, idealistic, and stoical) is the hitherto unrecognised counterpart to the heroism of men.

Vera Brittain discloses the modest and therapeutic aims behind her decision to write the text – to excise pain and record personal experience ('spiritual reassurance'). But these aims are quickly subsumed into a larger and more ambitious project. Her intention to inscribe women into the history of the war is married to the aim of investing the women's war effort with the heroic properties implicit in the term 'epic'. This is manifestly a term which Brittain could not have used had she had a different idea of the importance of women's part in the war or a less exalted notion of her own role as its chronicler and participant.

The importance of the idea of a uniquely personal voice ('my story is as interesting as theirs') and of a gendered viewpoint ('didn't women have

21. Brittain, *Testament of Experience*, pp.76–7.

their war as well?') is in its turn undercut by the weighty aim of representing a generation, and then of assessing the general significance of the war years. The focus of attention shifts from women to people, from women's war experiences to the war experiences of her own class. Consequently, attempting to weld together these very different elements, Vera Brittain constructs a text which is peculiarly fraught with tensions and contradictions. Not all these tensions and contradictions are peculiar to *Testament of Youth*. On the contrary, many are to be found in other memoirs of the 1914 war situated on the margins of the literary and the historical. Furthermore, in *The Great War and Modern Memory* Paul Fussell has noted that the special qualities of such memoirs have often been overlooked 'because too few readers have attended to their fictional character, preferring to confound them with "documentary" or "history".'[22]

Women's Autobiography, a set of essays edited by Estelle Jelinek,[23] is the first theoretical work to attempt to establish a distinct women's tradition of autobiographical writing and a useful starting point from which to explore some of the problems raised by *Testament of Youth*. Arguing that women's autobiographies may constitute 'if not a subgenre, then an autobiographical tradition different from the male tradition',[24] Jelinek suggests that there are important differences between autobiographies written by men and by women. Citing the critical consensus to the effect that 'a good autobiography not only focuses on its author but also reveals his connectedness to the rest of society; it is representative of his times, a mirror of his era',[25] Jelinek refers to a number of autobiographies by men. She observes that 'men tend to idealize their lives or to cast them into heroic molds to project their universal import'.[26] The life stories of men are often success stories and Jelinek notes that 'the proclivity of men toward embellishing their autobiographies results in the projection of a self-image of confidence, no matter what difficulties they may have encountered'.[27] She contends that 'the idealization or aggrandizement found in male autobiographies is not typical of the female mode'.[28] Women's autobiographies, she states, 'rarely mirror the establishment history of their times. They emphasize to a much lesser extent the public aspects of their lives'.[29]

22. *The Great War and Modern Memory* (Oxford: Oxford University Press, 1975), p.312.
23. *Women's Autobiography: Essays in Criticism* (Bloomington and London: Indiana University Press, 1980).
24. Ibid., p.6.
25. Ibid., p.7.
26. Ibid., p.14.
27. Ibid., p.15.
28. Ibid.
29. Ibid., p.7.

According to Jelinek, the distinctive emphasis of women autobiographers is on the personal, especially on other people. For the most part, her argument runs, women do not see themselves as legends or representatives of their times, as critics interpret the self-image in men's autobiographies. Instead, women write from a perspective adjacent or peripheral to men's experience. Jelinek argues that 'irregularity rather than orderliness informs the self-portraits by women'.[30] Women's autobiographies, she claims, may be discontinuous even when linear. These discontinuous forms are often not chronological and progressive but disconnected and fragmentary and thus analogous to the 'fragmented, interrupted and formless' nature of women's lives.[31]

But would a comparison of twentieth-century autobiographies with the lives of women written at times when women were denied access to the public sphere raise questions about the effects of diverse material conditions on women's lives? Are the differences that Jelinek cites in order to establish a specifically female mode of perception more properly understood as historical rather than sexual in nature? After all, psycho-sexual identity does not coincide with biological identity and, as Domna C. Stanton has shown, conventions about propriety in self-revelation are historically and culturally determined.[32] Does Jelinek's inclusion of diaries and memoirs stretch the autobiographical genre beyond its limits? Furthermore, have not large numbers of men also written diaries and journals and placed a high value on fragmentation, diffuseness and discontinuous forms? How do we explain the confessional mode of spiritual, romantic and sexual autobiography from St. Augustine to Rousseau? As Liz Stanley has argued, some autobiographies by men are overwhelmingly concerned with others, for example Henry James, with his brother William, while some autobiographies by women, for example Rosemary Manning's, are as egocentric as any man's.[33]

Notwithstanding the valuable insights generated by Jelinek's important attempt to displace existing paradigms, the generalisations in *Women's Autobiography* do not really measure up to careful scrutiny. Ultimately, one is forced to question the extent to which the autobiographies discussed have been selected precisely because they conform to her prescriptions. One suspects that the reason why there is hardly a reference to the most influential autobiography by a twentieth-century feminist, Simone de

30. Ibid., p.17.
31. Ibid., p.19.
32. Domna C. Stanton, 'Autogynography: Is the Subject Different?', in Domna C. Stanton (ed.), *The Female Autograph: Theory and Practice of Autobiography from the Tenth to the Twentieth Century* (Chicago: University of Chicago Press, 1984), pp.3–20.
33. 'Moments of Writing: Is There a Feminist Auto/Biography?', *Gender & History*, 2, 1, Spring 1990, pp.58, 65.

Beauvoir's *Memoirs of a Dutiful Daughter*, in *Women's Autobiography* is the difficulties that it would raise for anyone attempting to assimilate it into Estelle Jelinek's model.

However, it is possible to recognise major theoretical problems inherent in Jelinek's analysis yet still to find the criteria which she establishes useful when assessing specific biographies. *Testament of Youth* does not conform to her expectations of an autobiography written in 'the female mode'. This is very largely because the majority of women autobiographers do not project an image of self as representatives of their age nor, for that matter, do they claim the public significance for their work that Brittain does for *Testament of Youth*. It is also due in part to Brittain's passionate identification with the young men from the highly educated sections of her own social class who died in the 1914 war. The desire to commemorate the ideals for which Brittain believes these men voluntarily sacrificed their lives produces a self-image that is less diffident and more assertive than many images of self in women's autobiography. Moreover, because the source of Brittain's authority is her unswerving conviction in the rightness of her own beliefs, she produces a self-image that is the antithesis of that in many autobiographies which conform to 'the female mode' of autobiographical writing. As Martin Rintala has astutely, if somewhat unkindly, observed, 'Brittain's personalized writing was not simply the subconscious expression of a substantial ego. It was a conscious expression of a substantial ego.'[34]

Testament of Youth, for all its anti-war sentiments and its emphasis on the authority of a woman's perspective, ultimately belongs within the realm of 'dominant memory' as opposed to 'popular memory'. I use these two terms as they have been defined and elaborated by the Popular Memory Group.[35] The autobiography constructs a picture of autobiographical self in relation to society which, if it does not strictly mirror the thinking of the social and political establishment of the time, is still a picture that the establishment did not find uncongenial. *Testament of Youth* offers a view of war 'from above' which does not question the idea of nation or the ideology of Englishness under which the war is conducted, rather than a view which properly reflects the discontents and ambivalent feelings about the war of those 'below'.

An example of a 'popular memory' text written by a woman is Maya Angelou's autobiography, *I Know Why the Caged Bird Sings*.[36] To judge

34. 'Chronicler of a Generation: Vera Brittain's Testament', *Journal of Political and Military Sociology*, 12, Spring 1984, p.23.
35. 'Popular Memory. Theory, Politics, Method', in Richard Johnson et al. (eds), *Making Histories: Studies in History-Writing and Politics* (London: Hutchinson and Birmingham University Centre for Contemporary Cultural Studies, 1982), p.239.
36. *I Know Why the Caged Bird Sings* (New York: Random House, 1969).

from her autobiography, Angelou's *bios* (experience) and her *aute* (sense of identity) are clearly no less the product of her specific class and racial position than are Brittain's. *I Know Why the Caged Bird Sings* tells the story of a young, poor, black woman who was raped at the age of eight. It tells, movingly and searingly, the story of how Angelou later became pregnant as the result of a single, loveless sexual encounter at the age of sixteen. No matter how seriously Angelou takes herself, she remains poor, black, and a woman with multiple disadvantages. She cannot assume significance within the dominant order of white middle-class America except, somewhat ironically, as the author of a successful autobiographical text which vividly dramatises a black woman's experience of poverty, and racial and sexual prejudice. In the process of writing a past the author must inevitably write from the vantage point of a survivor. In this sense what holds true for Brittain also holds true for Angelou. But if the jettisoning of some, or all, of the conditions which motivated the writer to write does not itself necessarily invalidate her representations, we should perhaps ask what does? The answer, I think, is related to the text's reception; to its repudiation by readers who see themselves as subject to (and their own role as attempting to change) the myriad of oppressive ideologies which constrict the lives of women and from which success almost inevitably abstracts the autobiographer. This is the point at which the question 'when is a feminist text not a feminist text?' must be be put.

What ironically confirms Vera Brittain's membership of the dominant order is her perception of the world as hostile. This is most acutely felt after her return to Somerville College, Oxford, after the war. Yet the rebel whose text projects a hostile world against which she struggles to define her own identiy is only able to take herself seriously because her right to a place within the dominant order is *already assured*. It is only in the certainty of membership that the certainty of rebellion can be asserted. Objectively, there were few external barriers to prevent Vera Brittain becoming a success after leaving Oxford University. Maya Angelou's sense of the world as hostile is real not illusory. That reality is clearly not the projection of her subjective personal angst. It is the result of the deeply entrenched racist attitudes that her autobiography painfully evokes. Such racism is amply confirmed in countless oral and written testimonies which make up the 'popular memory' of black people in the southern states of America.

The central and founding myth on which *Testament of Youth* is based is the idea of the lost generation which is typified by Brittain's brother, Edward and her fiancé, Roland Leighton. In *The Generation of 1914*, the historian, Robert Wohl, has shown how the idea of a lost generation 'referred simultaneously to the severe losses suffered within a small and clearly defined ruling class and to the difficulties that survivors from this class (and others below it) had in adjusting to the political and social realities of postwar England'.[37] The myth of the missing generation provided an 'important self-image for the survivors from within the educated elite and a psychologically satisfying and perhaps even necessary explanation of what happened to them after they returned from the war'.[38] Wohl explains how the cult of the dead became for many who had been psychologically and physically injured by the war a means of accounting for the disappointments of the present: 'By focusing on the extraordinary virtues of those who fell . . . the survivors from within the privileged classes accounted for the depressing disparity between their dreams and their accomplishments.'[39]

Myths are the shared frameworks of explanation whereby cultures impose order upon potential confusion. But they are more than this. The myths of any community are the cement by which that community coheres as a whole and withstands the external pressures which threaten to pull it apart. As Frank Kermode has argued, 'we have a common project, truth in poverty, and a common need, solidarity of plight in diversity of state'. Therefore, the fictions that we live by must be complex enough to speak to our shared situations and to seek out the origins of our personal pain and confusion for 'without paradox and contradiction our parables will be too simple for a complex poverty, too consolatory to console'.[40] The real purpose of myth is to explain the inexplicable. In this sense neither the rational basis of the lost generation myth, nor its historical accuracy, is of immediate concern to us here. The myth was indubitably resilient not because it spoke to the intellect but because it spoke compellingly to the emotions. What matters about a social myth is not its foundation but its function. Accordingly, the myth of the lost generation (as we find it incarnated in *Testament of Youth*) can be properly understood only by analysing its specific ideological effects. My own interest in how the notion of the lost generation functions in the Brittain autobiography is not only in what the myth expresses, and in what it permits to be voiced, but also in what it represses and excludes.

One of the typical features of the autobiographical mode is that the

37. *The Generation of 1914* (London: Weidenfeld and Nicolson, 1980), p.120. Wohl points out that most men who served in the 1914 war returned. British casualties were fewer than any other major European nation. The lost generation, therefore, had a stronger basis in myth than fact.

38. Ibid., p.115.

39. Ibid., p.116. Wohl has been criticised for minimising the perspectives of non-combatants and for defining a generation not as a social fact but as an intellectual fantasy. See Simon Schama, 'To and From the Slaughter', *The Times Literary Supplement*, 16 May, 1980, p.559.

40. *The Sense of an Ending: Studies in the Theory of Fiction* (Oxford: Oxford University Press, 1966), p.164.

relationship between the authorial subject – the 'I' central to the narrative (and to a particular social group such as the working class) – and the narrative movement is peculiarly complex. As Julia Swindells notes, a class-conscious autobiographer 'invests in furthering not only the individual, the autobiographical self, moving through the narrative and through society'.[41] This type of autobiography 'carries the freight of a narrative direction which subsumes the autobiographical "I", with its conventional association with individualism, in the interests of a particular social group'.[42] In *Testament of Youth* the central figure claims a direct relationship to not one but two groups. The formulation 'my generation of obscure young women' harnesses 'my generation' and 'obscure young women' in an uneasy and somewhat incongruent union.

Let us examine the formulation carefully. In what, if any, sense might the privileged, middle class, Vera Brittain, a promising Oxford undergraduate in 1914 (and a published novelist and successful journalist when *Testament of Youth* was published in 1933) be said to speak for 'obscure young women'?[43] What it seems we are faced with is a double tension. There is a stress in these words on uniqueness, on subjectivity implicit in the dramatisation of self, and there is also a stress on representativeness, implicit in the obligation of the professional writer and social historian to produce an account of events which is ramifying and extends beyond its individual context. This double imperative, the impulse to merge the self with the group (and to mingle the unique and the representative) is perhaps the surest indicator of Brittain's dilemma in attempting to establish the discursive authority to interpret herself as a woman, and of her burning desire to write as a feminist which, until this point, I have acknowledged insufficiently.

For Vera Brittain, group identity defined both the parameters of oppression *and* of liberation. In the formulation 'my generation of obscure young women' there resides both an affirmation of the importance of the individual woman and a pointed resistance to the idea of individual destiny. Thus Brittain foreshadows the emphasis attached to personal liberation, and to the ideals of sisterhood and collectivity, which were to become the hallmarks of the women's liberation movement in the 1960s and 1970s. An exceptional woman writing as a woman, Brittain inscribes – with a confidence no longer possible – the claim to speak for other women. Thus

41. *Victorian Writing and Working Women: The Other Side of Silence* (Cambridge: Polity, 1985), p.139.
42. Ibid.
43. Brittain was not as consistently modest as this claim to obscurity might imply. She objected to being termed "a negligible writer" by Phyllis Bentley. See Alan Bishop and Terry Smart (eds), *Chronicle of Friendship: Vera Brittain's Diary of the Thirties, 1932–1939* (London: Gollancz, 1986), p.145.

the difficulties *Testament of Youth* presents for women of a later generation. Today women are positioned diversely by their gender, race, class, nation, age and sexual orientation – as were women in Vera Brittain's day. But the difference is that later feminists understand why this is the case. And from that knowledge comes resistance – to interpolation into collectivities of the kind which Brittain believed possible but to which feminists in the 1990s have ceased to subscribe.

At the level of autobiographical narrative the closed discourse focusing on the central figure is constructed out of the open facts of a real life. But, as Julia Swindells points out, the imitation of patterns of behaviour derived from literary sources, melodrama, romance, and so on, is an almost inescapable part of the construction of personal subjectivity.[44] The ordering of events in *Testament of Youth* follows the familiar literary pattern of stasis, disruption and closure whereby ideologically functional moments and images are dramatised into narrative coherence. The happy childhood of the young Brittain is tragically brought to an end by the outbreak of war, the idyll disrupted, the golden summer ended. Heeding her nation's call she serves her country as a nurse abroad. Returning home she finds an alien world. In this bright new world the survivors of Armageddon are no longer wanted.

This narrative pattern confirms in every detail the myth of the lost generation which was on the verge of hardening into a generally accepted interpretation of recent history by 1933. In *Testament of Youth* Brittain relays back to her generation a sharpened awareness of their common historical experience and of their common fate. The account in *Testament of Youth* both advances the collective consciousness of the social group and reflects for its approval that which the social group already wanted to believe was true. Thus *Testament of Youth* is at once constituted by and reconstitutive of the idea of the lost generation, reproducing the essence of that idea in its 'structures of feeling'. This is a term which Raymond Williams most concisely defined at the end of *Marxism and Literature* as 'confronting a hegemony in the fibres of the self and in the hard practical substance of effective and continuing relationships'.[45]

The role *Testament of Youth* performs in relation to women is altogether more complex because women were not combatants in the First World War and did not die in any sizeable numbers alongside the men whom they loved. There is no myth corresponding to the lost generation originating directly in women's first-hand experience of war. Although parts of the lost generation myth could be borrowed inventively for their purposes, the expectation of power, 'the promise of greatness' which the myth in its

44. Swindells, *Victorian Writing and Working Women*, p.140.
45. *Marxism and Literature* (Oxford: Oxford University Press, 1977), p.212.

essence promised, was largely irrelevant to women's lives. But in so far as they were left to face life after the war without those closest to them; the fathers, lovers, brothers, and sons who had died, the notion of a lost generation spoke articulately to their sense of anguish and was, for many women, not just a myth but reality. In the absence of any narrative able to sum up their situation more aptly, women were quick to utilise the lost generation myth imaginatively in their writing; assiduously perpetuating it in best-selling novels such as Ruth Holland's in *The Lost Generation* and May Wedderburn Cannan's *The Lonely Generation*. The literary mobilisation of the lost generation myth by women in semi-autobiographical fictions of this type often reveals a desire on their part to live vicariously through men, or some degree of male-identification, or else a strong sense of loyalty to the values of the élite of officers and gentleman from which some, albeit a minority, of the men who died belonged (as we have seen to be the case in *Testament of Youth*).

Until the development of her relationship with Winifred Holtby in the final sections of *Testament of Youth*[46] the accent in the autobiography falls very heavily upon the men in Vera Brittain's life. Apart from a teacher at school, and a don at Oxford, she had no women mentors. Women friends are a structuring absence in the autobiography. Both the war diary ('Alas! Sometimes it feels sad to be a woman! Men seem to have so much choice as to what they are intended for')[47] and the text of unpublished letters to Roland ('wish desperately that I were a man')[48] clearly intimate the young Vera's regret at having been born a woman. As Lynne Layton has suggested, it was the war itself which enabled Brittain to recover her sense of identification as a woman which she had hitherto repressed, and subsequently to form the working partnership with Winifred Holtby which was among the most important relationships in her life.[49]

Testament of Youth is the work of a feminist whose feminism began with an adolescent reading of Olive Schreiner's *The Story of an African Farm*.[50] Yet it is clear that Brittain, unlike her friend Winifred Holtby, does not view a desire for emotional closeness to other women as an essential component of her feminist conviction. In Holtby's short story, 'So Handy for the

46. I refer to this relationship only in passing here as Jean Kennard has analysed it in depth. See Jean E. Kennard, *Vera Brittain and Winifred Holtby: A Working Partnership* (Hanover: University Press of New England, 1989).

47. Brittain, *Chronicle of Youth*, pp.32–3.

48. Letter from Vera Brittain to Roland Leighton, dated 19 February 1916. Quoted Lynne Layton, 'Vera Brittain's Testament(s)', in Margaret Randolph Higgonet et al. (eds), *Behind the Lines: Gender and the Two World Wars* (New Haven: Yale University Press, 1987), p.73.

49. Ibid., p.82.

50. *The Story of an African Farm: A Novel in Two Volumes* (London: Chapman and Hall), 1883.

Funfair', a former WAAC uses the occasion of a week-end Bank Holiday excursion to Boulogne to slip away from her family and to re-visit the places where she was stationed happily during the war. On her precious day out she remembers affectionately the women with whom she once served.[51] Vera Brittain, on the other hand, expresses consternation at having to live in close proximity with 'VADs with strange accents and stranger underclothes'.(p.254) These women, we are informed, would have understood 'a sentimental, dependent sorrow, with hair-stroking at bedtime and hand-holdings in the dark'. But they were not unnaturally 'baffled by an aloof, rigid grief, which abhorred their sympathy, detested their collective gigglings and prattlings'.(p.274) The family servants during the war are 'ever-changing, inefficient', a 'rag-tag and bob-tail selection of girls'. Virtually all we are told about them is that one is 'several months pregnant' and that another is 'an amateur prostitute'.(p.429)

Winifred Holtby felt no need to create artifical barriers of this kind. She wrote that a former WAAF cook, Pugh, was 'older, and wiser, and stronger in almost any way than I am!' Asked to supply a testimonial for Pugh, who wanted to travel to New Zealand, Holtby remarked: 'Isn't it silly?'[52] Class divisions were, of course, rigid during the inter-war period and found outward expression through accent and dress. The point I make here is that Winifred Holtby's attitudes to working-class women were in many respects exceptional and that Vera Brittain's are those commonly found among members of her own class. While I do not dispute the inappropriateness of judging Brittain's conduct as a feminist by the standards of a later age, to judge her by the standards of her closest friend would seem perfectly in order. The obvious contrast to be drawn throws any theoretical claim to speak on behalf of other women seriously into question.

Vera Brittain's loyalty to the men of her generation is nurtured by an acute sense of grievance caused by her conviction that the excellence for which they stood has disappeared to be replaced by mediocrity. She paints a bleakly pessimistic picture of the post-war world as 'lacking first-rate ability and social order and economic equilibrium . . . spinning down into chaos as fast as it can – unless some of us try to prevent it' (p.472) and contrasts her own generation and the one below it which seems deficient in every respect. On Armistice day, she muses that 'already this was a different world . . . in which people would be light-hearted and forgetful, in which themselves and their careers and their amusements would blot

---

51. 'So Handy for the Funfair', in Winifred Holtby, *Truth is not Sober* (London: Collins, 1934), pp.151–72.

52. Letter from Winifred Holtby to 'Rosalind', dated 20 October, 1920, in Alice Holtby and Jean McWilliam (eds), *Letters to a Friend* (London: Collins, 1937), p.23.

out political ideas and great national issues. And in that brightly lit, alien world I should have no part.'(p.462)

In *Testament of Youth* Vera Brittain tells the story of how she was courted, first shyly, but later with growing persistence, by the young academic, George Catlin. She had until that point deliberately avoided the potential dangers of close emotional relationships, had dedicated herself to the memory of the dead, and reconciled herself to a life of loneliness. It was only because Catlin was of her age and generation – he was twenty-eight, she thirty when he proposed to her – that she felt able to marry him. She was certain in her own mind that, 'Had he been post-war I could not under any circumstances have married him, for within the range of my contemporaries a gulf wider than any decade divides those who experienced the War as adults from their juniors by only a year or two who grew up immediately afterwards.'(pp.617–18) What is mourned in *Testament of Youth* is not simply a set of lost friends but a set of lost class relationships as well. Examined closely, many of Brittain's affirmations of loyalty to her generation are also affirmations of loyalty to her class. One needs, I think, to be clear about what happens when Brittain carries élitist and hierarchical values beyond the grave as in *Testament of Youth*. In so doing she does not merely ask us to endorse such values in the context of the past; she asks us to affirm and perpetuate them in the present.

In the early parts of *Testament of Youth* the emphasis is on specific personal memories which reach back to a time prior to the deep and traumatic change brought about by the war. There is an emphasis here on Brittain's need to retain and to endorse a specific set of perceptions of the world which has vanished. George Lakoff and Mark Johnson have explained that 'as the circumstances of our lives change, we constantly revise our life stories, seeking new coherence'.[53] In *A Poetics of Women's Autobiography* Sidonie Smith describes how the autobiographer invests the past and the self with a coherence and meaning which may not have been evident before the act of writing itself. The autobiographer 'has to rely on a trace of something from the past, a memory; yet memory is ultimately a story about, and thus a discourse on, original experience'.[54] Attempts to recover the past, Smith continues, thus become 'not a hypostasizing of fixed grounds and absolute origins but, rather, an interpretation of earlier experience that can never be divorced from the filterings of subsequent experience or articulated outside the structures of language and storytelling'. The use of the past in *Testament of Youth* is often as a witness for conservative values and traditional ways of seeing.

53. *Metaphors We Live By* (Chicago: University of Chicago Press, 1980), pp.174–5.
54. *A Poetics of Women's Autobiography: Marginality and the Fictions of Self-Representation* (Bloomington: Indiana University Press, 1987), p.45.

It is recalled in what Roger Bromley has termed '"pressed flower" terms', that is to say that the past is 'torn from its roots and simply invoked as a witnesss for contemporary, dominant values'.[55]

One effect of Vera Brittain's attachment to the 1914 war is to render traumatic any encounter with antithetical perspectives which may require her to justify, rather than merely to rehearse or elaborate, her own position. Brittain provides two conflicting accounts of such a traumatic situation; a debate at Somerville in which she spoke and was resoundingly defeated. The first, the fictionalised account, is provided in her novel, *The Dark Tide*, in 1922, the second in *Testament of Youth* ten years later. In the later account Brittain is able to create considerable sympathy for herself by alleging that the Somerville debate was set up by other students specifically to ridicule her as 'neither a respect-worthy volunteer in a national cause nor a surviving victim of history's cruellest catastrophe' but 'merely a figure of fun, ludicrously boasting of her experiences in an already demode [sic] conflict'.(p.493)

However, the imperatives of fiction do not allow for the repression of antithetical perspectives in the same way as in autobiography. The credible presentation of the Oxford debate within a novel necessitates the reader being made aware of the views of characters other than the author's surrogate, Virginia, of whom a character in *The Dark Tide* remarks, '"the whole Third Year's just about sick of her; she treats all of us as if we weren't fit to black her stupid little boots"'.[56] The discriminating reader who comes to *Testament of Youth* after *The Dark Tide* will find a factual account of the Somerville debate in the autobiography which her previous reading of the dramatised account of the same event in the novel must lead her to conclude is singularly implausible. While Vera Brittain does recognise the gulf that separates her from other women, she makes no attempt to bring about reconciliation, simply rounding off the Oxford episode in *Testament of Youth* with the words: 'After that, until I left college, I never publicly mentioned the War again.'(p.493)

Paul Eakin has argued that it is as 'reasonable to assume that all autobiography has some fiction in it as it is to recognise that all fiction is in some sense necessarily autobiographical'.[57] Simone de Beauvoir, for example, candidly admits to self-censorship caused by her awareness of the existence of a critical reading public with the powers to repudiate or to reject her work: 'I cannot treat the years of my maturity in the same detached way – nor do I enjoy a similar freedom when discussing them

55. *Lost Narratives: Popular Fictions, Politics and Recent History* (London: Routledge and Kegan Paul, 1988), p.26.

56. Brittain, *The Dark Tide* (London: Richards, 1923), pp.44–5.

57. *Fictions in Autobiography: Studies in the Art of Self-Invention* (Princeton, New Jersey: Princeton University Press, 1985), p.10.

. . . There are many things which I firmly intend to leave in obscurity.'[58] Vera Brittain was clearly aware of the fictional elements in *Testament of Youth* ('as truthful as history but as readable as fiction').[59] She was also conscious of the impossibility of relying on memory for accurate recall of events which took place many years earlier. A diary entry of 1933 records the insecurity that leads her to engage in 'imaginary arguments' with supposed critics of her autobiography and admits to anxiety, '& fear of numerous inaccuracies through queer tricks of memory'.[60]

We may, of course, be no better placed as readers to verify the truth of an autobiographical act, i.e. an act of self-invention formalised in writing, than we are to verify the supposed truth of any author's past as narrated in fiction. On the contrary, our understanding of the extent to which an author manipulates her material, whether consciously or unconsciously, rather than casting doubts upon the authenticity or verisimilitude of the work in question, may actually help to endorse it. Indeed, the claims of truth and of the imagination involved in any attempt to tell a life history in narrative form may not be antithetical. For as Shari Benstock has put it, 'without *graphe* autobiography would not exist . . . it is known only through the writing'.[61]

Vera Brittain tells how in writing *Testament of Youth* she consciously kept close to the techniques of fiction, using the same graphic characterisation, the same direct presentation of scenes, the same arrangement of incidents in order to emphasise the drama and suspense of the story.[62] When asked by an American critic if she thought *Testament of Youth* "'a novel masquerading as autobiography'" she replied that she thought of it as "'an autobiography masquerading as a novel'".[63] The literary influences on *Testament of Youth* are pronounced. The literary itself provides the key to the construction in the text of self and loves, and it conditions, to a considerable degree, the actual presentation of the war. In contrast to Henri Barbusse (*Under Fire*) or Eric Mottram (*The Spanish Farm*), who recognised the messy business of war for what it was (and that recognition entailed a reluctance to simplify the complexities of human behaviour), Brittain clung to an essentially romantic concept of war as the locus of heroic acts.

As a writer Vera Brittain was drawn to literary traditions which translated the unpalatable facts of human suffering into lofty diction. Thus

58. *The Prime of Life*, Peter Green (trans.), (Deutsch and Weidenfeld and Nicolson, 1962), p.10.
59. Brittain, *Testament of Experience*, p.77.
60. Brittain, *Chronicle of Friendship*, p.147.
61. Benstock, *The Private Self*, p.30.
62. Brittain, *On Becoming a Writer* (London: Hutchinson, 1947), p.88.
63. Ibid.

she admires Charles Kingsley's *The Heroes*, with its stirring reference to those who are slain 'in the flower of youth on the chance of winning a noble name' which she had loved as a girl.[64] She found Rupert Brooke's *Sonnets* 'unhackneyed, courageous, and almost shattering in their passionate, relevant idealism'.(p.155) In three of Brittain's novels which make reference to the war, *The Dark Tide* (1923), *Not without Honour* (1924) and *Honourable Estate* (1936),[65] three characters who possess patriotic sensibilities, Virginia, Christine, and Ruth, are favourably contrasted to those who do not express feelings of loyalty to their country. In *Not Without Honour* the central protagonist, Christine, is converted into a passionate believer in the justice of the allied cause after the death of her fiancé, Albert. In a much later novel, *Honourable Estate*, the heroine, Ruth, cherishes the memory of her American lover, Eugene, who is also killed in action. In all of these novels Brittain manages to infuse a quality of absolute perfection into each doomed relationship.

As late as 1933 (*Testament of Youth*) and 1936 (*Honourable Estate*), Vera Brittain's love for the men she had lost in the 1914 war is responsible for literary representations of idealistic young soldiers virtually indistinguishable from the stereotypes of the English schoolboys who meet their deaths in battle in Ernest Raymond's popular patriotic novel, *Tell England*, a best-seller in 1922.[66] As remarkable as the relatively uncomplicated romantic chauvinism which surfaces in Brittain's writing is the fact that she never felt the need to repudiate it. *Testament of Youth*, written when Brittain was a pacifist in the 1930s, nevertheless defends and displays the patriotic sensibilities of two decades earlier. A Vice-President of the Women's International League for Peace and Freedom, Vera Brittain was, it appears, unable to see patriotic attitudes as a major impediment to the attainment of the goals to which the League aspired.

In an important essay, 'The Other Voice: Autobiographies of Women Writers',[67] Mary Mason has argued that the disclosure of the female self in autobiography is often linked to the identification of some 'other'. This grounding of identity through relation to the chosen 'other' enables women to write openly about themselves. This 'other' for Vera Brittain is her fiancé, Roland Leighton, a school friend of her brother, Edward. Poems signed RAL or VB introduce each chapter of *Testament of Youth*, allowing the reader a privileged entry into the intimate emotional world which Vera

64. Brittain, *Thrice a Stranger* (London: Gollancz, 1938), p.220.
65. Brittain, *Not Without Honour* (London: Richards, 1924), *Honourable Estate: A Novel of Transition* (London: Gollancz, 1936).
66. *Tell England: A Study in a Generation* (London: Cassell, 1922).
67. 'The Other Voice: Autobiographies of Women Writers', in James Olney (ed.), *Autobiography: Essays Theoretical and Critical* (Princeton, New Jersey: Princeton University Press, 1980); reprinted in Life/Lines, pp.19–44.

and Roland shared. As Ruth Higgins has noted, the irrregularity of the poems which date from 1913 to 1933, and the complex relationship between the poems and the narrative, means that the poems transcend the chronology of the autobiography and carry the authority of prophetic or retrospective insight.[68]

The elegaic and romantic qualities of *Testament of Youth* are closely bound up with the memory of Roland. Vivid prose describes the emotional intensity of the love affair, the high points of romantic feeling, and the features of the natural landscapes which they both loved. 'Down the long white road we walked together' (p.83) tells of the young lovers' first walk alone. Another poem, 'In the Rose-garden' (p.50), recalls the romantic setting of the rose garden of Uppingham School. Vera Brittain withholds the vital information that her fiancé has died in action just before their anticipated reunion. The overcast day on which she awaits his arrival mirrors Brittain's downcast, anxious frame of mind 'walking up and down the promenade, watching the grey sea tossing rough with white surf-crested waves, and wondering still what kind of crossing he had had or was having'.(p.236) The passages that precede the fateful telephone message from Leighton's sister are fraught with tension and suspense which heighten our sense of shock and loss.

In *Testament of Youth* Brittain's purpose is to convince the reader that Roland Leighton is intrinsically special publicly rather than special and unique to her alone. She even goes to the lengths of reproducing the emblematic proof of Leighton's academic progress, the Uppingham School list of prize-winners, as if to present documentary vindication of the subsequent claim which she wishes to make as to his extraordinary calibre.[69]

The means whereby Roland Leighton is differentiated from others is his close association with the concept of heroism derived from epic, myth and legend. In 1918 Brittain published *Verses of a VAD*, an anthology of war poems dedicated to Leighton, with an introduction by Roland's mother, the novelist, Marie Connor Leighton. Leighton is presented to the reader as the epitome of the knightly ideal, 'my pure and stainless knight' and 'Roland of Ronscesvalles in modern days' in the poem 'To Monseigneur'. The personal loss is subtly extended into the public domain in the words 'None shall dispute Your kingship'.[70] There is, we should be clear, an element of *conscious* distortion in Brittain's idealisation of Roland who, as Rebecca West pointed out in 1933, had matured and hardened

68. 'Testament of Youth', unpublished part 2 Tripos dissertation, Cambridge University, 1985. I wish to thank Ruth Higgins whose interest in Vera Brittain gave me many welcome opportunities to share and clarify my own ideas.
69. Higgins, diss., p.12.
70. Brittain, *Verses of a VAD* (London: Macdonald, 1918), p.18.

perceptibly during the course of the war. Like many another young soldier, Leighton had learned how to cope with the horrors of the trenches by repressing all deep emotion. As Rebecca West perceptively noticed, Leighton's letters home to Brittain displayed 'a kind of frozen remoteness' at which his fiancée railed, securing the required reassurances of his undying love.[71]

Vera Brittain had at one time toyed with the idea that all heroism was unnecessary, but eventually decided otherwise: 'but heroism means something infinitely greater and finer, even if less practical, than just avoiding blame, and doing one's exact, stereotyped duty and no more'.(p.243) It appears to have been an impetuous disregard for his own safety that had prompted Leighton to court death by venturing out in bright moonlight in full view of the enemy. Brittain goes to excessive lengths to establish the precise circumstances of Roland Leighton's death. There is, moreover, an obsessive quality in her desire to link her fiancé's name with heroism in the abstract, as she prises information about the circumstances in which Leighton dies out of his commanding officer, the Catholic padre, his colonel, his manservant, and a sympathetic fellow officer in turn.

In a recent biography, Hilary Bailey has drawn attention to discrepancies between the account of the scene in which the family disposed of Roland's blood-stained army kit given by Vera Brittain and the accounts given by his sister, Clare, in her introduction to *Chronicle of Youth* (1981) and in the biography of her mother, Marie Connor Leighton (1948). Furthermore, Bailey has pointed out that there is no mention of Vera Brittain being present in either of Clare Leighton's descriptions of the event.[72] As Ruth Higgins has observed, Vera Brittain's war diary records the 'aura of mortality and decay and corruption' which the rhetoric of heroism in the autobiography later blocks out. Brittain's retrospective and fictional perspective in *Testament of Youth* is, therefore, able to 'deny realities which the immediacy of the mode of journal cannot ignore'[73] and to produce a more aesthetic and pleasing, albeit cosmetic and sanitised, final impression of him in death.

It is entirely understandable that Vera Brittain, whose life was bifurcated with tragedy, whose brother, Edward, fiancé, Roland, and friend, Victor, all died in the war, should wish to dwell on the memory of the men she had loved. The losses she sustained were devastating, almost defying comprehension and aetiology. But if her personal circumstances merit our sympathetic attention the light in which she wishes to present the men who

71. West, 'The Agony of the Human Soul in War', p.10.

72. *Vera Brittain: The Story of the Woman Who Wrote Testament of Youth* (Harmondsworth: Penguin, 1987), pp.31–3.

73. Higgins, diss., p.19.

died must still be open to question. To be fair, one opens any anthology of war poems by women to find identical structures of feeling; the desire to cherish 'his' memory, to tend 'his' garden', to polish 'his' medals, to immortalise him through obedience to 'his' values.[74] For these women to have questioned the values of the men whom they had lost would have beeen tantamount to them questioning the necessity of the actual sacrifice, and subsequently having to live not only with the tragic consequences of war but with the tragic consequences of a war for which there seemed to be no purpose. Yet there is a line which others refuse to cross. This is the point beyond which grief becomes hagiography and beyond which something essentially human has been lost.

One of the undisputed facts of trench warfare was that it was no respecter of rank or person. The seasoned veteran and the raw recruit each went to his death in turn. For some imaginative writers, for example, Ernest Hemingway, particularly in *A Farewell to Arms*, and Stephen Crane in *The Red Badge of Courage*, the conditions of cowardice and courage are closely related. The experience of one does not necessarily rule out the possibility of ever experiencing the other. Would Vera have loved Roland less had he not acquitted himself as a hero? Is not the *only* purpose of the Uppingham School report to illustrate the promise of greatness? In the end is not such selective detail superfluous to emotional attachment?

Although the Great War had a deeply traumatic effect on many of its survivors it patently exercised no monopoly on grief and suffering. Moreover, as has often been observed, those who suffered the most in the war were often those who most fervently wished to forget. But Vera Brittain returned to the theme of the 1914 war in fiction, memoir and discursive writing with the persistence of a beachcomber searching for some detail which might have been accidentally overlooked. As striking as her attachment to the actual war, is her attachment to the notion that it somehow conferred an exalted status on those who took part. A sharply contrasting perspective may be found in Hugh MacDiarmid's poem, 'Another Epitaph on an Army of Mercenaries', written in 1935, in which the soldiers of 1914 are referred to as 'professional murderers'.

> It is a God-damned lie to say that these
> Saved, or knew, anything worth any man's pride.
> They were professional murderers and they took
> Their blood money and impious risks and died.

74. See Catherine Reilly (ed.), *Scars Upon My Heart: Women's Poetry and Verse of the First World War* (London: Virago, 1981).

In spite of all their kind some element of worth
With difficulty persists here and there on earth.[75]

Re-reading *Testament of Youth* one is struck by its distance from any objective assessment of the Great War. Vera Brittain is simply not interested in questioning why that war was fought nor is she much interested in how. Her autobiographical mode possesses the authority of personal memoir without the injunctions of a historical account which is expected to subsume opinions and impressions gained through first-hand experience at a higher level of generality. This is not, of course, specific to Vera Brittain; Maya Angelou does the same, and it may be a characteristic of autobiography. Nevertheless, Brittain is able to sustain purely subjective and personal judgements many years after the broad determinants of a situation hidden from the restrictive and partial viewpoint of the participants have become common knowledge. She tells us, for example, that 'I have never been able to visualise Lord Haig as the colossal blunderer, the self-deceived optimist, of the Somme massacre in 1916.' Instead, she prefers to remember Haig in the context of a specific Special Order issued during the war, 'for after I had read it I knew that I should go on, whether I could or not'.(p.420)

By stressing her emotional anguish and interpreting public events primarily in terms of their immediate impact on her life, Vera Brittain invites the sympathy of the reader. In so doing she constructs a specific role for herself which is analogous to the heroine of a novel, rather than to the narrator or the analyst of a work of history who is abstracted from the processes she describes. Thus what matters about the Somme is the 'conspicuous gallantry and leadership' (p.288) with which her brother, Edward, 'rallied his men after the panic' (p.285) for which he was awarded the Military Cross. 'Rallied his men after the panic' in this context is clearly a euphemism for Edward Brittain's actions in despatching unwilling and demoralized men to meet their deaths in a senseless assault on the enemy in which, from his own account, only some two officers and seventeen men of his regiment survived.(p.284) Although there is a reference to the battle as 'that singularly wasteful and ineffective orgy of slaughter' (p.276) in *Testament of Youth* no proper re-assessment of Haig, nor of the infamous battle of the Somme, in which four hundred thousand British soldiers died in a catastrophically ill-judged offensive against the Germans, is ever attempted. Such an assessment would, arguably, have fallen within

75. Hugh MacDiarmid, 'Another Epitaph on an Army of Mercenaries', in *Second Hymn to Lenin and Other Poems*, 1935; reprinted in Michael Grieve and W. R. Aitken (eds), *Hugh MacDiarmid: Complete Poems, 1920–1976*, 2 vols (London: Martin, Brian & O'Keeffe, 1978), vol. 2, p.551.

Brittain's self-set aim of making the autobiography 'as truthful as history and as readable as fiction'.

The version of the war repressed through Brittain's accent on the personal is the idea of the 1914 war which Vera Brittain found least palatable; the idea of the war as one long, extended botch-up or muddle, or what Rebecca West refers to as 'the vast and disgusting extent of its inefficiency'.[76] The death of the young Roland Leighton, for example, might well have been avoided had the commander of the outgoing regiment taken the elementary precaution of informing his successors that a specific tract of land came regularly under enemy fire. Significantly, Lloyd George was swept to power on the crest of a wave of public indignation at the bungling of his predecessors which was revealed by the findings of the Committee of Investigation into the débâcle of the Dardanelles.[77] The differences of opinion between Lloyd George and Haig about the conduct of British military operations were public knowledge during the war and afterwards. But contentious political and economic issues of this kind are avoided in *Testament of Youth*, largely through Vera Brittain's use of the autobiographical mode.

Vera Brittain switched from a degree in English to one in History on her return to Oxford after the war precisely because she believed that the study of history would enhance her understanding of recent public events. In *Testament of Youth* she usually insists upon the primacy of her subjective experience, but she does on occasion incorporate selective historical judgements when these are in line with her idea of her book as 'a vehicle for the picture of a vast age of transition'.[78] Thus she sometimes gives us retrospective information which fits her chosen self-image – social reformer or active campaigner for women's rights – or when such information accords with her broader representational perceptions of the significance of the war years. As an example, she states that the Representation of the People Bill, which gave women over thirty the vote, became law in 1918 (p.404) although she admits that she had been unaware of its passage at the time.

In *Testament of Youth* Vera Brittain is strongly critical of particular aspects of patriarchy, for example the lack of access to higher education available to women with academic abilities but she does not criticise the class system, nor does she recognise the inter-relationship between patriarchal and class-based forms of oppression. Thus the curious double standard which Brittain displays in criticising the sexual behaviour of her

76. West, 'The Agony of the Human Soul in War', p.10.
77. Arthur Marwick, *The Deluge: British Society and the First World War* (London: Macmillan, 1965), pp.218–19.
78. Brittain, 'War Service in Perspective', p.369.

family servants while at the same time welcoming the postwar freedom in sexual matters among her own class which ended the 'romantic ignorance' of 1914. 'Amongst our friends we discussed sodomy and lesbianism . . . compared the merits of different contraceptives, and were theoretically familiar with varieties of homosexuality and venereal disease of which the very existence was unknown to our grandparents.'(p.578) Such double standards were, of course, common. Virginia Woolf, although fond of her servants, Lottie and Nelly, nevertheless drew the line at any suggestion that each should have a room of her own.[79]

What Vera Brittain rebels against in *Testament of Youth* are the values of the provincial town, Buxton, in which she grew up ('To me provincialism stood, and stands, for the sum-total of all false values'). To understand the movement traced in *Testament of Youth*, we must understand that the trajectory described is essentially individualistic. It is above all else the small-minded attitudes of small provincial towns that Brittain detests. *Testament of Youth* shows how she distances herself from her locality and not from her class, for she was, in the final analysis, not mobilised into a critical relationship to her class, but in all the ways to which I have drawn attention, moved to defend its interests.

Where *Testament of Youth* does make references to the working class such references are often condescending. Vera Brittain's accounts of the poor in the East End of London are particularly revealing. Her preoccupation with the idea of generational conflict (which does not, of course, address questions of power or the unequal distribution of wealth directly) makes Brittain clearly impervious to the possibility that the workers might be instrumental in bringing about improvements in their own living conditions. Moreover, she was incapable of recognising the working class discontents of the early 1920s as symptoms of class conflict or of conceptualising social change as coming from below. In the elections of 1922 and 1923 Vera Brittain came into close contact with the homes of the poor in East London for the first time. She writes in *Testament of Youth* of 'the shock of poignant revelation' that comes from recognising 'the same humour, the same rough, compassionate kindness' that she had seen in the Tommies whom she had 'nursed for four calamitous years'.(p.576)

This is a view of the working class which is patronising and naïve in the extreme. It is a view which is difficult to square with any objective understanding of the social conditions of the 1920s, with the growing mood of working-class stridency throughout Britain, and with the general air of restlessness of the time. The year 1919 saw the outbreak of a series of important industrial strikes, demonstrations, and serious manifestations

79. Anne Olivier Bell and Andrew McNeillie (eds), *The Diary of Virginia Woolf*, 5 vols (Harmondsworth: Penguin, 1979–1985), vol. 2, p.281.

of working-class discontent which brought all the Clydeside area to a standstill and resulted in troops and tanks being despatched to Glasgow to restore public order. C.E. Montague's *Disenchantment*,[80] published in 1922, is the best known of many post-war examples of writing in which disillusioned ex-servicemen gave vent to their anger. Indeed, the veteran novelist, Mary Augusta Ward, attached sufficient importance to the visible signs of working-class discontent to make the fictional Dansworth riots a key episode in her penultimate novel, *Cousin Philip*.[81]

The patrician strain in Vera Brittain's social outlook is starkly revealed in a personal letter to Winifred Holtby written in 1935. She writes: 'I'm afraid I'm not really a good democrat, for there still doesn't seem to me anything quite equal to complete intelligence *plus* complete well-bredness.'[82] Vera Brittain's much vaunted ideal of a 'semi-detached marriage' – a marriage of two equal and independent partners as exemplified by her own marriage to George Catlin – was certainly advanced for its day. Its radical potential, is, however, considerably attentuated by the implicit understanding that the social changes advocated were intended to affect the lives of only a minority of women: 'The reorganisation of society in such a fashion that its *best* [my emphasis] women could be both mothers and professional workers seemed to be one of the most acute problems.'(p.610)

In view of Vera Brittain's professed feminism it is somewhat surprising that *Testament of Youth*, which is liberally sprinkled with references to authors and to famous people of her day, should scarcely mention other works about the war by women. Brittain certainly knew of such texts. In August 1932, for example, exactly a year before the publication of *Testament of Youth*, the novelist, Phyllis Bentley, had sent her a copy of Ruth Holland's war-time novel, *The Lost Generation*. But the latter acted primarily as a spur for Brittain to redouble her efforts competitively: 'If I don't hurry up some woman or other like Ruth Holland (whose novel obviously has an autobiographical basis) *will* do an autobiography instead of a novel – and then mine will have no merits or originality at all.'[83] Vera Brittain can hardly be held responsible for the fact that the popular reception of *Testament of Youth* obliterated other, diverse and contradictory, accounts of the women's war effort. However, she did collude with this by maintaining as late as 1968, when she was the only woman asked to

80. *Disenchantment* (London: Chatto and Windus, 1922).
81. *Cousin Philip* (London: Collins, 1919).
82. Letter from Vera Brittain to Winifred Holtby, dated 8 May, 1934, in Vera Brittain and Geoffrey Handley-Taylor (eds), *Selected Letters of Winifred Holtby and Vera Brittain 1920–1935* (London: Brown, 1960), p.280.
83. Ibid. Letter from Vera Brittain to Winifred Holtby, dated 26 August, 1932, pp. 222–3.

contribute to a commemorative symposium of essays, that there was one account of women's war experience which mattered. That was the account which she herself provides.[84]

But *Testament of Youth* is not the only account of the 1914–18 war by a woman. On the contrary, the impact of the First World War on the literary imagination was profound and far-ranging. To outline the ramifications of that war on women's writing would be to embark on an altogether different project. The connections between women's writing and the war are intimate and expansive as has been authoritatively shown in Claire Tylee's exemplary study, *The Great War and Women's Consciousness*.[85] And it is the richness, the breadth, and the complexity of much hitherto neglected writing by women which is central to my own re-assessment of the Brittain autobiography. The crux of my argument, the reason why a book which is highly critical of the practices of the male left begins with an assault on a woman which might appear to replicate them, is that the First World War and its representation in writing is no one's private property. Quite the opposite, the effects of the war may be traced, obliquely, directly, or subliminally on literally dozens of women writers all of whom were published before *Testament of Youth* in 1933, as Claire Tylee has reminded us.

To draw attention to the diversity and range of women's literary and discursive engagements with the war is not to detract from the indisputable strength of *Testament of Youth* as an eloquent evocation of that war. It is, however, to suggest that *Testament of Youth* is only one woman's account of the war, no more, no less. It is also to caution against the uncritical reception of that account as 'the war book of the women of England', the accolade conferred on it by Sir William Haley in *The Times*, the accolade which we will remember Brittain accepted without disclaimer,[86] an accolade by which the works of other women subsequently come to be regarded as less authoritative, less important.

Scrutinising the works that the monumental status of *Testament of Youth* has overshadowed, one is left with an overpowering sense that if the war belongs to anyone it belongs to May Sinclair with the relief contingent in Belgium, to Enid Bagnold nursing the wounded in London, to Sarah

84. See Brittain, 'War Service in Perspective', p.374.

85. *The Great War and Women's Consciousness: Images of Militarism and Womanhood in Women's Writings, 1914–1964* (Basingstoke: Macmillan, 1990). This excellent study is indispensable study for anyone interested in women's writing and the 1914 war. Women whose writing was influenced by the war included included Storm Jameson, May Sinclair, Winifred Holtby, Mary Borden, Dorothy Canfield, Rose Macaulay, Enid Bagnold, May Wedderburn Cannan, Rebecca West, Edith Wharton, Mary Augusta Ward, Sheila Kaye-Smith, Stella Benson, Beatrice Harradan, Elizabeth Von Arnim and Virginia Woolf.

86. Brittain, 'War Service in Perspective', p.367.

MacNaughtan tending the casualties of war in two continents, to Mary Borden helping the dying in France, to hundreds of forgotten women poets, story-tellers, diarists and letter writers. One is left with the certainty that it ultimately belongs to none of these women individually but to them all collectively. The restitution will not come about until the literary ownership of the First World War by Vera Brittain is contested, until her autobiography is read as a text and not a monument.

But to examine *Testament of Youth* closely is to understand precisely how much the status of the work as a monument rather than a text has obscured. It is – I say this tentatively – to see how much may be obscured by treating *any* work as a monument. It is to appreciate the need for careful historical analysis *and* for a rigorous critical methodology, and then to begin to see how they can work in harmony, how both are inseparable from the aims and objectives of feminist scholarship. It is to ask questions about ownership and restitution, about reading and writing, questions about the uses and misuses of power, about relationships between men and women, and about the past and the present. It is to remind ourselves again of the crucial importance of class and race and gender, and of the 'duplicitous and complicitous' relationship of life and art. For as Bella Brodzki and Céleste Schenck have put it so well, 'the duplicitous and complicitous relationship of "life" and "art" in autobiographical modes is precisely the point. To elide it in the name of eliminating the "facile assumption of referentiality" is dangerously to ignore the crucial referentiality of class, race and sexual orientation; it is to beg serious political questions.'[87]

The writings of feminists of an earlier day can sometimes exhibit contradictions and difficulties which present painful problems for women for whom they have claimed to speak. The crowning irony that attends the reception, production and re-production, of *Testament of Youth* is that all of this originates from *within* feminism. In writing *Testament of Youth* a socialist and a feminist has produced a text incompatible with the egalitarian ideals and democratic impulses underwriting both political philosophies; a text which obliterates and displaces accounts of the war reflecting other socialist and feminist positions. The irony is that the text has been read and enjoyed by countless feminists – that it has been read and enjoyed by the author of this book herself.

For in the end I believe that women have not been silenced only because they live in a world of men. To study women's history and literature is to understand how those silences have been broken and to learn how to break those silences ourselves. To do this women must accept responsibility for the part they have played in silencing themselves and other women. As Sally Alexander has reminded us, it was as a vindicator of women's rights

87. Bella Brodzki and Céleste Schenck, introduction to *Life/Lines*, pp.12–13.

that Mary Wollstonecraft refused to absolve women from culpability in their own history and could 'diatribe so thoroughly against the thrall of men's authority and desires over women's lives, because she herself fell so violently, and seemingly arbitrarily a prey to them.'[88]

To put our own house in order as feminist literary critics and historians is to make that house hospitable for other women. It is not to do the work of men.

88. Sally Alexander, 'Women, Class and Sexual Differences in the 1830s and 1840s: Some Reflections on the Writing of a Feminist History', *History Workshop Journal*, 17, Spring 1984, pp.128–9.

2

The Woman in the Little House: Leonora Eyles and Socialist-Feminism

Testament of Youth, as we have seen, sits awkwardly with socialist and feminist values. But how were feminist ideas expressed in the writing of other women who saw their fiction as part of a socialist political project? What follows is a case study of a forgotten writer, Leonora Eyles, about whom nothing has been written since her death in 1960. Leonora Eyles's first novel, *Margaret Protests*, set in the slums of East London,[1] was a best-seller in the 1920s and 1930s. The protest to which her title refers is double edged: directed both against the excesses of industrial capitalism and against masculinist ideas within socialist cultures. In this chapter I shall discuss how Leonora Eyles inherited and extended feminist traditions within socialist politics and explore some of the tensions and contradictions of her enterprise. *Margaret Protests* is not only concerned with questions of class but also concentrates on different aspects of women's struggles, particularly those related to motherhood and the protection of the environment, which were of crucial importance to women of the time.

My critique of *Margaret Protests* is concerned with how a novel seemingly belonging to nineteenth-century utopian traditions of writing, owing much to the 'mean streets' of Victorian and Edwardian fiction, is able to bring a new feminist perspective to the slum novel's familiar emphasis on urban poverty and to subvert the Victorian and Edwardian novel by giving some of its familiar elements a feminist specificity. I shall show how Eyles's writing exemplifies the ways in which women writers have eluded the terms of orthodox accounts of socialist fiction of the 1920s and 1930s. This has a bearing upon the critical reception of other women writers such as Rosamond Lehmann and Virginia Woolf. But before I turn to *Margaret Protests* and Eyles's and to other writings in more detail, I shall make some general observations about socialist and feminist approaches to neglected and forgotten works.

The enterprise of socialist literary criticism has its own temporalities

---

1. Leonora Eyles, *Margaret Protests* (London: Erskine Macdonald, 1919). All references are from the first edition and included in the main body of the text.

and histories which fall largely outside the scope of this chapter. However, the retrieval of lost texts and writers, an important aspect of feminist critical inquiry, has also constituted a major strand within socialist critical practice. Socialist critics have made a priority of questioning the hierarchies of literary value by focusing on writing with working-class authors or subject matter. Indeed, the revival of interest in texts as diverse as Charlotte Perkins Gilman's *The Yellow Wallpaper*, Lewis Grassic Gibbons's *A Scots Quair*, Lewis Jones's *Cwmardy*, and Kate Chopin's *The Awakening* is due to the efforts of feminists and socialists who have taken these novels, and others like them, as examples of a literary culture that may embody values radically opposed to the dominant literary culture.[2]

H. Gustav Klaus has been the prime mover of a number of initiatives which have questioned the existing constitution of the literary field by unearthing and analysing lost works. In *The Socialist Novel in Britain* he takes issue with the way in which the artistic triumphs of modernism have overshadowed a whole body of writing 'whose mere existence, given the difficult and discouraging conditions of production, is an achievement in kind'.[3] Neglected novels of the 1920s Klaus analyses include James C. Welsh's *The Underworld*, H.R. Barbor's *Against the Red Sky*, Ethel Carnie's *This Slavery* and Mary Agnes Hamilton's *Follow My Leader*. 'Extravagant' claims for this fiction are carefully avoided. Nevertheless, it is clear that these works are part of an evolving cultural and political project which would establish an alternative body of radical and socialist writing in which the socialist-realist writing of the 1920s would occupy a pivitol place.

This project has gathered momentum in recent years. The publication of several compilations of essays including Klaus's *The Socialist Novel in Britain*, *The Literature of Labour* and *The Rise of Socialist Fiction 1880–1914*; Jeremy Hawthorn's *The British Working Class Novel in the Twentieth Century*; Ken Worpole's *Dockers and Detectives*; and Andy Croft's *Red Letter Days*[4] has usefully augmented our understanding of the rise of socialist fiction, the literature of London's East End, and worker-writers

2. While I recognise the importance of arguments to the effect that realist modes and the novel genre are irretrievably contaminated by bourgeois ideology I have no space to engage with the complexities of such arguments here.

3. H. Gustav Klaus,'Silhouettes of Revolution: Some Neglected Novels of the early 1920s', in Klaus (ed.), *The Socialist Novel in Britain*, pp.90–110.

4. *The Socialist Novel in Britain. Towards the Recovery of a Tradition* (Brighton: Harvester, 1982); *The Rise of Socialist Fiction 1880–1914* (Brighton: Harvester, 1987); *The Literature of Labour: Two Hundred Years of Working-Class Writing* (Brighton: Harvester, 1985); *Dockers and Detectives: Popular Reading: Popular Writing* (London: Verso, 1983); *The British Working-Class Novel in the Twentieth Century* (London: Arnold, 1984); *Red Letter Days: British Fiction in the 1930s* (London: Lawrence and Wishart, 1990).

like the Tyneside novelist, Jack Common. These excavations have brought to light a rich and varied seam of socialist and working-class fiction of considerable length and complexity from the nineteenth century and earlier. These works allow us to glimpse a long ignored literary culture profoundly altering our sense of history and literature as a consequence. But in taking responsibility for the republication of forgotten texts, socialists have, by and large, proved much less successful than their feminist counterparts.

Many socialist writers remain out of print, and unknown, a fact that imposes severe limitations upon any counter-hegemonic project of retrieval. As Graham Holderness has put it, until 'working-class novels from the nineteenth and early twentieth-centuries are reprinted and educationally mobilized on a much larger scale, there can be no effective general recovery to shift radically the political balance of the literary tradition'.[5] How does the work of socialist critics concerned with working-class writing relate to feminism? The type of criticism that Gustav Klaus, for example, represents is political criticism originating from deep socialist conviction. His work is characteristic of a kind of intervention in cultural politics impelled by the desire to defend as well as explicate. The relationship of the critic to the text which Klaus himself exemplifies is essentially custodial, the critic exercising a kind of careful trusteeship over works of importance. Klaus's attitudes to literature are largely shaped by his attitudes to social class. As the literary is subsumed into the political in his criticism, what matters about a text is often the class of the writer and what it has to say to the class-conscious reader of our time.

What I wish to contest, however, is the way Klaus, and other critics with whom he is associated, reproduce through their own literary practice many of the most deeply ingrained and least constructive traditions of the organised labour movement. Although their literary criticism is neither overtly sexist nor overtly misogynistic, it nonetheless perpetuates a chain of assumptions which have the subordination of women at their centre. One example is the concept of the working class to which Klaus subscribes: the traditional concept of the working class aggregated, for the most part, in urban communities and prizing specific aspects of its own culture. The most highly valued aspects of working-class experience include the cult of masculinity which is often confused with working-class militancy. In giving primacy to male experience rather than to female, this concept clearly marginalises and excludes women.

Ken Worpole's *Dockers and Detectives* provides another example of an attempt at cultural reconstruction 'of some particular patterns of reading

5. 'Miners and the Novel: From Bourgeois to Proletarian Fiction', in *The British Working-Class Novel in the Twentieth Century*, p.19.

and writing during the past fifty years that conventional literary criticism has ignored'.[6] Worpole concentrates on analysing detective stories and escape stories, writing from London's Jewish East End, and working-class writers like James Hanley, Jim Phelan and George Garrett. It is true that Worpole volunteers the information that many women, including working-class women, feel estranged from popular vernacular writing because it clearly emanates from a world from which they have been historically and culturally excluded: 'They feel, no doubt correctly, that it reflects a certain kind of working-class male bravada which, by definition, is oppressive'.[7] Nevertheless, Worpole's deep commitment to the working man obliges him to defend, critically, vernacular realism 'because of its narrative strength and popular accessibility to the language of everyday life'.[8]

What have working-class women read? Worpole admits that women do not read stories of male bravura. What have they written? As the writers like Jim Phelan and George Hanley whom Worpole chooses to discuss are invariably male, we have no way of knowing from his account. Moreover, as he does not consider the question even to be worth exploring the reading and writing experiences of working-class women are a structuring absence in his study. Consequently, one is left with the impression that contemporary working-class culture and the popular fiction of the last fifty years consists exclusively of narratives in which labouring men read celebratory accounts of male prowess – precisely the image evoked by his title, *Dockers and Detectives*.

To take a final example, David Smith's discussion of Ellen Wilkinson's *Clash*, a novel set in part in a northern mining village after the General Strike, illustrates how gender-based notions of what may be considered appropriate subject matter for a political novel often hover below the surface of the male critic's writing. In *Socialist Propaganda in the Twentieth Century Novel* Smith begins his analysis of *Clash* by quoting Wilkinson selectively: 'it's no use my pretending that I'm more interested in A's falling in love with B and the possible reaction of C, than in politics, because I'm not. There isn't really anything I care as much about as politics, and there's no use in pretending there is!'[9]

Ellen Wilkinson's comments, which did not originally refer to *Clash*, are used to support David Smith's own argument that *Clash* is not really what it might seem to an unprejudiced reader, a romantic novel. The obvious implication is that romance somehow divests the novel of its

---

6. Worpole, *Dockers and Detectives*, p.9.
7. Ibid., p.47.
8. Ibid.
9. *Socialist Propaganda in the Twentieth Century Novel* (London: Macmillan, 1978), p.44.

political content. Far from constituting the essence of Wilkinson's novel, the presence of romantic and sexual interest in *Clash* amounts only to a distraction from more serious matters. What the critic clearly lacks is any understanding of the crucial importance of sexual politics in the lives of ordinary women and of how heavily sexual politics touched on Ellen Wilkinson's own life. As Betty Vernon's biography makes clear,[10] Wilkinson's personal dilemmas and choices (the conflicts arising from her view that a democratic and liberated sexual politics is only attainable as part of a more general political struggle) are clearly refracted in the dilemmas and choices of Joan Craig in her semi-autobiographical novel.

There is no reason, in principle, why socialist critics who are men should not be able to produce work with a satisfactory focus on women. Why, then, is the practice clearly so far removed from the possibility? Why has no work of socialist criticism so far engaged with Leonora Eyles, a popular and versatile socialist writer of the 1920s. I do not believe that Eyles has simply escaped the attention of those male socialist critics whose knowledge of the 1920s is exhaustive. Nor do I believe that she is simply considered to be too weak a stylist for discussion. The fact is that male socialist critics have consistently proved far more adept at recognising male aspirations than female, and have consistently failed to recognise the implications of much imaginative writing by women for those thinking creatively about human possibility. Yet it should be obvious, as Ethel Mannin pointed out in 1937, that women also dream.[11]

But collections like *The Socialist Novel in Britain*, despite their ritual disclaimers to the contrary, do not usually admit writing by women which does not reflect the more traditional concerns of the labour movement. Indeed, where they speak of radical imperatives or aspirations, the imperatives and aspirations of men are assumed to be the same as, or to stand in for, those of women. As *The Socialist Novel in Britain* is subtitled *Towards the Recovery of a Tradition*, feminists might well ask to whom this tradition belongs?

Feminist historians have drawn attention to the ways in which socialist traditions have systematically suppressed the voices of women. Barbara Taylor's ground-breaking study of the nineteenth-century co-operative movement, *Eve and the New Jerusalem*, is germane to my own argument. Taylor demonstrated how a scrutiny of the socialist tradition in the light of its contribution to the emancipation of women produces a rather different image from the one dominating most socialists' view of the past. *Eve and the New Jerusalem* outlines the consequences of the waning of the early utopian imagination and the death of the commitment to a new

10. *Ellen Wilkinson* (London: Croom Helm, 1982).
11. *Women Also Dream* (London: Jarrolds, 1937).

social order premised on equality between the sexes, two important elements in early socialist thinking:

> As the older schemes for emancipating 'all humanity at once' were displaced by the economic struggles of a single class, so issues central to that earlier dream – marriage, reproduction, family life – were transformed from political questions into 'merely private ones', while women who persisted in pressing such issues were frequently condemned as bourgeois 'women's rightsers'. Organised feminism was increasingly viewed not as an essential component of socialist struggle, but as a disunifying, diversionary force, with no inherent connection to the socialist tradition. And thus the present disowns the past, severing connections and suppressing ambitions once so vital to those who forged them.[12]

The narrow view of socialism so eloquently and authoritatively decried by Barbara Taylor is the narrow view of socialism so deeply inscribed in much socialist literary criticism. The writing of women which maintains that an essential aspect of the total transformation of society must be the transformation of relations between the sexes must to some degree be opposed to the traditional concerns of socialist men. Moreover, its visionary and utopian elements cannot be accommodated unproblematically within the the contracted socialist project which Barbara Taylor and others have shown to have systematically marginalised or excluded such visionary and utopian concerns. Furthermore, there is a danger of women's writing being omitted from general discussions of socialist writing, of its specific concerns not being properly addressed, or of it being subsumed within such discussion as a tributory of other more important currents.

That the 1920s was a time of great flowering and creativity on the part of women may be borne out not through lengthy excavations in the deposits of university libraries but simply by a scrutiny of the volumes currently on booksellers' shelves which have been re-issued by the feminist presses. On what grounds have works which are clearly of interest to feminism been excluded from discussion by socialists?[13] Why is Winifred Holtby, for example, not classified as a socialist writer of the 1920s?

---

12. *Eve and the New Jerusalem: Socialism and Feminism in the Nineteenth Century* (London: Virago, 1983), p.xvi.

13. Women writing in the 1920s, including Ethel Carnie, Ethel Mannin, Mary Agnes Hamilton, Gabrielle Vallings, Ellen Wilkinson and Amabel Williams-Ellis, had, of course, strong connections with the organised labour movement and wrote explicitly political fiction. See Ethel Carnie, *General Belinda* (London: Jenkins, 1924) and *This Slavery* (London: Labour Publishing, 1925); Ethel Mannin, *Venetian Blinds* (London: Jarrolds, 1932); Mary Agnes Hamilton, *Follow My Leader* (London: Cape, 1922); Ellen Wilkinson, *Clash* (London: Harrap, 1929); Gabrielle Vallings, *The Forge of Democracy* (London: Hutchinson, 1921) and *The Tramp of the Multitude: A Triptych of Labour* (London: Hutchinson, 1936); Amabel Williams-Ellis, *The Wall of Glass* (London: Cape, 1927)

Much of the fiction which in E.P. Thompson's useful phrase, has been rescued from the 'condescension of posterity',[14] relates to the limited range of writing usually discussed under the rubric of socialist writing of the immediate post-war period only in troubled and uneasy ways. The relationship between feminist and socialist writing would, of course, be a good deal less troubled and uneasy were the definition of socialist writing to be broadened along the lines suggested by Kiernan Ryan. The imaginatively all-encompassing definition of socialist writing offered by this critic breaks decisively with narrow, purely economic and prescriptively class-based definitions of socialism. Ryan begins by uncompromisingly rejecting 'the mere fictional reproduction of some ready-made, finalised version of socialist ideology' as totally inadequate to help bring about the 'emancipative transformation of the prevailing social relations into a more truly human socialist society'. The critic adds:

> The essential function and value of fiction as such, and of a *consciously* materialist and dialectical fiction above all, reside in its relentless, uncompromising interrogation of the received in the light of an ever-changing reality, its restless explorations beyond the given horizon of experience and knowledge – including, where truth and need demand, beyond the hitherto accepted formulations and prescriptions of socialism.[15]

As Carolyn Steedman reflected, when piecing together the patchwork of her mother's and grandmother's lives for her biographical work, *Landscape for a Good Woman*, 'it was the women who told you about the public world, of work and politics, the details of social distinction'.[16] Yet the literature of labour is manifestly a literature in which women do not tell their daughters or their sons about 'the public world of work and politics'. On the contrary, 'the public world of work and politics' is frequently represented as a world which women are assumed neither to enter nor to understand. As Steedman shows, the 'intelligent discontents' of working women, as revealed in their own accounts, are not the 'intelligent discontents' of working men, and these accounts shatter the glass in which men have all too often been able to contemplate their reflections as unique and indispensable providers and protectors of family. Moreover, they hold up for inspection men who in reality are able to offer little or no practical and emotional support to women and who are often engaged in love affairs with the hard traditions of manual labour which

14. *The Making of The English Working Class* (Harmondsworth: Penguin, 1968), p.13.
15. Kiernan Ryan, 'Socialist Fiction and the Education of Desire. Mervyn Jones, Raymond Williams, John Berger', in Klaus (ed.), *The Socialist Novel in Britain*, pp. 166–7.
16. *Landscape for a Good Woman: A Story of Two Lives* (London: Virago, 1986), p.33.

can *only* be conducted in the absence of women. Class consciousness, it turns out, is often, by a sleight of hand, male and not female consciousness, and far removed from feminist consciousness or consciousness of feminism.

In order to develop these points further I shall now focus upon Leonora Eyles, a curious and contradictory figure whose early novels concentrate critically on the narrowness of working people's lives and clearly place her on the side of those whose desire to interpret the world has been matched by a desire to change it.[17] The roots of Leonora Eyles's feminism may be found in nineteenth-century utopian traditions exemplified by women like Catharine Barmby, a founder member of the Communist Church, a small religious sect committed to feminist and co-operative ideals. The vision of socialism which we can see prefiguratively in her novels uncompromisingly rejects an economic and social order which is based on competition. Moreover, she insists that the relationships of subordination between men and women are no less inherently damaging and exploitative than the relations between those who own capital and those who sell their labour in the marketplace. All this must, of course, be deeply troubling to those whose idea of socialism is merely a reductive scientific materialism. The analysis of Leonora Eyles's early novels will show how her work generates a set of questions which reflect a feminist critique and sensibility. Furthermore, these questions provide a challenge not only to the canon of literature *but also to the literature of labour itself.*

In 1920 the critic, Reginald Brimley Johnson, summarised the post-war literary aspirations of the contemporary woman writer: 'She is seeking, with passionate determination, for that Reality which is behind the material, the things that matter, spiritual things, ultimate Truth. And here she finds man an outsider, wilfully blind, purposely indifferent.'[18] Brimley Johnson did not engage directly with Leonora Eyles's fiction, but his description certainly encompasses the spiritual quests of the heroines of her early novels. Each of these women, Margaret Wayre, Helen Clevion and Marcella Laschcairn, struggles to reclaim the identity which they believe a materialistic industrial system has unjustly denied her. Eyles dramatises the refusal and questioning of that system, not in the name of violent revolution or heightened class consciousness, but in the name of a radically

17. There are over twenty titles listed under Leonora Eyles's name in the British Library catalogue. I am able to refer selectively only to *Margaret Protests*, and to *Captivity* (London: Heinemann, 1922); *For My Enemy Daughter* (London: Gollancz, 1941); *The Hare of Heaven* (London: Melrose, 1924); *Hidden Lives* (London: Heinemann, 1922); *Unmarried but Happy* (London: Gollancz, 1947); *The Ram Escapes: The Story of a Victorian Childhood* (London: Nevill, 1953); *The Woman in the Little House* (London: Richards, 1922); *Women's Problems of To-Day* (London: Labour Publishing, 1926).

18. *Some Contemporary Novelists (Women)* (London: Parsons, 1920), pp.xiv–xv.

different social order which is predicated on the imagination, on liberty, and on beauty.

What would a feminist criticism wishing to illuminate feminist consciousness in socialist writing have to say about Leonora Eyles? In the first place, I think that we have to admit, as did Mary Agnes Hamilton in 1922, that Eyles is in many respects an exasperating writer, her potpourri of religious allegory, mysticism and social reform often uneasily conscripting naturalistic detail to a florid, and frequently overblown, prose style.[19] Yet even at those moments when Eyles's prose style fails to convince (for example, in the lofty, exalted passages of dialogue between men and women with heavy biblical overtones, which pretend to naturalism and break all its rules), much can still be found of interest. Leonora Eyles's women characters are often principled, strongly independent and proudly resilient. In the militancy of their unsupported motherhood, Helen in *Hidden Lives*, Margaret in *Margaret Protests* and Marcella in *Captivity* bravely defy convention. We should note as well that Eyles's fiction in many ways resembles the utopian fantasies of Victorian women novelists,[20] linking the sexual nonconformity and social dissidence within the fiction to a wider feminist and socialist vision. Finally, we would recognise the woman in the little house as a recurring image in Eyles's work. This metonymic projection of woman's isolation is used to stress each woman's distance from the collectivity of other women, to symbolise how patriarchal social relationships confine, divide, and isolate women.

Who, then, was Leonora Eyles? And what is her relationship to the overwhelmingly masculinist tradition of socialist writing? She was born Leonora Pitcairn in 1889 into a well-to-do family of Staffordshire pottery owners whose family fortunes subsequently declined. Leonora passed the examination which allowed her to stay at school as a pupil-teacher at the age of fourteen, but after both her parents died she was left in the care of a young stepmother whom she detested. Forbidden to take up a scholarship, which would have enabled her to achieve her ambition of training as a qualified teacher, Leonora ran away to London and from that day never saw her stepmother again. A naïve eighteen-year-old, exposed to all the potential dangers of the capital city, Leonora tried to cope as best she could and found work addressing envelopes in a basement office. Having to pay for her rent and coal out of her meagre wages left her hardly enough money for food and she was often hungry. Tempted by advertisements for domestic servants in Australia, she sold one or two possessions left to her by her mother to raise the passage money and sailed in 1907 with ten

---

19. 'Review of *Captivity*', *Time and Tide*, 12 May, 1922, pp.448–9.
20. See Nan Bowman Albinski, *Women's Utopias in British and American Fiction* (London: Routledge, 1988).

shillings in her pocket.[21]

In Australia she appears to have been happy, working hard all day on the land and living outdoors in a tent, with her nearest neighbour ten miles away. Later she dated her swift conversion to 'revolutionariness' to her days in Australia: 'When I had been there a few months I had changed from a timid-mouse sort of person into a fighter'.[22] She married A.W. Eyles and resolved at the same time that no man should ever support her. In 1926 she was able to record with some pride 'and no one ever has'.[23] Australia also gave her first-hand information for a novel, *Captivity*, and the account of Marcella's married life may well be based on Leonora Eyles's own marriage.

Since her autobiography, *The Ram Escapes*, ends on the eve of her departure to Australia, putting together the fragments of her life after that has not always been possible. We cannot be sure why or when Eyles returned to London. By the time she was twenty-four she already had three small children and was living in a little terraced house in Peckham struggling to earn sufficient money to support them all. Her husband 'W' having left her when the children were still very young, she was reduced to factory garment making, typing at ten pence per thousand words and whatever badly paid jobs she could find to do at home. The work exhausted her but hardly brought in enough money to feed or clothe her growing family.[24]

On the verge of despair, pushing her pram up Peckham Rye (where William Blake had once seen a tree of angels) she chanced to notice an advertisement in *The Times* for a young writer able to write appeals for a child-care organisation. Her career as a professional writer began when she was the successful candidate from among five hundred applicants for the post.[25] When war broke out she volunteered to become one of the two thousand women working on munitions in the Woolwich Arsenal.[26] After the war came a period of intensive writing during which she published most of her books, including her popular crime fiction, and was responsible for millions of words of journalism – writing for George Lansbury's *Labour Leader*, and the problem page of *Modern Woman* and the woman's page in *The Daily Herald*, and, under the pen name 'Martha', succeeding Winifred Horrabin as the woman's page editor of *The Miner* in 1927.

In the rapidly expanding market of women's magazines of the 1920s and 1930s Leonora Eyles was able to carve out a niche for herself as one

21. Eyles, *The Ram Escapes*, pp.197–200.
22. Eyles, *Women's Problems of To-day*, p.56.
23. Ibid., p.11.
24. Eyles, *The Ram Escapes*, pp.159–60.
25. Ibid., p.160.
26. Eyles, *For My Enemy Daughter*, pp.44–5.

of the country's best-known and most respected 'agony aunts'.[27] As Rosalind Coward has pointed out, the advice column now functions as a poor person's introduction to the world of professional therapy, but the centrality given to sexual problems, the exhortation to reveal the intimate details of sexual life, is a development dating only from the end of the Second World War.[28] It was through the advice column – a revealing mode of communication largely ignored by socialist historians and cultural critics of the inter-war period – that Leonora Eyles chose to reach out to thousands of women – as sisters and daughters, mothers and lovers, as workers in both the home and the public workplace, who read her columns avidly. A committed pacifist after the First World War, she argued the case for non-violent action in the *Labour Leader* and *The Daily Herald* whenever her editors allowed her, although like many women she abandoned pacifism at the start of the 1939 war.[29] The popular success of *Eat Well in War-Time* in 1940 was followed by a short-lived problem page in *Tribune* from April to July 1941. Here she offered advice on personal relationships badly disrupted by the war, nutrition, housing, health, birth control and the problems faced by evacuee families. A convert to vegetarianism and to theosophy in her later years, she remained a socialist until the end of her life in 1960.

Leonora Eyles's documentary study of working women's lives in Peckham, *The Woman in the Little House*, first appeared in serial form in the magazine, *Time and Tide* in 1922. *The Woman in the Little House* is a work of social investigation (Maud Pember Reeves's *Round About a Pound a Week* is a good point of comparison)[30] intended to bring the presence of inner-city poverty, poor nutrition and bad housing to the attention of a middle-class readership. The author was attacked by some women who felt that working women were responsible for their own living conditions. Honesty, thrift and cleanliness, they argued, should not be beyond the reach of any woman, however poor. Her critics pointed out that it was only because she had come from a very different social background that her reduced circumstances made her unhappy. Leonora Eyles responded that her neighbours in Peckham ('vaguely dissatisfied, uncomprehendingly bad-tempered') were all similarly discontented.[31] Her renewed defence of the woman in the little house was impassioned: 'I want

27. *Modern Woman* was founded in 1925, *Woman's Journal* in 1927, *Woman's Own*, amalgamating *Home Notes* and *Woman's Day*, in 1932, *Mother* in 1934, and *Woman* in 1937.

28. *Female Desire: Women's Sexuality* (London: Paladin, 1984), pp.136–7.

29. Eyles, *For My Enemy Daughter*, p.48.

30. *Round About a Pound a Week* (London: Collins, 1913, re-issued London: Virago, 1979).

31. Eyles, *The Woman in the Little House*, p.26.

her to *demand* life's best bargains, not its remainders; because she deserves the very best from life.'[32] The episode confirmed her deep hatred of the type of leisured, privileged woman who had been most vocal in her criticism. 'The dragon fly is beautiful, the ornithorhynchus is unexpected, the cow is useful . . . What are these women for?'[33]

In 1922 Leonora Eyles was at pains to stress that she was no rich woman slumming, no journalist descending into the underworld to jog the conscience of the rich. On the contrary, *The Woman in the Little House* was written from the first-hand experience of one who had lived in that house and known its misery. In that Peckham slum she had experienced discomfort, ugliness and irritation. In it two of her children had been born. For five years the conditions she shared with her young family effectively meant that she had no privacy whatsoever, 'in bed, in the kitchen, shopping, gardening, always was some-one very near to me, touching me most of the time. I felt sometimes as though I could come to hate these crowding people who were really so dear to me'.[34] Indeed, she had worked so hard and known so little pleasure as an adult that she had felt miserable if compelled to take a day's holiday.[35]

By 1932, however, Eyles's domestic circumstances had obviously changed for the better. Happily married to David Murray (editor of *The Times Literary Supplement* from 1938 to 1944), she had managed to re-enter the world of middle-class comfort. The first of her regular 'Life and You' personal columns, in the inaugural issue of *Woman's Own*, introduced Eyles to readers of the new magazine as 'the woman who understands' and referred briefly to her history of personal hardship in order to gain the trust and confidence of potential correspondents.[36] The 'happy snapshots' of Eyles taken in the library or in the 'charming orchard' of her country home in Sussex, in subsequent issues of *Women's Own* project a radically different image and speak of a gracious mode of living which the woman in the little house could not hope to emulate. For despite the first-hand knowledge of working women's conditions in Eyles's writings they also exhibit the unmistakeable hallmarks of a woman cut adrift from her own class. The distaste that she felt for the meanness of East End streets, her deep sense that what the East Enders needed was art, beauty and poetry, confirm her impressions as being those of an outsider. However well-disposed towards the women she described, she did not, in the final analysis, belong, although her own experience of slum life and her feminist militancy clearly distanced her from other middle-class women.

32. *Time and Tide*, 14 April, 1922, p.360.
33. Ibid., 5 January, 1923, p.12.
34. Eyles, *The Woman in the Little House*, p.54.
35. *Women's Problems of To-day*, p.11.
36. *Woman's Own*, 15 October, 1932, p.40.

After the war, probably because hundreds of women who read her columns in *The Daily Herald* and *Labour Leader* wrote to her, Leonora Eyles was often asked to speak at trade union recruiting meetings. The factory women who drifted into these meetings seemed to her to be utterly worn out, some taking needlework home to complete, although this was illegal. Eyles was deeply moved by their condition, and came in time to believe that women should stay at home and look after their children. Women were under great pressure to return to the home at this time, and many feminists were fighting for women's right to paid work,[37] but she still defended her position: 'They should be free to work away from home or not as they like, but they should not be driven by poverty into factories.'[38] For a time Eyles had herself worked for the children's charity, Dr. Barnardo's. Looking through their archives she had noticed that almost every unruly, neglected, or destitute child was the child of a woman who went out to work.[39] She believed that full equality for women must involve the reconstruction of society so that the needs of women and children were placed at the centre of the social agenda. For her it was never just a question of rights to be bargained for or legislation to be won. Motherhood could be made efficient only if the state recognised its importance. She objected to the phrase 'the endowment of motherhood' with its clear suggestion of charity or largesse: 'women don't want charity. They want and deserve wages.'[40]

In 1926 the publication of *Women's Problems of To-day* triggered an acrimonious correspondence between Marie Stopes, the pioneering advocate of family planning methods, and Leonora Eyles. Stopes, who claimed to have 'the intimate confidence of hundreds of thousands of working class women',[41] objected to the 'reactionary and misleading' statement in the book: 'when men and women are no longer dispossessed the problem of Birth Control will cease to exist,'[42] wrongly supposing Leonora Eyles to be associated with the Catholic opposition to birth control in the Labour Party. This was far from the case. In fact, Eyles was prepared to offer contraceptive information to any woman who wanted it and was in the habit of referring her London readers to family planning clinics for

37. See Jane Lewis, 'In Search of A Real Equality: Women Between the Wars', in Frank Gloversmith (ed.), *Class, Culture and Social Change* (Brighton: Harvester, 1985), p.212.
38. Eyles, *Women's Problems of To-day*, p.11.
39. Eyles, *The Woman in the Little House*, p.63.
40. Ibid., p.161.
41. Letter from Marie Stopes to Leonora Eyles, 28 May, 1926, PP/MCS/A84. Stopes collection, Contemporary Medical Archive Centre (hereafter cited as CMAC) Wellcome Institute, for the History of Medicine, London. I wish to thank Dr Lesley Hall for drawing my attention to this correspondence.
42. Letter from Marie Stopes to Leonora Eyles, dated 21 May, 1926, PP/MCS/A84, CMAC.

advice. As a result of her own unhappy experiences, ('married when a child, to a dipsomaniac and kept having babies'),[43] she feared that birth control might sink women into 'the dreary morass of sex obsession' by encouraging them to believe that sex was the most important aspect of woman's existence. However, her conviction that contraception might make working class women vulnerable to sexual exploitation at the hands of men ('there is so much more in life than sexual connection, even the modern type with pessary all complete')[44] was always coupled to a deep concern about the plight of poor women burdened with unwanted children. In 1927 the correspondence between the two grew appreciably warmer as it became clear that both recognised the necessity for clinics to be set up as a matter of urgency to help women in the mining districts after the miners' lock-out which followed the General Strike of 1926.[45]

These feminist and socialist concerns inform *Margaret Protests*, Eyles's first novel and her most important. A best-seller in 1919, it remained popular with the reading public as late as the 1960s when it was reprinted as a Portway imprint, a label under which books in demand in public lending libraries were occasionally re-issued.[46] This account of a woman's voyage through the social and cultural order traces the route of Margaret Wayre, a young woman who marries 'beneath her proper station' and charts her growing disillusionment with a life of domestic drudgery. The novel highlights the dichotomy between the Victorian ideal of womanhood and the degrading reality Margaret experiences. The subtext of *Margaret Protests*, published shortly after Marie Stopes's *Married Love* and *Wise Parenthood* (1918)[47] is birth control, a subject about which Leonora Eyles had learned from reading Havelock Ellis and then Marie Stopes.[48] At its simplest, the novel tells how a young widow is driven by poverty to set up a business dealing in abortion-inducing medicines in order to support her family. Though her illicit business flourishes, Margaret suffers deep

43. Letter from Leonora Eyles to Marie Stopes, dated 20 December, 1927. Add. Mss., 58680-738, 58702, vol CCV1, British library (hereafter cited as BL).

44. Letter from Leonora Eyles to Marie Stopes, dated 22 May, 1926. Add. Mss. 58701, vol CCL111, BL.

45. Letter from Marie Stopes to Leonora Eyles, dated 28 December, 1927, PP/MCS/A84. CMAC. The first family planning clinic outside London was set up during the seven months of the miners' lock out in 1926 in the colliery district of Cannock Chase and was visited by some 140 miners' wives. See Peter Fryer, *The Birth Controllers* (London: Secker and Warburg, 1965), p.253.

46. There is no entry for this imprint in either the Cambridge University or British Library catalogues.

47. *Married Love: A New Contribution to the Solution of Sex Difficulties* (London: Fifield, 1918); and *Wise Parenthood: The Treatise on Birth Control for Married People, a Practical Sequel to Married Love* (London: Putnam's, 1918).

48. Letter from Leonora Eyles to Marie Stopes, dated 20 December, 1927. Add. Mss., 58680-738, 58702, vol CCV1, BL.

pangs of conscience about how her profits are being made. After the death of her young son and the defection of her partner, Kitty, she decides to trek out to the depths of the countryside to begin her life afresh. It is an extraordinary tale, one which includes features of melodrama, of the social exploration commonly found in the industrial and urban novels of the nineteenth century and aspects of feminist utopianism. Margaret's is the story of any woman who fights back and breaks out of the patriarchal incarceration which decrees rigid roles for women. The novel vividly dramatises the possibility of questioning and refusing these roles.

To understand how *Margaret Protests* relates to other slum novels we need to remind ourselves that such novels are almost entirely a product of the male imagination as the overwhelming majority of novels published about the slums have been written by men. If we were asked to draw up a list of late nineteenth-century and early twentieth-century slum novelists the names of authors who immortalised working class London, and the East End in particular, would probably include Walter Besant, George Gissing, Arthur Morrison, William Pett Ridge, Henry Nevinson, Somerset Maugham, Jack London, Edwin Pugh and Clarence Rook.[49] Women's names do not feature among the lists of writers who mythologised the East End by exploiting, as Walter Besant and others became famous for doing, the romance of the area. Nor are they to be found as authors of the so-called social realism of the 1890s with its booze and *bonhomie*. Margaret Harkness (pseudonym, John Law) is better remembered as the recipient of Engels's celebrated letter explaining his preference for Balzac over Zola than for her novel *A City Girl* (1887) which prompted Engels's correspondence with her. Harkness's contemporary, Constance Howell, is today unknown.[50]

Margaret Protests contains many recognisable features of Edwardian and Victorian representations of urban working-class life; echoes of slum novels such as *The Hole in the Wall* or *Neighbours of Ours* will be obvious.

49. Walter Besant, *All Sorts and Conditions of Men. An Impossible Story* (London: Chatto and Windus, 1882); George Gissing, *The Nether World* (London: Smith and Elder, 1889), and *Thyrza* (London: Smith and Elder, 1887); Arthur Morrison, *A Child of the Jago* (London: Methuen, 1896) and *The Hole in the Wall* (London: Methuen, 1902); William Pett Ridge, *Mord Em'ly* (London: Pearson, 1898); Henry Nevinson, *Neighbours of Ours* (London: Arrowsmith, 1895); Somerset Maugham, *Liza of Lambeth* (London: Fisher Unwin, 1897); Jack London, *The People of the Abyss* (London: Macmillan, 1903); Edwin Pugh, *A Street in Suburbia* (London: Heinemann, 1895); Clarence Rook, *The Hooligan Nights* (London: Richards, 1899).

50. John Law, *A City Girl* (London: Vizetelly, 1887); Constance Howell, *A More Excellent Way* (London: Sonnenschein, 1889). For Margaret Harkness, see John Goode, 'Margaret Harkness and the Socialist Novel', in Klaus (ed.), *The Socialist Novel in Britain*, pp.45–67. For Constance Howell, see Brunhild de la Motte, '"Radical-Feminism-Socialism": The Case of the Women Novelists', in Klaus, (ed.), *The Rise of Socialist Fiction*, pp.28–49.

Yet the novel has a number of features which clearly set it apart from such representations. Extending and developing the traditions of radical protest exemplified by writers such as William Blake, who used industrial artifacts like the factory or the mill as powerful symbols of oppression, Leonora Eyles, as we have seen, found an iconography better suited to expressing the servitude of woman. The elements of overt social protest in the novel centre on the little house as a supreme symbol of women's subjugation. In *Hidden Lives*, her second novel, the little house is personified, the slum Ruthers Row is 'twelve small cottages, with earth floors and gaping walls, their heads propped despondently in the smoky air, their feet ankle-deep in ashes and garbage'.[51]

The usual distinctions between the workplace and the home are questioned in her writing. For women, the workplace is the home, and the home the workplace, as we are continually reminded through the careful selection of social-realist detail in *Margaret Protests*. The only men at home during the day are the very young, the sick or the old and the only well-dressed men to be found in the labyrinth of streets in South London in which *Margaret Protests* is set are harbingers of trouble of some sort. Many women writers such as Kathleen Woodward, whose autobiography, *Jipping Street*, describes the experience of growing up female and working class in pre-war Bermondsey, or Kathleen Dayus, whose book, *Her People*, is a vivid account of day-to-day life in the city of Birmingham early in this century, have provided illuminating insights into working-class experience.[52] However, Eyles belongs to the select company of novelists for whom the concentration on women's lives is such that the working class *is* effectively female. Margaret Harkness, Constance Howell, Olive Birrell, Emma Leslie and Isabella Ford had all written of slum conditions before her.[53] But a writer who used her anomalous identity as a mother of three and a refugee stranded between cultures and classes to describe slum life from the perspective of a working mother is a rarity indeed.

The following extract from *Margaret Protests* is taken from a point midway in the narrative when Margaret (Leonora Eyles gives her heroine her own middle name) has returned to her former home in order to take an observer, Falcon Smith, on a conducted tour of the area. The fact-finding journey through the slums of London – bounded by The Elephant and Castle, Camberwell Green, and Walworth Road – corresponds to the

51. Eyles, *Hidden Lives*, p.8.
52. Kathleen Woodward, *Jipping Street* (London: Harper, 1928, reissued London: Virago, 1981); Kathleen Dayus, *Her People* (London: Virago, 1982); *All My Days* (London: Virago, 1988).
53. Olive Birrell, *Love in a Mist* (Smith and Elder, 1900); Emma Leslie, *The Seed She Sowed: A Tale of the Great Dock Strike* (London: Blackie, 1891); Isabella Ford, *On the Threshold* (London: Arnold, 1895).

literary exploitation of uncharted London from the Victorian writers James Greenwood and George Sims onward.[54] However, we should note that it is a woman's first person-narrative which is at the centre of interpretation. This constitutes a departure from the conventions of the mid- and late-Victorian classic journeys of exploration in which we would expect the burden of exposition to fall upon a man:

— We went away leaving Mrs. Quinn dishing up the 'stoo' so that Mr. Quinn could fall on it the moment he came in – and Falcon Smith, with a deep breath, said, as he stood on the pavement:
— 'Where can we get a taxi?'
— 'Not here, I'm afraid. We'll have to get the tram to Camberwell Green.'
— So we went along little shabby streets to the tram – past green grocers who shouted their wares aggressively, past the usual fried fish shops, past butchers' shops with meat piled in the open window, where frowsy looking women pawed and mauled it.
— We said nothing until, passing one of these shops, where we could hear the man arguing with a woman about a piece of bone which she thought ought not to 'count' – I said, bitterly:
— 'That's the sort of thing women live for – that's working women's life – haporths of bone! pennorths of cabbages, pennorths of meat! Washing dirty clothes – in tiny sculleries where they can't get enough water at work to wash a doll's handkerchief decently! Drying them in smuts until they're grey and everything's grey. Fretting and worrying because 'he' likes 'stoo' and Doll likes bloaters. Oh, can't you see the appallingness of it! And then men have the impudence, the cruelty to say that women are petty! Good heavens, can you take a man from selling farthing candles behind a little village counter, and make him a successful Chancellor of the Exchequer? Then how can you take a woman from dirty washing, cooking food, and all the petty, material things you can think of, and expect her to be big?'
— 'You feel this very much,' he said, quietly.
— 'Yes, I do. I'm hot about it. That house of Mrs. Quinn's – it was mine in replica. Except for this, Mrs. Quinn is quite a skilful housewife. I never was. So my house was probably worse than that, on washing days especially. Then – Mrs. Quinn hasn't the living to earn. There's a 'abby there, as beast of burden, you know. So there again her place is probably better than mine.' (pp.207–8)

While the detail of this passage, with its emphasis on ugliness, its 'ill-kept sordid shops', and 'frowsy looking women' who 'paw' and 'maul' meat, is clearly reminiscent of turn-of-the-century naturalism, we should also notice that it contains inflections indigenous neither to turn-of-the-century naturalism nor to the slum novel which have clearly been imported to serve feminist ends. Margaret's laboured explanations about the lives of the poor, ostensibly addressed to the spectator, Falcon, are clearly

54. George R. Sims, *How the Poor Live* (London: Chatto and Windus, 1883); James Greenwood, *A Night in a Workhouse* (London: *Pall Mall Gazette*, 1866).

intended for the consumption of the reader. Were we to come across them elsewhere the message which our reading of the Victorian slum novel has habituated us to expect would be different. Having once apprehended the true horrors of the slums we would expect to be asked to do all within our power to bring them speedily to an end.

Margaret's speech is predicated not on the question of poverty in the midst of plenty, which preoccupied the Victorians, but on 'the woman question' (the debate about the rights of women and the nature and role of women). Its purpose is to question deep-rooted ideas relating to 'natural' female inferiority by attaching the spiritual impoverishment of the working-class woman to the material conditions to which she is subject. Just as a man cannot be transformed overnight from someone who earns a living by selling candles into a successful Chancellor of the Exchequer, Margaret argues, so a woman cannot be transformed from someone whose existence is restricted to cooking meals and washing dirty clothes into a person of stature. Consciousness of gender, the awareness of belonging to an oppressed group, pervades the passage and becomes the key organising principle of the work, the central difference upon which all other psychological, moral and social distinctions turn. Leonora Eyles here makes us aware not merely that women are corrupt but of the specific processes whereby women have come to be corrupted. She sees, moreover, how men and women have come to be imbricated in their material circumstances, and with each other, and also the pitfalls that may destroy a politics of resistance that, if it is to exist at all, must grow out of the intimate relationships lived within an oppressed community. The solidarity she seeks does not exist naturally but has to be constructed. In seeking to build such a solidarity, Leonora Eyles clearly inherits and continues the feminist traditions that have existed within socialist politics.

The detail we are given about Mrs Quinn, Margaret's neighbour, is carefully selected to avoid condescension. Margaret points out specific facts that have emotional significance for women. We are told that Mrs Quinn is a better manager, a more skillful housewife than Margaret, whose own house is a replica of hers. Yet if it is easy to detect a note of sisterhood (if that term is not too modern in its connotations) it is also easy to detect the imposition of artificial values upon working-class characters. Leonora Eyles will never allow her working-class women characters to express hopes, ideals or aspirations which might detract from our understanding of working-class conditions as inexorably tragic or pathetic. The differences in background which separate her from the working-class women she describes thus ensure that whatever bonds of sympathy might exist between the two, her writing discloses not the closeness but the distance between the author and the women she describes.

The opening paragraphs of her second novel, *Hidden Lives*, although lacking Eyles's characteristic focus on women, introduce us not to a London slum but to an industrial town in the Midlands, also situating us at a kind of horrified distance from ugliness:

> To the right stretched the town shawdruck, a horror of desolation, of brokenness. Always when Francis Reay crossed the shawdruck he closed his eyes for an instant, and had a vision of Job the Patient, tormented by pain and ill counsellors, sitting among the potsherds of his ancient city; but the sky above Job was a burning blue, to which he might have turned for cheer. The sky above Shellpit was hidden by the dank smokes and vapour of many industries that stripped the beauty from the stunted trees, making men's souls and bodies stunted and unbeautiful.[55]

Here the corruption that hangs over Shellpit is specified as industrial in character. The sky above Shellpit is concealed by 'the dank smokes and vapour of many industries'. Thus a cancerous and deeply ominous aspect of urban existence is introduced, a landscape insidiously, hideously, altered and corroded through the processes of industry. Indeed, in a literal sense the shawdruck *is* the waste of industry and the power of the passage resides in the metonymy. Standing in for the industry which is the *raison d'être* of the urban slums, the shawdruck (an industrial waste tip) is presented to us with a double perspective. It is part of a specific mode of production, a material fact, and it is also a phantasm that turns into the waking nightmare of the clergyman Francis Reay. In his troubled imagination the waste tip of a small town in the Midlands is compared to the devastation of an ancient biblical city. Such is the magnitude of the disaster for humanity that it represents.

Leonora Eyles's insistence that the shawdruck be seen as part of an economic system which must be held responsible for producing such abominations is a recognition of the power of the industrial colossus to dwarf and dominate the lives of those who live under its shadow. The emphasis on illusion in the passage makes the shawdruck something of a chimaera, a figment of the imagination of a sick society. The hope is that its members may one day awake to the possibilities of other things. Eyles's own hatred of the advanced capitalist processes of production is evoked through omniscient narration. Words such as 'dank', 'stunted', 'stripped' and the clumsy 'unbeautiful' underscore the narration and are used to produce a sense of moral abhorrence in the reader, a hard condemnation of industrialism which is almost Dickensian in character. At the same time the explicit parallel with Job, the good man overtaken by calamities not of his own making, the archetype of patience under misfortune, produces a notion of industry as a kind of alien force weighing down a helpless people. It is a monster which could be vanquished but not economically

55. *Hidden Lives*, p.7.

contested. It cannot be transformed or re-possessed and re-organised for the common good. There follow only two possible responses to the catastrophe. One is the idea of escape, a solution in several of Eyles's novels; the other, stoic endurance of the kind exhibited by the majority of urban slum dwellers.

The rhetoric of passages like these carries us beyond realism to focus on the unbridgeable chasm that separates the world as intended by God and the world defiled by man. The presence in the text of specific images like the shawdruck or the woman in the little house, to which a whole complex of different meanings attach, alerts us continually to questions of good and evil and of right and wrong. The narrative logic of these works leads to the conclusion that human suffering is inextricably linked to the man-made industrial world which produces it. There are strong utopian elements in Eyles's early novels and the utopian mode predominates at the end of *Margaret Protests* when Margaret sets off with her young family to live in rustic simplicity in a place so remote that money does not change hands, in which exploitation is unknown: 'A fantastic thing – a woman with two children, in the twentieth-century, setting out to find an ideal world in England – was it too fantastic, too visionary? Was I mad? Ought I instead of setting off along the country lanes to-morrow, to be locked up in an asylum where dreamers so often end, crushed?' (p.325)

What choices exist for Margaret, cursed with a feckless husband, an unhappy marriage, and unexpected widowhood? The text strongly implies that the choice between urban degradation and the good life away from the city is open to any-woman or to every-woman. At least it is open to her once she has come to understand how sterile and self-deluding is the notion that material progress alone will improve women's lives. The ending of *Margaret Protests* is not intended to offer a literal answer to the problem of women's exploitation. Instead, Eyles appropriates the discourses of utopian enthusiasm to express an intensity of aspiration for which there is simply no secular language available. In *Margaret Protests* Eyles symbolically affirms every woman's potential to cut free of bondage and through her own determined efforts to build a New Jerusalem ('the House Made Without Hands') at which Margaret arrives at the end of the novel. Here at last the good do not suffer and the purest of human emotions may be expressed without fear.

The tone of protest in Eyles's early novels conveys a feminism which in concentrating, and rendering powerfully, the injustices suffered by women, is intended to heighten the desire of women to take control over their own lives. Yet it also leads Eyles to simplify what is complex and in so doing she clearly displays the weakness of the inexperienced novelist. For a tendency to simplistic naturalism, to present women as the hapless victims of circumstances, is a major recurring problem in her fiction.

Sarah, the arsonist in *Hidden Lives*, Annie, the prostitute in *The Hare of Heaven*, Kitty, the thief in *Margaret Protests*, are all unconvincing character studies clearly revealing the limitations of this kind of misplaced sympathy. Only perhaps in *Captivity*, a novel in which Eyles describes the vivid details of a man's drunken behaviour in order to convey precisely what this means for the woman nearest him, is oversimplification avoided. Eyles's hatred of the industrial system also led her into some of the same pitfalls as the early Chartist writers, which Martha Vicinus has described: 'This insistence upon a better future, rather than exploring and validating the here and now, no matter how grimy and degraded, prevented authors from treating seriously contemporary working-class life and from developing character and conflict within the existing world.'[56] Leonora Eyles cannot strike a balance between the requirements of feminist politics and those of artistic form.

The quest for 'authenticity', a *leitmotif* in Eyles's fiction, results in fixed patterns of behaviour for many of her women characters, sending Margaret in *Margaret Protests*, Helen in *Hidden Lives*, and Marcella in *Captivity* into the depths of the countryside in pursuit of their deeper, spiritual selves. Moreover, hatred of the industrial world produces a travestied picture of the London slums in her writing. If the urban slum were nothing more than an abomination, it would, of course, be impossible for any sensitive writer to tell of what goes on there without disapprobation. To suggest that slum dwellers can still lead reasonably human lives, to describe factories as if some good might come from them, would be to imply that the slums themselves are justified. Yet capitalism is contradictory, and its social relations no less so, and such complexities cannot be presented merely in terms of juxtaposition; *either* the slums of Shoreditch *or* the moors of Bedstone in *The Hare of Heaven*; *either* Ruthers Row *or* the mountains of Lashcairn, in *Hidden Lives*; *either* outcast London *or* a rural paradise in *Margaret Protests*.

In fact, the demolition of Ruthers Row (and its replacement by any of the woman-based options in the novels, whether Lady Carradon's village homes or Helen's refuge for working women, Bethesda, is only made possible by the affluence generated by the productivity of factories. The garden city of Eyles's vision is not a utopia, but has its own well-documented problems too – the deracination and anguish that is often experienced when old communities are broken up and Londoners find themselves dispersed, often against their wills, to characterless new housing developments situated far from home in an unfamiliar countryside. Such contradictions are obscured and concealed by an exclusive emphasis

56. Martha Vicinus, 'Chartist Fiction and the Development of a Class-Based Literature', in Klaus (ed.), *The Socialist Novel in Britain*, p.23.

on the passive and downtrodden aspects of life in the East End, in which the sense of community, the neighbourliness and warmth we find in discursive accounts of life in the East End in this period, is missing.

The novelist's focus on the middle classes, often professionals like the doctor, Helen Clevion, reinforces the reader's sense of the urban poor as the objects of compassion or reform. Though middle-class characters may live in working-class neighbourhoods, they manifestly do not share the working classes' living conditions. Seldom in any of Leonora Eyles's novels do working-class characters talk of more than 'stoo' or 'bloaters', and there is often a thinly-veiled pity for their limited intellectual capacities. That Eyles sees the working class as having no collective voice or class-based sense of identity is exemplified in the dramatic clash in *Hidden Lives* between the classic Victorian landlord Jonathan Ruthers ('what people want to call the submerged tenth are only fit to be submerged')[57] and Helen Clevion, the classic reforming Victorian heroine who believes the working classes deserve better than his hovels. There is not the slightest suggestion in this dramatic confrontation that the submerged tenth should speak for themselves.

In 1922 Eyles became conscious of the simmering working-class discontent manifested in a series of major strikes and urban disturbances and responded in characteristically domestic and personal terms: 'I firmly believe that the only thing to get at the root of the industrial unrest to-day is happiness in the little homes. This unrest, if one studies it from the point of view of the restless ones, is so much less political than domestic and neurotic.'[58] She adds: 'If something is done to make the women better in health and spirits, the men will simmer down, for the women set the note of a nation as they do of home.'[59] The unrest gave her a welcome opportunity to canvas support from *Time and Tide*'s respectable and socially-concerned female readership for the endowment of motherhood 'as a national service, to be paid for as the army and navy or the civil service are paid for'.[60] Seriously worried by the prospect of cracks in the social fabric in the period leading up to the General Strike, she appealed to women to stay calm: 'Revolution in its finest and constructive sense – will begin in the homes of the people.'[61]

Towards the end of 1925 a series of articles headed 'Oh That I Knew Where I Might Find Him' began to appear regularly in *The Daily Herald*, continuing throughout the first few months of 1926. Curiously juxtaposed to another regular feature in the newspaper, a daily column, 'From the

57. Eyles, *Hidden Lives*, p.138.
58. *Time and Tide*, 14 April, 1922, p.360.
59. Ibid.
60. Ibid.
61. Eyles, *Women's Problems of To-day*, p.13.

Workers' Point of View', each religious piece contained a personal acccount of the different churches, chapels and religious meeting houses which the writer had visited in her quest for God. The author was none other than Leonora Eyles, for whom Anglicanism, Nonconformity, Catholicism, Quaker Meetings and Socialist Sunday Schools had all at some time provided hope and enlightenment. The end of the spiritual journey of the woman for whom socialism seems to have been meaningful only if informed by a particularly literal kind of Christianity was to come much later with Theosophy. In 1926 Eyles was alarmed at the prospect of bloodshed and conscious of how far removed she was as a woman from the sources and centres of economic and political power. From this perspective, what could make more sense than to remind the labour movement of the presence of God? Today when one reads the lofty Victorian earnestness of these religious pieces, written in a daily paper of the labour movement at a time of almost unprecedented political crisis, one is left wondering whether they tell more about the state of the labour movement in 1926 or about Leonora Eyles.

In the end, Leonora Eyles's key criticism of industrial society was largely the same as her criticism of patriarchal society, that it forced women to deny their feminine natures. The freedom her women desire, when closely analysed, is really a desire for freedom to display a nature that is essentially *more* serene and *more* beautiful than industrial society will permit. And the flight of her characters from the city to the country conveys the impression that women may find happiness only by turning their backs upon the industrial world. The femininity to which Eyles's characters aspired and the Victorian ideal of unblemished womanhood, it would seem, are in many respects alike. Failing to question the origins of her ideal of womanhood, Eyles's writing, in the end, represents an escape from, rather than an assault upon, patriarchal values. Like Vera Brittain, Leonora Eyles appeared to be unaware of the contradictions inherent in some of her most cherished convictions.

3

'Nothing is Impracticable for a Single, Middle-Aged Woman with an Income of her Own': Literary Spinsterhood in the 1920s

In Katherine Mansfield's short story, 'Miss Brill' (1922), a genteel, English spinster domiciled in France assumes a practised air of *joie de vivre*. The shabby fox-fur ('dear little thing!') fondly paraded by Miss Brill in all weathers is a totem belying the reality of its ageing owner's poverty and loneliness. But the truth of her situation is brought home to Miss Brill by a courting couple overheard in the park. The boy resents the 'silly old mug' of the 'stupid old thing' and the girl callously mocks the faded fur which looks to her 'exactly like a fried whiting'. The story ends pointedly. Miss Brill carefully returns her cherished fur to its box: 'but when she put the lid on she thought she heard something crying'.[1]

The disparity between how the spinster sees herself and how she appears to others is the essence of this short story as it is of much imaginative writing on spinsterhood published in the 1920s. Individual women writers had long been concerned with the plight of the spinster, a concern reaching back to *Shirley* (1851) and resurfacing with Mona Caird's *The Morality of Marriage* (1897), Cicely Hamilton's *Marriage as a Trade* 1909), and Elizabeth Robins's *Way Stations* (1913), as well as F.M. Mayor's *The Third Miss Symons* of the same year. The situation of the 'redundant' single woman had much preoccupied the Victorians in the 1840s and 1850s and the 'Odd Woman' had come widely to be regarded as a demographic, economic and moral problem in the 1890s. But the topic of spinsterhood recurs in the 1920s with a frequency and insistence that can only be understood in its historical specificity. For most of the inter-war period about one-third of all women who had not married by the age of twenty-nine did not marry during their reproductive years.[2] As Billie Melman has

---

1. *The Collected Short Stories* (London: Constable, 1945). pp.335 and 336.
2. Jane Lewis, *Women in England 1870–1950: Sexual Divisions and Social Change* (Brighton: Wheatsheaf, 1984), p.4.

pointed out, the socio-demographic imbalance was widely 'interpreted as a sign of universal disequilibrium – a fall as it were, from a 'natural' state of harmony between males and females'.[3] With unmarried women of marriageable age far outnumbering men in the same age group, the meaning of spinsterhood became a site of contestation between those who wished to objectify the spinster and others who saw her as a person with needs, desires and potential of her own. From the beginning of the decade the terms 'superfluous woman' and 'spinster' became interchangeable and 'spinster' to be widely used as a pejorative term.[4]

The 1920s is often contrasted unfavourably with the decade of intense feminist activity which preceded it. Organised feminist activity was at a low ebb, and, in many respects, the 1920s were inauspicious years for women. But bleak though it might appear, this picture does not tell the whole story. If much that was written in the 1920s was unashamedly hostile to the spinster, there was also a strong drive towards self-assertion on the part of the spinster herself to which the texts I discuss bear powerful witness.[5]

But the writings of Ivy Compton-Burnett, Radclyffe Hall, Winifred Holtby, Katherine Mansfield, F.M. Mayor, Dorothy Richardson, May Sinclair, and Sylvia Townsend-Warner are diverse, and cannot, without gross distortion, be assimilated to any common label. There was not, nor could there have been, sufficient consensus, aesthetic or political, among women writers to make a uniform approach to spinsterhood possible. Nevertheless, common interests, for example in the wider options that should be open to the increasing numbers of women whose minds did not travel along the smooth road to matrimony, are explored across a wide spectrum of literary texts. And a number of oppositions are frequently

3. *Women and the Popular Imagination in the Twenties: Flappers and Nymphs* (Basingstoke: Macmillan, 1988), p.18.

4. The word 'spinster' had no pejorative overtones before the Industrial Revolution. It acquired them only in the eighteenth and the nineteenth century. Today the term has virtually gone out of use.

5. Novels with sympathetic attitudes to the spinster in the 1920s include E.M. Delafield, *Consequences* (London: Hodder and Stoughton, 1919); *The Pelicans* (London: Hodder and Stoughton, 1918); Radclyffe Hall, *The Unlit Lamp* (London: Cassell, 1924); Winifred Holtby, *Anderby Wold* (London: Lane, 1923); *The Crowded Street* (London: Lane, 1924); Sylvia Lynd, *Swallow Dive* (London: Cassell, 1921); Katherine Mansfield, 'The Daughters of the Late Colonel' and 'Miss Brill', in *The Garden Party and Other Stories of Katherine Mansfield* (London: Constable, 1922); F.M. Mayor, *The Rector's Daughter* (London: Hogarth, 1924); *The Squire's Daughter* (London: Constable, 1929); Sheila Kaye Smith, *Joanna Godden* (London: Cassell, 1921); May Sinclair, *Life and Death of Harriett Frean* (London: Collins, 1922); *Mary Olivier: A Life* (London: Cassell, 1919); Sylvia Stephenson, *Surplus* (London: Fisher Unwin, 1924); Sylvia Townsend Warner, *Lolly Willowes; or the Loving Huntsman* (London: Chatto and Windus, 1926); E.H. Young, *The Vicar's Daughter* (London: Cape, 1928); *The Bridge Dividing* (London: Heinemann, 1922); *Miss Mole* (London: Cape, 1930).

invoked: movement or stasis? duty to self or to others? freedom or imprisonment?

In 1921 the demographic issue acquired a new significance after the census disclosures of the late summer and the reporting of Northcliffe's public references to 'Britain's problem of two million superfluous women' during a visit to the United States.[6] Speculation on the future prospects of two million 'superfluous women' became a national pastime. *The New Statesman* highlighted the difference between its own liberal attitudes and those of other publications in this unsigned editorial piece on 24 September:

> Hence we think it absurd on the part of the Press to talk so much of the two thousand [sic] 'superfluous women', or 'thwarted women', as though 'superfluous', 'thwarted', and 'unmarried' were convertible terms . . . We have known a considerable number of married women who were at least as superfluous as St. Teresa, and there are married men of our acquaintance who live thwarted lives in comparison with William Pitt. Who, indeed, is to decide what is a thwarted life? Was Swift's a thwarted life? Or Ruskin's? If so, it seems clear that thwarting may be merely a means to completer fulfilment.[7]

The flavour of the debate may be gleaned from the correspondence in *The Daily Telegraph* in August and September. Among the better-known contributors were the novelists Beatrice Kean Seymour and Sheila Kaye Smith, the first woman M.P., Lady Astor, and the veteran suffragist, Millicent Garrett Fawcett.[8] While many correspondents argued that society was ethically and economically endangered by the demographic imbalance, others made the point that many spinsters had acquitted themselves patriotically in the war or that many were already self-supporting. There is 'not a village, not a prison, hardly a workhouse or hospital that would not be better for the service that educated women could render' enthused Edith Picton-Turbervill.[9] 'I am also a "working lady" thrust out into the world to work for my living by the maelstrom of war', wrote one woman, 'and must protest against being termed as "an abomination"'.[10]

The tone in which the public debate was conducted was not to every woman writer's taste. Some, including May Sinclair, whose novels *Mary Olivier: A Life* (1919) and *Life and Death of Harriett Frean* (1922) are

6. Melman, *Women and the Popular Imagination in the Twenties*, p.19.

7. 'Woman', *New Statesman*, 24 September, 1921, p.669.

8. See *Daily Telegraph*, 1921, Beatrice Kean Seymour 30 August, Nancy, Viscountess Astor 1 September, Millicent Garrett Fawcett 12 September, Sheila Kaye Smith 13 September.

9. Ibid., 16 September, p.9.

10. Ibid., 'Betwixt and Between', 13 September, p.10.

concerned with the effects of sublimation and repression on the life of the spinster, pointedly refused to participate. When Sinclair, who was living in genteel poverty with her mother at the time, was asked to write for the newspapers she answered: 'I'm not interested in the Superfluous 2,000,000! If they *are* superfluous, let them emigrate. But they don't and won't.'[11]

The notion of the state-directed emigration of women to the colonies was perhaps the most authoritarian of many 'solutions' to the demographic imbalance. But when *The Times* of August 1921 advised women to travel to the colonies to find a husband, as Adela Quested does in E. M. Forster's *A Passage to India* (1924), Vera Brittain wrote to Winifred Holtby ('as one superfluous woman to another') making her feelings clear: 'Personally I haven't the least objection to being superfluous ... though I shall be delighted for any work I may do to take me abroad, it will not be because I shall thereby be enabled the better to capture the elusive male.'[12]

However, the life of the spinster in the family home was still often one of unrelieved domestic servitude. Radclyffe Hall, visiting a Devon resort in 1921, was distressed by the sight of an old lady waited upon by her ageing daughter: 'ghastly to see these unmarried daughters who are just unpaid servants', and the old people, 'sucking the life out of them like octopi'.[13] Hall later discarded her first title for *The Unlit Lamp*, 'Octopi', but retained the metaphor of strangulation from which the novel's social satire derives much of its strength. The inter-war novels of Ivy Compton-Burnett, who had experienced psychic subjugation at the hands of her widowed mother, are peopled with insupportable autocrats of the breakfast table. Domestic tyranny exercised over their young by matriarchs – the egocentric, Sophia Stace in *Brothers and Sisters* (1929), the sharp-tongued Harriet Haslam in *Men and Wives* (1931) – is a commonplace.

The loosening in the 1920s of sexual taboos extended only to non-marital heterosexual activity.[14] It was of little benefit to the many unmarried women with neither the desire nor the opportunity to form sexual relationships with men, or whose sexual orientation was to women. Indeed, the revolutionary feminist historian, Sheila Jeffreys, has claimed that the hostile attitudes to the spinster were deliberately aggravated by sex reformers who stressed women's right to experience sexual pleasure in

11. Quoted by Hrisey Dimitrakis Zegger, *May Sinclair* (Boston: Twayne, 1976), p.128.
12. Brittain, *Testament of Youth* (London: Gollancz, 1933), pp.577–8.
13. Una, Lady Troubridge, *The Life and Death of Radclyffe Hall* (London: Hammond, 1961), p.69.
14. Linda Gordon, *Woman's Body, Woman's Right: A Social History of Birth Control in America* (Harmondsworth: Penguin, 1977), p.194.

marriage, reviling earlier feminists as prudes and puritans.[15] This claim should, however, be viewed with caution.

The taboos on homosexual activity, exemplified in the trial of *The Well of Loneliness*, intensified considerably during the decade, doing much to break the patterns of emotional dependency between women in the 1914 war. Moreover, a woman attempting to escape from the traditional limitations of domestic obligations might well find herself thrust into them again by the authority of the psychologist. Winifred Holtby noted with dismay that women everywhere were being told to 'enjoy the full cycle of sex-experience, or they would become riddled with complexes like a rotting fruit'.[16]

In particular, there was a vogue for psychoanalytic ideas after more of Freud's works, available since 1913, came to be translated in the 1920s. Katherine Mansfield rebelled openly against the sexualisation of literary sensibility: 'I shall *never* see sex in trees, sex in the running brooks, sex in stones and sex in everything.'[17] But for many women writers the confusion and conflict stirred by the cross-set of taboos and new modes of analysis was deeply distressing, and, as Winifred Holtby commented, 'the wonder is that any woman continued to write novels at all'.[18]

Hostility to the spinster was at its most vitriolic in the Catholic social theorist, A. M. Ludovici. Ludovici combined his onslaughts upon 'thousands of bitter or sub-normal women' who had 'thwarted or deficient passions' with contradictory attacks on 'Feminist propaganda in favour of sterile Free Love, Restricted Fertility and Birth Control'.[19] Even the seemingly innocuous idea of careers which would help women to support themselves came under fire from Ludovici as a 'hopeless last resource, or else as a means of disposing merely of those girls who belong to an inferior biological class'.[20] In *Lysistrata* he objected to those who argued that the bodily destiny of their sex was a matter of no consequence.

And yet to anyone who reveres the body, and who knows how the spirit is tortured by a body unsatisfied and neglected, how thoroughly unfounded does this claim appear! A thwarted instinct does not meekly subside. It seeks compensation and damages for its rebuff. True sublimation, except through

15. *The Spinster and Her Enemies: Feminism and Sexuality 1880–1930* (London: Pandora, 1985), p.155. See also Margaret Hunt, 'The De-Eroticism of Women's Liberation: Social Purity Movements and the Revolutionary Feminism of Sheila Jeffreys', *Feminist Review*, 34, Spring 1990, pp.18–23.
16. *Virginia Woolf: A Critical Memoir* (London: Wishart, 1932), p.29.
17. Letter to Beatrice Campbell, dated May 1916. C. K. Stead (ed.) *The Letters and Journals of Katherine Mansfield: A Selection* (London: Allen Lane, 1977), p.76.
18. Holtby, *Virginia Woolf*, p.30.
19. *The Future of Woman* (London: Kegan Paul, Trench, Trubner, 1936), p.70.
20. Ibid., pp.78–9.

whole-hearted and unremitting religious practices, is rare. What then is the fate of these 2,000,000 women?[21]

In an earlier work, *Woman: A Vindication*, Ludovici had uttered this stern warning:

> Since the spinsters of any country represent a body of human beings who are not leading natural lives, and whose fundamental instincts are able to find no normal expression or satisfaction, it follows . . . that the influence of this body of spinsters on the life of the nation to which they belong, must be abnormal, and therefore contrary to the normal needs and the natural development of that nation.[22]

'Natural Lives', 'normal expression', 'abnormal' influence and 'natural development'. The play on the idea of 'the natural' in this litany of deviance reveals an obsessive interest in exorcising difference. In a labyrinth of connection, interrelation and extension, the spinster is transformed into an agent of perverse subversion, a fifth columnist, an enemy of the state. Ludovici's views on spinsterhood are clearly extreme, but even so repay careful attention as symptomatic of the opinions expressed commonly, if less virulently, at the time. As late as 1935 Dorothy Sayers's detective, Harriet Vane, investigating a spate of poison-pen letters in an Oxford college, 'could think of whole sets of epithets, ready-minted for circulation' for their author, among them are 'soured virginity' – 'unnatural life' – 'semi-demented spinsters' – 'starved appetites and suppressed impulses'.[23]

But ironically those like Ludovici who labelled the spinster deviant, and malignant, conferred an authoritative right to speak upon the woman thus travestied. This accelerated the process whereby the derogatory image of the spinster came to be contested, and in the end transformed, largely as a consequence of the objections voiced by spinsters themselves. The spinster, according to Ludovici, is defined by 'want' or 'lack'. The spinster must have some 'wants' but is denied others. The spinster must 'want' a husband. This 'want' is confidently refuted in *Lolly Willowes*, *The Crowded Street*, *The Unlit Lamp*, *Surplus* and *Joanna Godden*. It is beautifully subverted by E.H. Young's *soi-disant* spinster, Hannah Mole, *Miss Mole*, (1931) jauntily sailing under spinsterhood as a flag of convenience and wondering why so much importance was attached to the chastity of women.

Although there is always a ricochet between lived experience and

21. *Lysistrata: Woman's Future and Future Woman* (London: Kegan Paul, Trench, Trubner, 1925), p.35.
22. *Woman: A Vindication* (London: Constable, 1923), p.231.
23. *Gaudy Night* (London: Gollancz, 1935), p.81.

literary experience, the literary and lived experience of women in the 1920s reveals a particularly intense interchange. In *Time and Tide* the journalist, Rosaline Masson, characterised the plight which commonly befell the dispossessed daughter in an arresting image: 'Much of the home-life of our country is built up on a substratum of obscure martyrdoms . . . until the family home is broken up by death. And then the luxurious, hospitable family home belches forth dismayed spinsters into an unsympathetic world, to wander about as aimlessly, and seek cover as nervously, as do the wood-lice when the flower-pot is lifted.'[24]

Sylvia Townsend Warner's heroine, Lolly Willowes, is twenty-eight and must 'make haste if she were going to find a husband before she was thirty'.[25] When her father dies, a bemused Lolly, 'feeling rather as if she were a piece of family property forgotten in the will, was ready to be disposed of' (p.6) as her relations should think best. Like Lady Slane in *All Passion Spent* (1931) Lolly believes it 'best as one grows older to strip oneself of possessions, to shed oneself downwards like a tree, to be almost wholly earth before one dies'.(p.106) When she wishes to leave his London town house for the countryside, brother Henry is aghast. But kneeling thankfully among the cowslips, 'the weight of all her unhappy years' behind her at last, Lolly trembles with relief, 'understanding for the first time how miserable she had been' (p.149) before her release from the wretchedness of dependence.

The myths that passed for truth about the spinster's life were not merely journalistic excesses, nor simply the currency of notorious misogynists. On the contrary, they were so resilient and so common that it was all but impossible for the spinster to escape the socially imposed expectations of the dominant sex. The spectre of loneliness, the chimaera of romantic love, the reality of interminable waiting, for a husband who never quite materialises on the threshold, and for a life that consequently never quite begins, all these found resonances in women's fiction. The symptoms of women forced to repress deep emotional and sexual needs were vividly evoked by May Sinclair. The sickness of Aunt Charlotte in *Mary Olivier* is clearly related to her unrequited longing for marriage. Harriett Frean's lingering illness is the learned helplessness of one who thinks of herself as a girl long after becoming a woman. In later years if Harriett were introduced to any stranger 'she accounted for herself arrogantly: "My father was Hilton Frean".'

The red campion outside Harriett's house symbolises the passion forbidden her, the brittle blue ornamental egg, a wedding present to her

24. 'Dark Stars (Unpaid), 2, Unmarried', *Time and Tide*, 11 March, 1921, p.227.
25. Townsend Warner, *Lolly Willowes*, p.2. All quotations are from the first edition and page references are given in the main body of the text.

parents, the fertility she is never to know. In quiet desperation Harriett clings to the image of her lost mother, 'and always beside it, shadowy and pathetic, she discerned the image of her lost self'.[26] The mental disintegration that gradually overtakes Harriett nearly befalls Mary Olivier, who cannot marry because mother 'needs her' but just escapes Harriett's unhappy fate through sublimation, in philosophy and poetry, of the kind Ludovici did not believe to be possible.

Yet women writers did not all create spinster protagonists content to submit meekly to their lot. Some chose to become actively engaged in a protracted struggle for self-realisation. People might speak pityingly of the nation's spinsters: 'nothing for them except subjection and plaiting their hair'. (*LW*, p.235) But many a spinster was confident that the last thing she required was pity. And a succession of sympathetic works all reject the prevalent condescension and contest the simple caricatures of the man-hating old maid and the old maid desperate to find a man.

As women's literary resistance to patriarchal values took subtle and diverse forms, the presence of a 'strong' or overtly rebellious character is clearly inadequate as a yardstick of feminist consciousness. It is not, after all, Mansfield's timid and ineffectual spinster sisters in *The Daughters of the Late Colonel* (1922) who exemplify resistance to the crushing weight of patriarchal authority, but the sensitive atomising of the sisters' predicament which makes possible the story's incisive analysis of patriarchy. And the cumulative power of the narration, symbolism and imagery which pinpoints the 'sunlessness' of Josephine and Constantia's drab existence, and intimates that freedom, like the reprieve that arrives after the executioner's axe has fallen, has come too late to be of use.

The more resolute sister, Constantia, is allowed one brief act of self-assertion; locking the drawer upon her father's belongings (at a symbolic level locking her father's lingering presence out of her life). Constantia's gesture of defiance is uncharacteristic, unexpected. It does, however, illustrate that routine submission to authority need not exclude the possibility of occasional resistance, any more than discomfort with patriarchal values need imply their complete or irreversible rejection on a woman's part.

The lives of dependent unmarried women were not merely restricted, they were potentially shot through with pain. To track the life of the spinster from childhood was to choose to explore why women beyond the usual age of marriage, 'growing old, as common as blackberries, and as unregarded' (*LW*, p.234) had quietly resigned themselves to their lot. Moreover, in so doing the woman writer affirmed the importance of workaday lives often considered too dull to merit attention: ('to sit half

26. Sinclair, *Life and Death of Harriett Frean*, p.99.

an hour by an elderly lady getting deaf, another half an hour by some awkward spectacled girl . . . such was generally Mary's fate').[27] The effect was subtly to shift responsibility, and therefore blame, for her unwanted dependency from the spinster herself to her circumstances.

Simply acknowledging the importance of moments of being and incandescence in the life of a character, who might otherwise be represented as wholly pitiful, can in itself be a mark of respect.[28] 'One writes (*one* reason why is) because one does care so passionately that one *must* show it – one must declare one's love',[29] was Katherine Mansfield's tellingly simple reply to John Middleton Murry's praise of her loneliest spinster, Miss Brill. Yet, astonishingly, it is only recently that Mansfield's short stories on the 'dame seule' theme, have been exonerated from the charge of 'cruelty' to their central characters frequently levied against them in the past.[30] As Kate Fullbrook has argued, recognition of the late short stories as 'unremittingly critical accounts of social injustice grounded in the pretence of a "natural" psychological and biological order' is overdue.[31]

By paying attention to the twists and turns of a spinster's life a literary work need not trade in commonplaces and abstractions about spinsterhood. Nor need it ignore the enriching and worthwhile 'voyages of discovery into new ideas and energetic practices in art or social welfare, education or religion' with which Muriel Spark observed that countless women like the redoubtable Scottish schoolteacher, Jean Brodie, filled 'their war-bereaved spinsterhood'.[32] Sarah Burton, the singleminded teacher in *South Riding*, does not bemoan the lack of opportunities for relationships with men. Their presence would merely distract attention from her work: 'And a good thing too, I was born to be a spinster, and by God, I'm going to spin.'[33] The occupations of schoolteacher or governess provided an attractive vocation for the spinster intent on economic self-sufficiency or on making her influence felt. Indeed, the spinster-companion governess figure is sometimes the most positive, perceptive and independent-minded figure in the dramatis personae of Compton-Burnett's fiction. As Marlon

27. Mayor, *The Rector's Daughter*, p.82. All quotations are from the first edition and page references are given in the main body of the text.

28. Rhiannon Williams, '"Hit or Miss": The Middle Class Spinster in Women's Novels 1913–1936', unpublished part 2 tripos dissertation, Cambridge University, 1985.

29. Letter to John Middleton Murry, dated 21 November, 1920. John Middleton Murry (ed.), *Katherine Mansfield's Letters to John Middleton Murry: 1913–1922* (London, Constable, 1951), p.598.

30. See, for example, Margaret Drabble 'Katherine Mansfield: Fifty Years On', *Harpers & Queen*, July 1973, pp.106–7.

31. *Katherine Mansfield* (Brighton: Harvester, 1986), p.127.

32. *The Prime of Miss Jean Brodie* (London: Macmillan, 1961), p.52.

33. Winifred Haetley, *South Riding: An English Landscape* (London: Collins, 1936), p.57.

B. Ross has observed, to Compton-Burnett, the 'governess represents a way of living, an ideal condition of wise contentedness to which the marginal manless women is best able to aspire'.[34]

Many spinsters' closest and most enduring relationships were with their sisters and the adventures of siblings often provided the staple plots of popular fiction, for example, of E.M. Delafield's lightly satirical novel based on the exploits of two sisters, *The Pelicans* (1918). Deirdre, the narrator of Rachel Ferguson's whimsical *The Brontës Went to Woolworths*, scoffs at the 'kind of novel called *They Were Seven*, or *Three – Not Out*,' in which 'one spends one's entire time to sort them all, and muttering, "Was it Isobel who drank, or Gertie?"'[35] Loving and committed relationships between women are dramatised between Joan Ogden and Elizabeth Rodney in *The Unlit Lamp*, between Muriel Hammond and Delia Vaughan in *The Crowded Street*, and between Averil Kennion and Sally Wraith in *Surplus*. In this forgotten lesbian novel the heroine asserts that 'to limit the fullest manifestation' of the power of love to 'beings, between whom the physical tie of matehood or parenthood exists, is like declaring that electricity can only be generated by one particular kind of dynamo'. *Surplus* ends with Sally wondering whether her role in life is really 'to teach some other unmated woman that she hasn't missed the greatest thing in the world, if she's had a great friendship?'[36]

Many of these women writers rejected the convention of concentrating on one key incident in a single woman's life, usually a proposal of marriage, and although marriage is often her family's preferred option it is manifestly not the spinster's. Indeed, for several heroines – Miriam Henderson, Muriel Hammond, Lolly Willowes, Joan Ogden, and Joanna Godden – marriage is rejected precisely because it is seen as an imposed rather than a natural condition, a threat to their precious sense of personal autonomy. Flouting convention, Miriam Henderson in *Pilgrimage*, plays billiards, smokes in public, wears trousers, rides a bicycle and conceives a child with no thought of acquiring a wedding ring: 'If you define life for women, as husbands and children, it means that you have no consciousness at all where women are concerned.'[37] For Muriel in *The Crowded Street* to marry Godfrey would be 'to give up every new thing

34. 'Contended Spinsters: Governessing and the Limits of Discursive Desire in the Fiction of I Compton-Burnett', in Laura A. Doan (ed.), *Old Maids to Radical Spinsters: Unmarried Women in the Twentieth-Century Novel* (Urbana and Chicago, University of Illinois Press, 1991), pp.39–65.

35. Rachel Ferguson, *The Brontës Went to Woolworths* (London: Benn, 1931), p.7.

36. Sylvia Stephenson, *Surplus* (London: Fisher Unwin, 1924), pp.294, 313.

37. Dorothy Richardson, *Pilgrimage* (13 vols), vol. 3, *Deadlock* (London: Duckworth, 1921), p.298.

that has made me a person'.[38] The Redland sisters in *The Rector's Daughter*, whose little house is a hive of good works, have 'not a low, but a poor opinion' of men as 'incapable, forgetful, tactless, capricious – rather the view of the Cranford ladies. They did not care for men's society. This was fortunate, for, as is usual with spinster households, they saw few.' (p.225)

Lolly Willowes feels shy and unnatural in the company of the laywers whom her in-laws have earmarked as potential husbands: 'Their jaws were like so many mousetraps, baited with commonplaces.'(p.55) In her in-laws' household Lolly seems not to be herself but to have become 'two persons, each different'. One is Aunt Lolly, 'a middle-aging lady, light-footed upon stairs and indispensable for Christmas Eve and birthday preparations'. The other is 'my sister-in-law Miss Willowes', whom Caroline introduces and then abandons to a 'feeling of being neither light-footed nor indispensable'.(p.61) Only when well away from the influence of her family is 'the true Laura' able to to discover her real identity, to pour out her soul to her confidant, the devil, and to discover and relish her real identity. As Jane Marcus has noted, *Lolly Willowes* revives the ancient equation of chastity with female freedom and posits chastity not as the absence of experience or sexuality but as a positive state of wholeness for women.[39]

To permit one's heroine to be on such splendidly good terms with the devil, to question and to challenge without hint of punishment, especially in the troubled area of male control and female submission, *is* to rebel against the dominant social relations, irrespective of the extent to which a rebellion like Lolly's must depend upon an independent income (and not just on an independent mind) and irrespective of how circumspect this may appear today. As Muriel's mentor in *The Crowded Street* says, 'the thing that matters is to take your life into your own hands and live it, accepting responsibility for failure or success. The really fatal thing is to let other people make your choices for you.'[40]

The joy of these texts for the many women who still read them avidly in modern editions is that, once free, there is never a real danger within the narrative that the heroine can ever be boxed back again into the kinds of domestic relationships that define and constrict women's lives. As Lolly Willowes reminds us 'nothing is impracticable for a single, middle-aged woman with an income of her own'.(p.102) The emphasis of these literary

38. Winifred Holtby, *The Crowded Street* (London: Lane, 1924), p.305.

39. 'A Wilderness of One's Own: Feminist Fantasy Novels in the Twenties: Rebecca West and Sylvia Townsend Warner', in Susan Merrill Squier (ed.), *Women Writers and the City: Essays in Feminist Literary Criticism* (Knoxville: University of Tennessee Press, 1984), p.135.

40. Holtby, *The Crowded Street*, p.261.

works on the heroine's longing for freedom generates an excess of desire which the narrative is at moments hard pressed to contain. In women's fictions, as Nancy K. Miller has argued, the reader's sense of security, itself dependent on the heroine's, 'comes from feeling not that the heroine will triumph in some *conventionally* positive way but that she will transcend the perils of plot with a self-exalting dignity'.[41] Even when a character fails dismally, when the free girl with a burning hope of womanhood becomes, like Joan Ogden, in *The Unlit Lamp* a 'funny old thing with grey hair', contemplating spirited women of the type she had once been, and thinking of herself sadly as 'a forererunner, a kind of pioneer that's got left behind',[42] the novel in question can still be read as a tribute to the vanguard who fell.

Today we see the category of the frustrated spinster as a fabrication, a severely limited, deficient work of definition, but in the 1920s it passed for truth. At a time when the popular perception of the spinster was deceptively simple: 'all those girls are just as like one another as two peas', a matron observes with 'married hardness' in *The Rector's Daughter* (p.30), the very diversity of literary representation in the 1920s introduced a welcome complexity. There is much in these novels to suggest that their heroines are typical. May Sinclair, for example, in framing her heroines' predicaments within the paradigms of Freudian theory, makes it clear that what is true for them is true of other women of their backgrounds. But there is also much that focuses on what is atypical and unique.

Women writers felt personally the weight of ideologies which constantly threatened to reduce the spinster to the status of object. Their response, in the idiom of the nineteenth-century, took the form of a 'covert solidarity that sometimes amounted to a genteel conspiracy' between the writer and her women reader. In the idiom of the present we may choose to refer to this as sisterhood. Specifically, what Elaine Showalter has termed as 'active unities of consciousness'[43] are manifested in the empathy between the woman writer who had broken free from convention and her character whose life is still hemmed by it: 'There was a moment when I first had "the idea" when I saw the two sisters as *amusing*; but the moment I looked deeper (let me be quite frank) I bowed down to the beauty that was hidden in their lives and to discover that was all my desire',[44] wrote Katherine Mansfield of Josephine and Constantia Pinner. Not all the authors to whom I have referred were spinsters. But with the exception of

41. 'Emphasis Added: Plots and Plausibilities in Women's Fiction', *PMLA*, vol. 96, no. 1, January 1981, p.40.

42. Radclyffe Hall, *The Unlit Lamp* (London: Cassell, 1924), p.301.

43. *A Literature of their Own: British Women Novelists from Brontë to Lessing* (London: Virago, 1978), pp.15–16.

44. Letter to W. Gerhardie, 23 June, 1921, John Middleton Murry (ed.), *The Letters of Katherine Mansfield*, 2 vols (London: Constable, 1928), vol. 2, p.120.

Katherine Mansfield and Dorothy Richardson, those of most interest today; Ivy Compton-Burnett, Radclyffe Hall, Winifred Holtby, Flora Mayor, May Sinclair and Sylvia Townsend Warner wrote from first-hand experience. Moreover, the desire of these women to speak from their own personal knowledge of spinsterhood occasionally slips into their texts in untoward ways. Mary Jocelyn, is not Flora Mayor's surrogate, despite the fact that her own father was a clergyman of considerable intellectual distinction. But one clergyman's daughter's understanding of the heartache of another (the 'odd cry from the heart, or whatever there is beyond the heart', p.337), nevertheless permeates the novel. At times in the narrative each of these authors appears to be working through some painful personal response to external circumstances, to be tracing or contemplating her own flight path of escape: 'My Muriel is myself – part of me only – the stupid frightened part', wrote Winifred Holtby.[45]

Individually, as literary works, only *The Rector's Daughter, Lolly Willowes, Pilgrimage, Miss Brill,* and *The Daughters of the Late Colonel* are of significant interest. But read together, and in context, the women's novels of the 1920s acquire new meanings as symptoms of women's unwillingness to submit uncomplainingly to those values, images and ideas, which ensure either that the dominant social relations are perceived by most people to be 'natural' or are not perceived at all. And collectively, when each work is read with reference to the others, they delineate a form of resistance, albeit at times hesitant and ambivalent, to the distorting ideologies of the day.

The sympathetic literary representation of spinsterood can perhaps be examined most interestingly in the least explicitly feminist of these women's fictions, *The Rector's Daughter.* This is a highly contradictory text which articulates the problems of the spinster more movingly than the others. But its outlook, consciously outmoded at the time, severely restricts the contemplation of ways of ameliorating her plight. As the title of *The Rector's Daughter* indicates, the relationship between Mary Jocelyn and her erudite, but increasingly cantankerous, father is central to this novel. The Rector of Dedmayne is a Victorian patriarch and his unmarried daughter utterly at the mercy of his whims. The village's name is symptomising: 'dead' plus 'mayne' – a signification between might and main: dead man, deadening power. There is more than a suggestion in the novel that the cost of Canon Jocelyn's magisterial learning has been extracted heavily from his family; Canon Jocelyn's children have never felt at ease with their father and he, in his turn, has never felt able to accept his children as they really are. Jocelyn behaves frostily to his mentally-

45. Letter from Holtby to 'Rosalind', dated 28 October, 1924. Alice Holtby and Jean McWilliam (eds), *Letters to a Friend* (London: Collins, 1937), p.288.

handicapped daughter, Ruth, and indifferently to his exiled son, William, and perhaps what Mary feels most deeply of all is her father's lack of feeling.

But in contrast to May Sinclair, who casts the Vicar of Garth as a paterfamilias with a rod of iron in *The Three Sisters* (1914), Flora Mayor avoids any simple dichotomy between father as oppressor and daughter as victim. While Mayor is critical of specific aspects of the Canon's personality, she is also sympathetically aware of the reasons for his intellectual and moral rigidity, namely the intellectual and moral legacy of the world in which he was young, and the querulousness, peccadillos and infirmity of old age. What complicates interpretation of the personal relationship between Mary and her father is their relationship to the community at large in which both have clearly defined public roles.

From the opening pages of *The Rector's Daughter* Mary Jocelyn is a loved, loving, and altogether indispensable member of her little community: 'In a sense the whole village adored Mary, but quietly'.(p.22) Mary patiently presides over bible classes, gently officiates at mothers' meetings and harvest festivals and trains the church choir. Mothers are offended if she is not the first to welcome new arrivals. The Rector's daughter is 'as much a part of her village as its homely hawthorns' (p.7), adept at patching up the differences between various layers of society which make up the excitement of village life.

Unlike other women novelists of her day, Flora Mayor never questioned the role of family as the basic unit of authority in society. Ivy Compton-Burnett, for example, drew clear parallels between the abuse of power by the head of the household and by the head of the state: 'The assumption of divine right and the acceptance of it takes things further along the same line. History gives us examples that are repeated in smaller kingdoms.'[46] Compton-Burnett is forthright in condemning the power adults exercised over children in the Victorian home: 'I write of power being destructive and parents had absolute power over children in those days.'[47]

But in *The Rector's Daughter* the Jocelyns father and daughter, serve as a model for the harmonious relationship between the individual and the community in which Mayor strongly believes. This relationship is essentially deferential; supportive of and supported by the allegiances of tradition and hierarchy which the Canon's unstinting devotion to classical scholarship, and Mary's unstinting devotion to the welfare of his

---

46. I. Compton-Burnett and M. Jourdain – 'A Conversation', *Orion*, 1, 1934, reprinted in Charles Burckhart (ed.), *The Art of I. Compton-Burnett: A Collection of Critical Essays* (London: Gollancz, 1972), p.29.
47. Quoted in Hilary Spurling, *Secrets of a Woman's Heart: The Later Life of Ivy Compton-Burnett 1920–1969* (London: Hodder and Stoughton), p.174.

parishioners, respectively embody.

Although it is in the home that much of Mary's work is done, it is outside it that her full worth as a human being is recognised. To register the devastating effect of Mary's death from influenza on the tightly-knit community to which she belonged the novel subtly changes direction. Narrative progression gives way to retrospective probing in order to record, delicately and reconditely, the significance of a life, abruptly and tragically cut short at the age of thirty-nine. The full impact of her loss is deeply felt at the end of the novel as the shock of Mary's death is allowed to reverberate. It was 'crazy' and 'tragic' (p.336) that Mary did not marry and find happiness in the usual way: 'You feel it, Miss Dora, same almost as me, because you've been about the world just as I've done, and I know ladies, and there never will be any one like her again' (p.334), utters the good-hearted countrywoman, Cook.

There is an overwhelming sense of sadness and wasted potential in *The Rector's Daughter* achieved largely through quiet understatement. As a lonely child who longed for friends 'but friend-making needs practice' Mary 'retired within herself, and fell in love instead with Mr Rochester, Hamlet and Dr. Johnson'.(p.14) The absence of the formal schooling denied to Mary – which was provided, as a matter of course, for each of her three older brothers – leaves her with much time for dreaming and thinking during solitary girlhood walks: 'She had much seething within her waiting for an outlet. She wrote her thoughts down to get rid of them.'(p.19)

The cumulative effect of the minutely-observed inventory of every day-to-day task ('solace') which occupies Mary's time in the middle years she spends in tending to Aunt Lottie – winding up clocks, letting the cat and dog in and out of the house – emphasises the tedium of her existence more tellingly than any protest. No sooner is each duty performed than, as is the punishing nature of such things, it must needs be done all over again. Observation of character ('Aunt Lottie, though not deaf, was inquisitive and inattentive'; p.325) is precise. Mary finds one outlet to express her intelligence and creativity, her writing, but the worth of her writing is never properly recognised. The woman poet is lost – both to herself and to the world – her poems, about which we are left in ignorance, are airily dismissed at the end of the novel as 'just the Anglican spinster warbling' (p.337) – albeit by a character whom we know to be incapable of doing them justice.

In 'Miss Brill' an impoverished spinster ekes out a living as best she can by giving lessons in English. The governess, Doris Kilman in *Mrs. Dalloway* (1924) is highly intelligent. But she is poor, moreover degradingly poor, and impeccable though her academic credentials may be, is economically beholden to an employer whom she despises, consoling herself with her tea, her chocolate éclairs and her hot-water bottle at night. In *A Room of One's Own* (1928) the narrator survives in the only ways open to a respectable, middle-class woman before 1918. Addressing envelopes, reading to old ladies, making artificial flowers, and teaching the alphabet to small children, Mary Beaton had 'always to be doing work that one did not wish to do, and to do it like a slave'. One corrosive simile sums up her weary labours: 'like a rust eating away the bloom of the spring, destroying the tree at its heart'.[48] Mary Jocelyn's friend, Dora Redland, 'the UF.' or 'Unnecessary Female', (p.39) paints an idealistic, optimistic gloss on servitude – 'the wonderful desire which is so strong in English spinsters to serve, to help, to be perhaps almost too busy in other people's affairs'.(pp.223–4) But serving others is not enough to make Mary Jocelyn feel fulfilled. Mary's life is a chastening example of how emptily spinsters have been forced to spend their lives – in the routine exercise of chores that time and duty have drained of meaning, or made the sole repository of meaning. In this respect Mayor shares the concerns of, and is writing in conversation with, her sister authors in the 1920s.

The essence of Mary's labour is that it is freely given. At her lowest ebb she ventures out in the pouring rain to visit a new-born baby: 'But I can't bear the people to think I don't care.'(p.206) Caring of this kind, of the order Mary epitomises, is clearly intended to make literal and specialised (to women) the qualities of compassion and love: 'Mary had a pull over us in a way', says a character, Brynhilda; 'she cared, and we can't care, not much, and never for long'.(p.336) The far-reaching ethical ramifications of Mary's concern is explained by Mayor's biographer, Sybil Oldfield: 'To refuse to do this work . . . is to force the unwanted failures of the earth to feel the full depth and extent of their unwantedness. It is to kill their spirit.'[49]

A key episode in *The Rector's Daughter* shows how expertly Mayor controls the readers' response. The Rector has delivered a carefully prepared Lenten address to a disappointingly sparse congregation, and has wreaked his irritation on his daughter by contradicting her timid remarks on the way home ('old remarks, which she had often made because he liked them' pp.215–16). In the privacy of her bedroom Mary rummages around to find a letter from Mr. Herbert and then breaks down in uncontrollable tears – a rare moment at which Mayor allows a real, if momentary, tension between submission to duty and longing for freedom ('if only the door had never been unlocked', pp.215–16). At this point in the narrative it is

48. Virginia Woolf, *A Room of One's Own* (London: Hogarth, 1929), p.57.

49. *Spinsters of this Parish: The Life and Times of F.M. Mayor and Mary Sheepshanks* (London: Virago, 1984), p.237.

the Rector, but at others it may be the self-opinionated Aunt Lottie, the lonely schoolmistress, Miss Gage, or any one of her father's importunate parishioners, who demand and secure Mary's concentrated attention. It is precisely because Mary's patience had hitherto seemed limitless that the surge of emotion between evensong and dinner is so powerful. But even Mary's patience can be stretched to its limits – to breaking point. As the virtuous woman that she is, Mary needs no telling that the married clergyman who is the cause of her anguish is beyond her legitimate aspirations and implicitly accepts the need to subdue her passions. The Canon speaking of George Eliot says that 'to indulge in love for a married man is always illicit'.(p.199) But even in cherishing in her heart a forbidden love Mary is allowing herself a liberty which would have shocked her father's generation.

Mayor vividly dramatises the distress Mary experiences in trying to live in a principled way, feeling deeply and yet, in the main, managing successfully to repress her deepest feelings. For were Mary's emotional needs to be less sensitively drawn, or their containment more mechanical, the degree of sympathetic attention we accord her would be correspondingly less: 'It is like a bitter *Cranford*. Mrs. [sic] Mayor explores depths of feeling that Mrs. Gaskell's generation perhaps did not know and certainly did not admit to knowing', wrote Sylvia Lynd in *Time and Tide* in 1924.[50]

Mary's day-to-day existence amply corroborates Rosaline Masson's view that the home life of the country was based upon 'a substratum of obscure martyrdoms'. But this is not the case that Mayor wants to make. Personal anguish in *The Rector's Daughter* is not evoked to explore the social structure which makes it feature large in women's lives. On the contrary, it is evoked, as by Charlotte Brontë in *Jane Eyre*, primarily to induce our identification with the heroine in her suffering. Throughout the novel Mary's are the *only* standards – deeply caring, unselfish, finely discriminating, painfully sensitive, unfailingly generous and compassionate – by which we are asked to judge the behaviour of others.

Cecily Palser Havely, writing on another text, summarises the general issues which *The Rector's Daughter* also raises for women:

> There can be nothing wrong with any writer's desire to give the fullest possible account of an exclusively female experience or point of view. But the danger in the situation is that so much women's writing about women tends to consolidate the unhappy status quo, and not to advance the claims of women to a fuller life in every respect.

50. *Time and Tide*, 18 July, 1924, p.691.

> The better the thing is done, the easier it is to believe that this is the thing
> that women do best, and from there it is too easy a step to believing that it is
> the only thing they can do.[51]

In analysing *The Rector's Daughter* I make no criticism of the desire
to care for others, quite the opposite. But it is, nevertheless, true that society
does not reward 'caring' as it rewards all else it values – with money, power
and status – and that society teaches girls to care, and requires this of
women, in ways not expected of boys and men. While there is some ironic
awareness of this discrepancy in the text ('she knew she excelled in one
branch of knowledge – old ladies', p.106) the view that caring is women's
special province, often used to impede women's progress to full equality,
is one the novel in its entirety endorses.

This is certainly not the case in other novels published in 1924, *The
Unlit Lamp, Surplus, Lolly Willowes* and *The Crowded Street*, nor is it true
of May Sinclair's earlier novella, *Life and Death of Harriett Frean*. The
heroine of *Surplus*, Sally Wraith, who sets up a motor vehicles business,
admits to having as much inclination and aptitude for work with the sick
and the poor 'as the pirate chief has for assuming the cassock'.[52] In the
beech forests of the Chilterns Lolly Willowes is determined to resist the
temptation to do good which pursues her relentlessly. She declaims that
she did not opt to become the village witch in order 'to run round being
helpful', to become 'a district visitor on a broomstick' (pp.238–9), but to
'escape all that – to have a life of one's own, not an existence doled out to
you by others'.(*LW* p.239)

Neither Radclyffe Hall nor Winifred Holtby consider speaking up for
women to be a sufficient end in itself. They both plumb the source of
women's problems in the unreasonable expectations of her family. Muriel
in *The Crowded Street* – originally called *The Wallflower* – turns her back
on the relentless tedium of her life at home in the suburb of Marshington
(Cottingham where Holtby grew up) to work for a women's organisation
in London and put into practice 'an idea of service – not just vague and
sentimental, but translated into quite practical things'.[53]

In *The Unlit Lamp* the personal attention Joan Ogden's selfish, ailing
mother demands effectively wrecks her daughter's promising career as a
doctor. The irony of medicine never being recognised as caring work
(because it falls outside the ambit of traditional work for women) is heavily
underscored. Try as she might Joan cannot free herself from the kindly

51. 'Carson McCullers and Flannery O' Connor', in Douglas Jefferson and Graham
Martin (eds), *The Uses of Fiction: Essays on the Modern Novel in Honour of Arnold Kettle*
(Milton Keynes: Open University Press, 1982), p.118.
52. Stephenson, *Surplus*, p.309.
53. Holtby, *The Crowded Street*, p.305.

tyranny of family interest and in the end is forced to relinquish not just the hope of a career but also all hope of ever being able to establish any kind of independent existence for herself. Like Lalage Rush in *Ordinary Families* (1933) Joan can offer no convincing reason for wanting to leave home. In *Ordinary Families* the narrator tartly notes how 'in very few of the thousands of good homes, from which the children struggle to escape, can the truth ever be told . . . even in the heat of a family row'.[54]

Lolly Willowes, The Unlit Lamp and *The Crowded Street* are all a good deal more critical of middle-class family expectations and a good deal more scathing about domestic obligations imposed upon the unmarried daughter than is *The Rector's Daughter*, in which there is a strong suggestion that Mary would have made a good wife and a loving mother, but little suggestion that she might ever have become anything else.

One question that arises is why Mayor conflates the important work of caring for others – which most readers would agree is genuinely life-enhancing – and the routine performance of household duties which may appear to the reader merely as domestic drudgery passed off as caring in a thin disguise. If, as would appear to be the case, we are expected to respect the selfless way that Mary performs *all* the work required of her, why is this dedication to domestic duty so frequently lauded in literature only when exemplified by women? The truth is that *The Rector's Daughter* is profoundly ambivalent on the question of self-sacrifice. As Merryn Williams succinctly puts it, Mayor did not want to 'denounce the traditional Christian and womanly virtue of self-sacrifice, although she did not recommend it to all and sundry'.[55]

Flora Mayor admits that the psychological toll extracted from Mary as a 'dutiful daughter' is too high, but she will not generalise from that to the patriarchal system. In the end, the paternal order that the novel embodies both establishes an authoritative system of values and abolishes the apparent discrepancy between individual desire and social respons-ibility. What is absent in *The Rector's Daughter*, but markedly present in other texts about spinsters of this period, *Lolly Willowes, Life and Death of Harriett Frean, The Crowded Street*, is the potential for changing the ground rules of domestic attitudes and for questioning the relationships between women and men. Mayor is out of step, and probably out of sympathy, with other women writers who want to question these values or who may want to suggest that some restructuring of society's expectations of women may be necessary.

In the matter of the Lenten Sermon we have seen the clergyman depicted at his worst, but the portrait of Canon Jocelyn is not unmitigatedly

54. Eileen Arnot Robertson, *Ordinary Families* (London: Cape, 1933), p.217.
55. *Six Women Novelists* (Basingstoke: Macmillan, 1987), p.52.

severe and dexterous touches soften the general picture of unbending rectitude. Despite his lack of feeling for his other children, he is genuinely fond of Mary, and tries to console her when he senses her disappointment in love. But he cannot help patronising even when well-intentioned: "'It's an excellent wine, and" (in the warmth of his feeling he said "and", not "but") "it is particularly well suited to ladies"'.(p.143) An entry in her father's journal expressing remorse over the death of his younger daughter, Ruth, which Mary discovers after his death – 'I feel no grief. How should I? I have not deserved to grieve' (p.313) – also presents the Canon in a more sympathetic light.

Selective details of this kind generate the novel's representation of values. They present the Rector to us in a more human light and rub out any lingering suspicion that Jocelyn may really be little more than 'an ogre father battening on his daughter's vitality' (p.217), subtly erasing the traces of any substantive conflict that may have existed between Mary and her father. Whatever their differences, we are left in no doubt that the two members of the Jocelyn family are cast in the same mould and that *both* epitomise all that is precious and worth cherishing in the little community: 'The Jocelyns must have been wonderful, and the people were dreadfully upset when they heard she had passed away.'(p.335) This epitaph, with its elision of father and daughter, shows the joint esteem in which both were held by the ordinary folk in the village. The realisation that something precious and irreplaceable, the old-fashioned love of learning and the elevated heights of classical scholarship which the Canon embodies, is about to disappear forever (to be replaced by democratic and potentially unsettling ideas about education being ordinary and commonplace?) ultimately matters more to the parishioners in Dedmayne than any differences between the different generations of the Jocelyn family.

There is an elegaic, contemplative tone to *The Rector's Daughter* and the first impressions that we have of Dedmayne in this extended rural retrospect are the ones that remain with us. The emphasis is on a vanishing world: 'what has been known from childhood must be lovable, whether it is ugly or beautiful' (p.6), and on an old-fashioned little community, just on the verge of extinction, its fragility sensitively evoked. Mary's home, the Rectory, is a 'frail, frail survival, lasting on out of its time, its companions vanished long since' which would 'fall at a touch' (p.12) when the Canon himself died. The middle-aged feel the Canon to be 'a belated traveller'.(p.317) Mrs. Plumtree is a 'faded specimen of the generation that is almost gone'.(p.106)

The parishioners, Miss Gage and Mrs. Davy, are finely drawn, their tiny ambitions and harmless affectations gently ridiculed, but only from a perspective that is essentially affectionate. Any humour derived at their expense is, like Elizabeth Gaskell's in *Cranford*, always an expression of the author's enjoyment of their idiosyncracy and of her desire to leave the objects of her humour essentially unchanged.

In throwing a ladder back to before 1914, to an isolated hamlet where time stands still, Flora Mayor denies Mary options she knew were open to educated women in the 1920s. Her avoidance of the difficult questions that Freudian theory and feminism, in their different ways, were raising for women marks Mayor's difference in outlook from other women writers. The life and expectations of Mary Jocelyn correspond to the social position and subjective experiences of women in an earlier age. This is essential to the realisation of a caring society and the avoidance of vexed issues that might otherwise have to be confronted. For the relationship of a text to the values and ideas of its time is illustrated by what it says and by what it does not.

It is in the 'significant *silences* of a text, in its gaps and absences, that the presence of ideology can be most positively felt'.[56] The real effect of dwelling upon a caring society in the past, as Raymond Williams astutely points out in *The Country and the City*, is often withdrawal from a full response to existing society. 'Value', he writes, 'is in the past, as a general retrospective condition, and is in the present only as a particular and private sensibility, the individual moral action'.[57]

At one level of argument a text illustrates nothing beyond itself. To value it for its referential qualities, as a response to social realities, is to say that it has failed to transcend its material. 'Real art,' as Susan Sontag explains, always 'has the capacity to make us nervous. By reducing the work of art to its content and then interpreting that, one tames the work of art.'[58]

But to understand the relationship of any work of art to the ideologies current at its moment of production is a different objective. This must involve closely examining the specific material conditions, the actual relations, and the deeper contradictions out of which both works of art and specific ideologies have emerged. As we have seen, *The Rector's Daughter* emerged in the context of the national preoccupation with two million supposedly superfluous women. But here lie problems for the feminist reader. For many of the impulses informing the text, particularly in relation to its defence of family, the position of women, and the kind of society Mayor upholds, are deeply conservative.

One major achievement of *The Rector's Daughter* is to create a heroine who, on the surface, appears nothing more than a garden-variety Anglican spinster, but whose life is acknowledged to be exemplary by the

56. Terry Eagleton, *Marxism and Literary Criticism* (London: Methuen, 1976), p.35.
57. *The Country and the City* (London Chatto and Windus, 1973), p.180.
58. *Against Interpretation and Other Essays* (London: Eyre and Spottiswoode, 1969), p.8.

community in which she lives. In the context of the dominant public attitudes to the spinster in the 1920s this is significant. Mary is clearly in no way 'superfluous' or 'useless' or 'abnormal'. The radical potential of this representation is, however, contained and attenuated by Mayor's affirmation of the importance of traditional family values and of heterosexual, romantic love.

The ideological project of *The Rector's Daughter* is to stress the need for personal responsibility in a changing world. To do this Mayor must either simplify or exclude that world. For, as Raymond Williams observes, it is a contradiction in the form of the novel (as received and developed by George Eliot) that the 'moral emphases on conduct – and therefore the technical strategy of unified narrative and analytic tones – must be at odds with any society – the "knowable community" of the novel – in which moral bearings have been extended to substantial and conflicting social relationships'.[59]

The only values offered that jar with those of Dedmayne are voiced by Brynhilda Kenrick and her fashionable circle who had 'shaken off their families and united in light elastic unions with friends'.(p.95) Wives without husbands and husbands without wives – this travesty of the Bloomsbury circle could easily be recognised and dismissed by the first readers of the work. It is the only challenge to the caring community admitted to the work – and no real challenge at all.

The Rector's Daughter is a product of the anxieties besetting Mayor's class and the social milieu represented in the novel is similar to her own. In this respect it may be usefully contrasted with a short story by D.H. Lawrence, 'Daughters of the Vicar' (1914), in which Lawrence describes a vicar's family isolated and surrounded by working-class people who have scant regard for their social superiors. The church at Aldecross stands '*buried* in its greenery, *stranded* and *sleeping* among the fields, while the brick houses elbow nearer and nearer, *threatening* to crush it down' [my emphases].[60] This short story indicates Lawrence's own keen awareness of the existence of communities which may be unknowable to outsiders and deeply threatening to middle-class sensibilities. We have only to put it beside *The Rector's Daughter* to be made aware of that novel's silences in relation to class and to sexual politics, and of the social tensions which Flora Mayor refused to face.

My reading of *The Rector's Daughter* – a conservative text which I have not rashly attempted to present as radical – has identified the specific points at which that text was allied to the common ideologies of the day and the

59. Williams, *The Country and the City*, pp.168–9.
60. 'Daughters of the Vicar', in *The Tales of D.H. Lawrence* (London: Martin and Secker), p.47.

specific points at which it departed from them. I have also outlined the ways in which this, and other texts of the time, may have acted as a focus of recognitions which helped contemporary readers to understand and resist the ubiquitous preconceptions about spinsterhood which had entered, infiltrated and violated the recesses of women's inner lives.

Much of this chapter has concentrated on the discussion of character but the 'exemplary character' we have recognised in Mary Jocelyn raises questions about how literary texts are read, about what constitutes a progressive text, and about how we recognise one. Is it possible for characters like Mary to serve as positive role models for women? as alter-egos? or even ego-ideals? Judith Kegan Gardiner has suggested that the 'woman writer uses her text, particularly one centering on a female hero, as part of a continuous process involving her own self-definition'.[61] Feminists have argued that in some respects the relationship between the woman reader and a fictional character resembles the interactions commonly found in friendships between women. As the psychoanalytic writer, Carol Gilligan, has explained, 'women replace the bias of men toward separation with a representation of the interdependence of self and other, both in love and in work'.[62] Simone de Beauvoir, for example, tells how she came to recognise a fictional character as an alter-ego and how this recognition strongly influenced her own personal development.

> About this time I read a novel which seemed to me to translate my spiritual exile into words: George Eliot's *The Mill on the Floss* made an even deeper impression on me than *Little Women* . . . Maggie Tulliver, like myself, was torn between others and herself: I recognised myself in her. She too was dark, loved nature and books and life, was too headstrong to be able to observe the conditions of her respectable surroundings, and yet was very sensitive to the criticism of a brother she adored.[63]

Notwithstanding de Beauvoir's eloquent testimony, it is not clear how the lives of 'strong' or 'exemplary' women in fiction affect women's lives for better or worse. Within fiction 'exemplary' characters can and do inspire others to change their lives. Muriel in *The Crowded Street* resolves, albeit temporarily, to become a mathematician after reading *The Life of Mary Somerville*. It is also true that in the process of reading we may sometimes revise our sense of self, retaining or relinquishing old

61. 'On Female Identity and Writing by Women', *Critical Inquiry*, 8, Winter 1981, p.357.
62. *In a Different Voice: Psychological Theory and Women's Development* (Cambridge: Mass.: Harvard University Press, 1982), p.170.
63. *Memoirs of a Dutiful Daughter*, (trans.) James Kirkup (London: Deutsch and Weidenfeld and Nicolson, 1959), p.141.

understandings in the light of the new. But as no two individuals are ever identical the recognition of similarities between ourselves and a fictional alter-ego must also entail the recognition of *differences* – of temperament and situation, of race, sexual orientation and class. 'We may stress the value of sympathy,' observed Virginia Woolf, 'we may try to sink our own identity as we read. But we know that we cannot sympathise wholly or immerse ourselves wholly.'[64] It is also possible that studies of rebellious,'strong' or 'exemplary' women may reconcile women readers to their lot by presenting them with images of womanhood which appear highly remote and unattainable. For however much they would like to be 'strong', many women are acutely conscious of the compromises which they have had to make in their personal lives and may consequently feel deeply ambivalent about images of 'the exemplary' and the 'powerful' in which they fail to recognise their existing or potential selves. If literary representations do not make sufficient allowance for women's weaknesses and vulnerability and do not adequately 'reflect the diversity and complexity of our desires'[65] they may be of limited value to the woman reader attempting to come to a fuller understanding of herself through the literary text.

No work of fiction can ever be interpreted as progressive merely on account of the characters within it; other factors must also be taken into the reckoning. A character, 'strong' or 'weak', must always be assessed within the narrative and structures in which she is contained. In much the same way no work of fiction text can be ever regarded as progressive simply as an effect of its content but only as a result of its intersection with other discourses and institutions. The test of any text's progressiveness always take place, to some extent at least, outside the text, within political discourse and in generic, semantic and readerly interchange. And the political function and effectivity of any text must always depend on its socio-historical conjuncture and on an informed understanding of the conditions in which it comes to be written and read.

In evaluating the texts on literary spinsterhood in the 1920s from a feminist perspective much will depend on our understanding which discourses have been displaced and to what effect. Read alongside Freudian ideas about sexuality ('a woman, must enjoy the full cycle of sex-experience, or she would become riddled with complexes like a rotting fruit') as Winifred Holtby understood them at the time, or beside A.M. Ludovici's misogynistic prejudice about supposedly surplus women ('not

64. 'How Should One Read a Book?', in *The Common Reader*, second series (London: Hogarth, 1932), p.268.
65. Elizabeth Wilson, *Mirror Writing: An Autobiography* (London: Virago, 1982), p.155.

leading natural lives . . . able to find no normal expression or satisfaction'), *The Crowded Street, Lolly Willowes, The Rector's Daughter* and other texts which invest the life of the spinster with dignity, come to acquire a new significance for us. Whatever their starting point these texts were progressively aligned within the wider social and political debates of the day.

As Pierre Macherey has reminded us, literature comes into being, 'not by magic, but by a real labour of production' in determinate conditions.[66] But the conditions which give rise to literary texts, though clear enough at the time, may not be evident later, and the full significance of texts may therefore be lost. Only when literary texts are restored to their histories, when, for example, fictional and discursive accounts of spinsterhood are placed side by side, can works of fiction be properly understood as pictures of reality which have been produced by women and men living in specific historical circumstances, and which men and women living in later and different historical conditions are then free to refuse, to question, or to appropriate as they wish.

66. *A Theory of Literary Production*, (trans.) Geoffrey Wall (London: Routledge and Kegan Paul, 1978), p.67.

4

Lesbian Representation: *Orlando* and *The Well of Loneliness*

I do not believe in shutting our eyes to social tendencies; it is not 'natural' to have 2,000,000 more women than men, and 'this sort of thing' was bound to arise from the state of affairs. Therefore any girl in these days is liable to form friendships or make acquaintances which may lead to undesirable relations, and it is just as well that she should be warned.

A.P. Herbert[1]

The context of the words above is the trial of *The Well of Loneliness*. The connections Herbert made between that which is 'not natural' (the demographic imbalance) and 'this sort of thing' (lesbianism) were common. Like many who defended *The Well of Loneliness*, A.P. Herbert appears to have seen its primary value as a cautionary tale.

I wish to discuss the relationship between feminist and lesbian consciousness by comparing two texts published in 1928. At a superficial level *Orlando* and *The Well of Loneliness*[2] appear to have little or nothing in common. I shall, however, argue that *Orlando* is both a feminist text and a lesbian text – that it is a text in which feminist and lesbian ideas can be seen to be inextricably intertwined. The bracketing of feminist and lesbian concerns is common in the 1990s. This was not the case in 1928 when, as we have seen, the meanings attached to spinsterhood were a site of impassioned contestation, and the literary representation of lesbian sexual practice a matter for the courts. Today many feminists view lesbian relationships as subversive because they demonstrate the existence of female sexual desire outside male control. Such links between lesbianism and feminism had not been theorised in 1928. Feminists like Vera Brittain who defended *The Well of Loneliness* did so as enlightened citizens and

---

1. Quoted by Angela Ingram, '"Unutterable Putrefaction" and "Foul Stuff": Two 'Obscene' Novels of the 1920's', *Women's Studies International Forum*, vol. 9, 4, 1986, p.348.
2. Virginia Woolf, *Orlando: A Biography* (London: Hogarth, 1928), Radclyffe Hall, *The Well of Loneliness* (London: Cape, 1928); reprinted uniform edition (London: Hammond, 1956). All quotations are from the first edition of *Orlando* and the 1956 edition of *The Well of Loneliness* and page references are given in the main body of the text.

not because they could see any connection between the patriarchal oppression of women and the patriarchal repression of lesbian sexuality.[3]

For much of its history *Orlando*, until recently one of the most neglected of all Virginia Woolf's novels, was not deemed to be feminist or political. Makiko Minow-Pinkney has pointed out that precisely because feminist critics have been 'eager to dispel the old image of ethereal aestheticism' much of the feminist critical work on Virginia Woolf of the 1970s and 1980s has been at its weakest in relation to the experimental novels between *Jacob's Room* and *The Waves*.[4] A re-reading of *Orlando* is therefore necessary to recover the radical strain that runs through *all* Woolf's writings, even the most experimental and ostensibly non-politicised.

Virginia Woolf began *Orlando* on 8 October, 1927 and finished it on 18 March, 1928. *The Well of Loneliness* was published on 15 July and withdrawn from circulation on 21 August. Woolf privately thought *The Well of Loneliness* a 'meritorious dull book'.[5] Aware of the ironies of linking her own name with E.M. Forster (who 'thought Sapphism disgusting: partly from convention, partly because he disliked that women should be independent of men'),[6] she, nevertheless, agreed to sign a joint letter of protest to *The Nation and Athenaeum* on 8 September ('it appears that I, the mouthpiece of Sapphism, write letters from the Reform Club!').[7] On 24 September she set out for a week's holiday in France with Vita Sackville-West, the model on whom the character of Orlando was based, and one of Radclyffe Hall's most committed and energetic supporters. They returned to England on 1 October in time for the publication of *Orlando* on 11 October (the novel ends sonorously on that date at the twelfth stroke of midnight).

In late October Woolf read the two papers which were later to become

3. Brittain carefully distinguishes between 'women of the type of Stephen Gordon', whose 'abnormality' is 'inherent' and who 'deserve the fullest consideration and compassion' and others whose lesbianism is 'merely the unnecessary cult of exotic erotics'. See Vera Brittain, *Radclyffe Hall: A Case of Obscenity* (London: Femina, 1968), pp.49–50.

4. Makiko Minow-Pinkney, *Virginia Woolf and the Problem of the Subject: Feminine Writing in the Major Novels* (Brighton: Harvester, 1987), p.x.

5. Anne Olivier-Bell and Andrew McNellie (eds), *The Diary of Virginia Woolf*, 5 vols (Harmondsworth: Penguin, 1979–1985), vol. 3, p.193. All further references in footnotes are to *The Diary* and give the volume number.

6. Ibid.

7. Letter from Virginia Woolf to Vita Sackville-West, dated 9 September, 1928. Nigel Nicolson and Joanne Trautmann (eds), *The Letters of Virginia Woolf*, 6 vols (London: Hogarth, 1976–1980), vol. 3, p.530. Radclyffe Hall and Virginia Woolf both try to avoid the use of the term lesbian. Hall uses the term 'invert' which has clinical overtones and Woolf, as in this letter, uses the term 'sapphist' which has poetic ones. All further references in footnotes are to *The Letters* and give the volume number.

A Room of One's Own to audiences from both of the Cambridge wom
colleges, at Newnham on 20 October, and in the presence of Vita, at Gi
a week later on 26 October. The trial, at which Sir Chartres Biron acte
presiding magistrate, was clearly at the forefront of her mind on t
occasion: 'Are there no men present? . . . the figure of Sir Chartres Bir
is not concealed? We are all women you assure me?'[8] According to Ja
Marcus, Virginia Woolf had originally contemplated making her women
scientists, Chloe and Olivia, share 'the obscenity trial for a novel', before
settling for the words 'shared a laboratory together' which appear in *A
Room of One's Own*.[9] On 7 November she attended a meeting of artists
and intellectuals convened to discuss questions of censorship and artistic
freedom arising out of *The Well of Loneliness* trial.

Although Virginia Woolf went to court ready to speak for the defence,
having drafted a statement to the effect that *The Well of Loneliness* 'treats
a delicate subject with great delicacy and discretion',[10] she was not called
upon to testify. The trial took place on 9 November. An order banning *The
Well of Loneliness* was obtained on 16 November and an appeal turned
down on 14 December. But the trial clearly made a strong impression. An
entry in Virginia Woolf's diary refers to the presiding magistrate ('like a
Harley St. specialist investigating a case') in language which brings to
mind Sir William Bradshaw in *Mrs. Dalloway*.[11]

In 1928, as Virginia Woolf was clearly aware, neither the critical
establishment nor the reading public was ready for the intimate relations
between women in *The Well of Loneliness* nor, for that matter, were they
ready for the explicit sex of *Lady Chatterley's Lover*. *Orlando* contained
specific and satiric references to Lawrence's banned work: 'the
gamekeeper will whistle under the window . . . the very stuff of life . . .
the only possible subject of fiction',(p.242) Her own novel escaped the
attention of the censor only because Woolf entertained no illusions about
the power exercised by those who decreed the limits of what was
permissible in literature and life.

As sheer fantasy she knew that *Orlando* would give her the freedom
to mock and bend the conventions of the established order with impunity.
And having made peace with her age she would be left free to write: 'The
transaction between a writer and the spirit of the age', as the narrator of
Orlando knowingly observes, 'is one of infinite delicacy' and 'upon a nice

8. Virginia Woolf, *A Room of One's Own* (London: Hogarth, 1929), p.123.

9. 'Sapphistry: Narration as Lesbian Seduction', in Jane Marcus (ed.), *A Room of One's Own*', in *Virginia Woolf and the Languages of Patriarchy* (Bloomington: Indiana University Press, 1987), p.169.

10. Quoted by Angela Ingram, '"Unutterable Putrefaction" and "Foul Stuff": Two "Obscene" Novels of the 1920's', p.349.

11. *The Diary*, vol. 3, p.206.

arrangement between the two the whole fortune of his work depends'. (pp.239–40) We may read *Orlando* as Woolf's *modus vivendi* with her times, as a pragmatic acceptance of the limits of the contemporary 'horizon of expectations'. *Orlando* allowed its author to be of her age without submitting to it, and to remain true to herself without exposing herself to the pain of public controversy.

Virginia Woolf's reticence about speaking directly on sexual matters was intimately connected to her fear of male censure. In 'Professions for Women' (1931), she explained how women writers were inhibited 'by the extreme conventionality of the other sex. For though men sensibly allow themselves great freedom in these respects, I doubt that they realize or can control the extreme severity with which they condemn such freedom in women.'[12] The magical change of sex in *Orlando* was the perfect stratagem which enabled her to write about sexuality at a safe distance from the censoring voices whose power to silence women writers dealing directly with lesbian subject-matter was proved by the fate of *The Well of Loneliness*.

In the preface to her engagement with Woolf's major novels, the critic, Makiko Minow-Pinkney, appears to find modernism and feminism, if not commensurate, at least to be working in a harmonious partnership: 'Woolf's experimental novels can . . . best be seen as a feminist subversion of the deepest formal principles – of the very definitions of narrative, writing, the subject – of a patriarchal social order.'[13] Yet at the end of *Virginia Woolf and the Problem of the Subject* Minow-Pinkney reverts to the view that feminism and modernism are in some senses incompatible: 'On the other hand, modernism and feminism are in some way at odds: the symbolist version of modernism, which Woolf embraced, rejects feminist anger, "self-consciousness", explicit polemical statement, all of which supposedly denature writing. But the historical and personal pressures of the 1930s . . . prompted Woolf to write her most outspokenly feminist books, *The Years* and *Three Guineas*.'[14]

In referring to 'feminist anger' in this passage Minow-Pinkney would seem to endorse Jane Marcus's well-known argument that anger is a primary source of creative energy for women, that it is almost synonymous with feminist writing, and that its suppression in Woolf's writing was detrimental to her creativity.[15] While anger may certainly be a key component of feminist writing it is not a *sine qua non*, and it is often

12. Leonard Woolf (ed.), *The Collected Essays of Virginia Woolf*, 4 vols (London: Hogarth, 1966–1967), vol. 2, p.288. All further references are to *The Collected Essays* and give the essay title and volume.

13. Minow-Pinkney, *Virginia Woolf and the Problem of the Subject*, p.x.

14. Ibid., p.187.

15. 'Art and Anger', *Feminist Studies*, vol. 4, 1, February 1978, pp.69–98.

irrelevant to feminist art. *Orlando* is a celebratory, playful, exuberant testing and parading of feminist possibilities. A serenely contented text of fun and fantasy, it is no less a feminist text for the absence of anger.

The Well of Loneliness is the best-known lesbian text in English but is *Orlando* a lesbian text? The definition of a 'lesbian text' is contentious.[16] However, irrespective of whether we define it as a text written by a lesbian, a text which represents erotic or physical relationships between women, or a text which expresses a lesbian vision, my contention is that *Orlando* should be regarded as a 'lesbian text'. Although Virginia Woolf's own relationship with a woman, and her representations of the love of her own sex in *Orlando*, are not exclusively physical, they include a physical dimension. As is well known, *Orlando* resulted directly from Woolf's physical and romantic attachment to Vita Sackville-West.[17] Although Quentin Bell informs us – with the absolute confidence of one who has no way of knowing – that 'the love affair – or whatever we are to call it' had ended in 1935,[18] this is not the case. On the contrary, the romantic attachment to Vita Sackville-West lasted all Virginia Woolf's life. It was the thought of Vita that sustained her through the bleak, lonely days of the war: 'And there you sit with the bombs falling round you. What can one say – except that I love you and I've got to live through this strange quiet evening thinking of you sitting there alone?'.[19]

In her diary Virginia Woolf initially mentions 'a biography beginning in the year 1500 and continuing to the present day, called *Orlando: Vita*; only with a change about from one sex to another'.[20] The novel's general themes of history and sexual identity are consistently pointed towards a description of personality: 'The book necessitates a double reading; its fantasy and pageantry are being used as the material of a love letter which tells the loved one the writer's opinion of her.'[21] Woolf's diary tells us that she is writing *Orlando* 'half in a mock style very clear & plain, so that people will understand every word. But the balance between truth &

16. See Bonnie Zimmerman, 'What Has Never Been: An Overview of Lesbian Feminist Criticism', in Gayle Greene and Coppélia Kahn (eds), *Making a Difference* (London: Methuen, 1985), pp.177–210, and Catharine R. Stimpson, 'Zero Degree Deviancy: The Lesbian Novel in English', in Elizabeth Abel (ed.), *Writing and Sexual Difference* (Brighton: Harvester, 1982), pp.243–59.

17. Nigel Nicolson, *Portrait of a Marriage* (London: Weidenfeld and Nicolson, 1973), p.204.

18. *Virginia Woolf: A Biography*, 2 vols (London: Hogarth, 1972), vol. 2, *Mrs. Woolf 1912–1941*, p.183.

19. Letter from Virginia Woolf to Vita Sackville-West dated, 30 August, 1940. Louise DeSalvo and Mitchell A. Leaska (eds), *The Letters of Vita Sackville-West to Virginia Woolf* (London: Hutchinson, 1984), p.465.

20. *The Diary*, vol. 3, p.161.

21. Hermione Lee, *The Novels of Virginia Woolf* (London: Methuen, 1978), p.140.

fantasy must be careful.'[22] Her original conception of the novel was somewhat different. The diary records the outlines of a novel, *The Jessamy Brides*, based on the lesbian couple in Elizabeth Major's *The Ladies of Llangollen*: 'Sapphism is to be suggested. Satire is to be the main note – satire & wildness.'[23] In switching to *Orlando* she disguised rather than altered the lesbian basis of her work. *Orlando* was the outcome of a 'perfectly definite, indeed overmastering impulse' for fun and fantasy and she wanted to write a history of Newnham or the women's movement in the same vein.[24] Woolf linked *Orlando* with this future project to indicate that she did not believe that fantasy was inimical to a fundamentally serious enterprise.

The textual strategies of *Orlando*, its use of multiple perspectives, shifts and changes in subject position; caprice, repetition, exaggeration, parody and whimsy, do not represent the loss of an insurgent project; fun and fantasy are also potentially subversive. Virginia Woolf rejected the surface realism of nineteenth-century fiction ('for us those conventions are ruin, those tools are death').[25] Her quest for new literary forms reflects her interest in literary experiment as gendered experiment and in *Orlando* her feminism finds expression in her narrative, style and point of view. As Gillian Beer puts it, 'for women under oppression such needs can find no real form within an ordering of plot which relies upon sequence, development, the understanding and renunciation of the past, the acceptance of the determined present.'[26] The literary techniques in *Orlando* are not simply decorative devices; rather, they dramatise Woolf's argument in her style. For the writer's aim was to set precisely at the centre of the text the essential device on which so much else hinges – Orlando's dramatic change of sex. This fantastical sex-change allows her to describe same-sex love with simplicity and directness as the natural human response which it is. The passage which follows the metamorphosis is unequivocal in its affirmation of Orlando's love for Sasha:

> And as all Orlando's loves had been women, now, through the culpable laggardy of the human frame to adapt itself to convention, though she herself was a woman, it was still a woman she loved; and if the consciousness of being of the same sex had any effect at all, it was to quicken and deepen those feelings which she had had as a man. For now a thousand hints and mysteries became plain to her that were then dark. Now, the obscurity, which divides the sexes

22. *The Diary*, vol.3, p.162.
23. Ibid., p.131.
24. Ibid., p.203.
25. Woolf, 'Mr. Bennett and Mrs. Brown', in *The Collected Essays*, vol. 1, p.330.
26. 'Beyond Determinism: George Eliot and Virginia Woolf', in Mary Jacobus (ed.), *Women Writing and Writing about Women* (London: Croom Helm, 1979), pp.88–9.

and lets linger innumerable impurities in its gloom, was removed, and if there is anything in what the poet says about truth and beauty, this affection gained in beauty what it lost in falsity.(p.147)

The Russian Sasha by whom the male Orlando was first enchanted is bewitchingly seductive. Images and metaphors 'of the most extreme and extravagant twined and twisted' in Orlando's mind. She becomes for him 'a melon, a pineapple, an olive tree, an emerald, and a fox in the snow all in the space of three seconds'.(p.36) Orlando did not know whether he had 'heard her, tasted her, seen her, or all three together'.(p.37) The passages in which Orlando, hot, 'with skating and with love', courts Sasha are awash with sensual detail, the feelings of physical passion as the ice 'did not melt with their heat' (p.43) are notably stronger than anywhere else in Woolf's writing.

When Orlando changes sex, 'through the culpable laggardy of the human frame to adapt itself to convention' (p.147) she is still able to retain and rationalise her love for Sasha. The self-conscious language of narration here is carefully juxtaposed to the simple utterances in which Orlando's deepest feelings are expressed. In the extraordinary metamorphosis Woolf is able to represent attraction to members of her own sex as no more surprising than the distance between the sexes which patriarchally organised societies ordain as natural. The conflict between constraint and desire momentarily disappears, our sense of social prohibitions merely sharpening our pleasure in transgressing them. On first seeing Sasha, Orlando had feared for a moment that Sasha was of his own sex and that all embraces were out of the question. Later, Orlando becomes bolder and more animated: 'If the consciousness of being of the same sex had any effect at all, it was to quicken and deepen those feelings which she had had as a man.' It is not the love of one's own sex which appears aberrant but its repression. Thus Orlando's affection 'gained in beauty what it lost in falsity'.(p.147)

Orlando is about intimacy between women ('the relationship so secret & private compared with relations with men. Why not write about it? truthfully?')[27] Writing 'truthfully' for Virginia Woolf involved acknowledging that erotic attraction is often part, if not all, of the reason why women enjoy the society of their own sex. When Orlando takes up with a young prostitute, Nell, and then reveals herself to be a woman, she and Nell are able to relate with warmth and candour despite the fact that Mistress Nell had 'not a particle of wit about her.'(p.197) The relationship with Nell frees Orlando from the need to be competitive, allows her to speak honestly and to savour the delights of sisterhood. After 'the sneer

27. *The Diary*, vol. 2, p.320.

of Mr. Pope . . . the condescension of Mr. Addison . . . the secret of Lord Chesterfield' (p.198) the poor girl's talk refreshes Orlando like wine. Indeed, the hours spent with Nell pass so quickly and merrily that Orlando actually comes to prefer her company to that of wits.

To some extent *Orlando* is all the things that others have seen in it; literary history, biography, parody, fantasy, feminist satire, a gentle mockery of literary convention, a 'satirical phantasmagoria of the mind of its author'.[28] But it is more; a most original and public declaration of same-sex love. That remains true even if the textual and sexual lyricism and vitality of *Orlando* cannot be contained by reference to the original subject of Woolf's passion. One may reject Nigel Nicolson's hyperbole – 'the longest and most charming love-letter in literature'[29] and still agree that the whole of *Orlando* is there to show how deeply Woolf was capable of feeling love for another woman:

> Must it then be admitted that Orlando was one of those monsters of iniquity who do not love? She was kind to dogs, faithful to friends, generosity itself to a dozen starving poets, had a passion for poetry. But love – as the male novelists define it – and who, after all, speaks with greater authority? – has nothing whatever to do with kindness, fidelity, generosity, or poetry. Love is slipping off one's petticoat and – But we all know what love is. Did Orlando do that? Truth compels us to say no, she did not.(p.242)

As Maria DiBattista notes, 'What is Love?' is the first question posed in *Orlando*.[30] The narrator, seeking a deeper definition of love, equates it with kindness, faithfulness, generosity, and the passion for poetry. As the narrator's irony insists, love is emphatically not, as the male novelists define it, 'slipping off one's petticoat'. The satiric references to *Lady Chatterley's Lover* in *Orlando*, 'the gamekeeper will whistle under the window . . . the very stuff of life and the only possible subject for fiction',(p.242), underline Virginia Woolf's acute awareness that the fashionable Lawrentian eroticism of her day positions women still at the service of men, and only in relation to men. She could be content neither with a Lawrentian view of sexual behaviour patterns nor with the male-modelled lesbian behaviour patterns of *The Well of Loneliness*.

Virginia Woolf had no wish to escape from sexuality, as her erotic passion for Vita Sackville-West illustrates. On the contrary, her letters to Vita reveal a deeply sensual and romantic nature.[31] But what she did wish

28. A.D. Moody, *Virginia Woolf* (London: Oliver and Boyd, 1963), p.43.

29. Nicolson, *Portrait of a Marriage*, p.201.

30. *Virginia Woolf's Major Novels: The Fables of Anon* (New Jersey: University of Yale Press, 1980), p.127.

31. See letter from Virginia Woolf to Vita Sackville-West, dated 24 August, 1925. *The Letters*, vol. 3, pp.197–8.

to escape from was the Procrustean bed of heterosexuality. Winifred Holtby explained Woolf's position on these matters very clearly: 'She does not simplify life by saying that sex is unimportant. She proclaims its importance, but denies the implications usually derived from its significance.'[32] Sexuality and heterosexuality are not the same and should not be confused. The moment in *Mrs. Dalloway* when Sally Seton kisses Clarissa – one of the very few moments of physical love in all Woolf's fiction – is 'the most exquisite moment of her whole life,' a moment when 'the whole world might have turned upside down!'.[33]

Virginia Woolf wrote *Orlando* wishing to acknowledge the benefits that membership of her sex conferred upon her, not least women's capacity to feel for and care for one another. It was her appreciation of what being a woman meant, of the pleasures as well as the pain, that made her defend her sex so passionately. Orlando's change of sex allows the author to deconstruct the sexist assumptions her age believed to be 'natural'. For who is better qualified to comment on the disqualifications that society imposes upon woman than one who has lived as a man for thirty years? On returning to sixteenth-century England, Orlando, who in his previous incarnation as a man has insisted that women should be 'obedient, chaste, scented and exquisitely apparalled' finds that she has to 'pay in my own person for those desires'.(p.143) When, for example, a fetching pair of ankles threatens to distract an honest seaman in *The Enamoured Lady* and send him tumbling to his death Orlando realised that she 'must, in all humanity keep them covered'. To her intense disappointment all she can do once she sets foot on English soil in her incarnation as a woman is to 'pour out tea and ask my lords how they like it'.(p.144) The cliffs of England, Orlando glumly reflects, 'meant conventionality, meant slavery, meant deceit, meant denying her love, fettering her limbs, pursing her lips, and restraining her tongue'.(p.149)

Skirts which collect damp leaves, thin shoes which are quickly soaked, and crinolines which restrict free bodily movement are the least of Orlando's problems. In the eighteenth century she is informed that as a woman she can hold no property whatsoever and that to enjoy the company of her own sex is impossible for 'when they lack the stimulus of the other sex, women can find nothing to say to each other. When they are alone, they do not talk, they scratch'.(p.199) In the nineteenth century her children are disinherited by Lord Palmerston. The twentieth century, with its Lawrentian ideas of literature and women's sexuality, threatens to seduce Orlando away from her writing, 'since she is a woman, and a beautiful

32. *Virginia Woolf: A Critical Memoir* (London: Wishart, 1932), p.180.
33. *Mrs. Dalloway* (London: Hogarth, 1925; reprinted Harmondsworth: Penguin, 1980), p.40.

woman, and a woman in the prime of life, she will soon give over the pretence of writing and thinking and begin at last to think of a gamekeeper'.(p.242)

Orlando, then, ridicules all the anti-feminist sentiments that Woolf had encountered in her own life, the prohibitions which prevented women from dressing, writing and thinking as they wished without fear of censorship: 'But hist – they are always careful to see that the doors are shut and that not a word of it gets into print.'(p.198) *Orlando* gives voice to the unspoken desires that women have felt, to the passions that men have repressed, and to the words that men have taken out of women's mouths: 'All they desire is – but hist again – is that not a man's step on the stair? All they desire, we were about to say when the gentleman took the very words out of our mouths. Women have no desires, says this gentleman.'(pp.198–9)

In Virginia Woolf's work as a whole there is a continual representation of gender difference, produced not as in *The Well of Loneliness* through exclusive concentration on female subjectivity, but often, as in *Orlando*, through insistence on multiple viewpoints. From Mr. Ramsay in *To the Lighthouse* to Bart Oliver in *Between the Acts* and across a spectrum of male characters (William Dodge in *Between the Acts* and Bernard in *The Waves* are the exceptions) the male mind is invariably represented as egocentric, overbearing, reductive and insensitive. The men in *Orlando* belong to this wider pattern.

Such observations need not imply that Virginia Woolf is lacking in admiration for the male intellect. The opposite is true; it is from the great men of letters of the eighteenth century, Pope, Swift and Addison, that Orlando learns 'the most important part of style, which is the natural run of the voice in speaking'.(p.192) But Woolf's appreciation is tempered, subtly, by the feminist insight that reminds us, presciently, that the intellect, divine as it might be, 'has a habit of lodging in the most seedy of carcases'.(p.193) It is qualified too by the wit that casts Orlando in the role of tea-maker extraordinaire to a motley collection of sages. A flourish of the sugar tongs accompanies Orlando's ironic delivery of the satirical line 'how women in ages to come will envy me!'(p.193) In *To the Lighthouse* Woolf suggests that Mr Ramsay's prodigious intellectual performance is made possible only by Mrs Ramsay's practical support. The co-option of Orlando as tea-maker by the literary giants of the eighteenth century makes much the same point.

Such gender-conscious ironies in *Orlando* serve as a continual reminder of Virginia Woolf's desire to show the lived experience of being a woman as different from the lived experience of being a man. In writing approvingly of the androgynous mind (Shakespeare, Coleridge and Proust), or in choosing to create attractive and sexually ambiguous characters (Orlando, Shelmerdine and Sasha) she is admiring the ability to feel empathy with the experience of the other sex without attempting to erase the difference between the sexes. The concept of androgyny should not be relegated to a passing fancy that occurred to Woolf while thinking about *A Room of One's Own*, and of no importance thereafter. But neither should it be divorced from the basis of lesbian experience from which Virginia Woolf wrote *Orlando*.

Orlando, with its pretence to scholarship, its rejection of biographical conventions, and its mischievous appendix which contains material not in the text, obviously mocks established biographical traditions. For example, the 'obligation' of the biographer 'to plod, without looking to right or left, in the indelible footprints of truth' (p.62), even when recounting such outrageous events as those in Constantinople, is made impossible by the fire that 'had its way withall such records'. Only 'tantalising fragments which leave the most important points obscure' – a much defaced letter to a recipient in Tunbridge Wells and the diary of an English naval officer – remain to tell 'the very famous, and indeed, much disputed incident'.(p.116) Woolf made it clear that she wished *Orlando* to be the antithesis of traditional biography and that she was also correcting and parodying the *new* social history, particularly Trevelyan's social histories with their lack of reference to women other than queens.

There are specific problems for feminism raised by readings of *Orlando* divesting it of its innovativeness and iconoclasm by placing it in a line of traditional historical biography. Avrom Fleishman and Leon Edel, for example, have both attempted to assimilate *Orlando* to a largely irrelevant grid by tracing and establishing paternal precursors, ignoring the evidence of Woolf's troubled relationship to the men around her including Lytton Strachey and her father, Leslie Stephen, first editor of *The Dictionary of National Biography*, against whose influence she had reacted.[34]

Avrom Fleishman diligently searches for male influences despite the fact that *Orlando* clearly severs many such connections. He mentions 'The Art of Biography' which Virginia Woolf wrote in 1929 while working on *Roger Fry: A Biography* but he does not discuss 'The New Biography' which Woolf published in *The New York Herald Tribune* in October, 1927.[35] This omission can give the impression that *Orlando* is a riposte to Harold Nicolson's *The Development of English Biography* which was published by the Hogarth Press in 1928. 'We may assume that they influenced each other', writes Fleishman[36] without telling us that 'The New Biography'

34. 'His life would have entirely ended mine. What would have happened? No writing, no books; – inconceivable' reads a diary entry on what would have been her father's 96th birthday. *The Diary*, vol. 3, p.208.
35. *Virginia Woolf: A Critical Reading* (Baltimore: Johns Hopkins University Press, 1975), p.136.
36. Ibid.

was published first. Leon Edel tellingly suggests that we think of *Orlando* as 'grandfathered and uncled by a group of biographers', particularly by the 'pre-eminent figure in modern biography', Lytton Strachey.[37] Edel stresses Strachey's influence on *Orlando* ignoring the other influences such as *The Ladies of Llangollen* which are clear from Virginia Woolf's diary. David Daiches fails to see the satiric purpose of the citations of Defoe, Sir Thomas Browne, Sterne, Emily Brontë, Sir Walter Scott, Lord Macaulay, DeQuincey and Walter Pater in the preface to *Orlando*.[38] As J.J. Wilson points out, the only male literary figure to emerge untarnished at the end of *Orlando* is Shakespeare.[39]

In 'Women and Fiction' Virginia Woolf asserts that women writers wish 'to alter the established values – to make serious what appears insignificant to a man, and trivial what is to him important'.[40] In *Flush* she mischievously undermines Strachey's resolutely iconoclastic form of biography by taking seriously the life of a dog. In *Orlando* she systematically rejects the idea that history is the study of great men. A prime target of her satire is the propensity to reduce truth to a set of hard, logical facts. She refused the office of 'gadfly to the state' which was 'so far a male prerogative' saying that she preferred the butterfly to the gadfly, 'that is to say, the artist to the reformer'.[41] The techniques used in *Orlando* are those that had eluded most biographers and suited her feminist satire. The authorial self, which is absent from the tightly-crafted structures of her experimental novels, is present in *Orlando*, directing our attention to the processes of writing. In 'The New Biography' she perceives truth 'as something of granite-like solidity and of personality as something of rainbow-like intangibility'.[42] *Orlando* represents 'that queer amalgamation of dream and reality, that perpetual marriage of granite and rainbow',[43] at once bold and subtle, which Woolf hoped would characterise the art of the new biographer. *Orlando* is a *new* biography.

In *Feminism and Art* the critic, Herbert Marder, identified the general movement from repression to freedom in *Orlando* arguing that the scene that ushers in the elaborate change of sex is an 'elaborate ritual of liberation'.[44] David Daiches observes that 'the paradox about the Mask

37. *Literary Biography: The Alexander Lectures 1955–1956* (London: Hart-Davis, 1957), pp.93, 94.
38. *Virginia Woolf* (New York: New Directions, 1942), p.94.
39. 'Why is *Orlando* Difficult?', in Jane Marcus (ed.), *New Feminist Essays on Virginia Woolf* (London: Macmillan, 1981), p.178.
40. 'Women and Fiction', in *The Collected Essays*, vol. 2, p.146.
41. Ibid., p.147.
42. 'The New Biography', in *The Collected Essays*, vol. 4, p.229.
43. Ibid., p.235.
44. *Feminism and Art: A Study of Virginia Woolf* (Chicago: University of Chicago Press, 1968), p.111.

is, that though it may be used as a means of conveying suggestions too subtle for more naturalistic means of communication, it is itself so rigid and inflexible that unless you have seen its meaning beforehand you can never be persuaded of it by watching the Mask. The Mask is most effective as a means of communication between those who have the same insights.'[45] John Graham, discussing Woolf's irony in *Orlando*, notes that 'all forms of irony seem to assume the hypothetical existence of someone who knows the secret, the real meaning, and someone else who does not'.[46]

Is it merely an accident that the movement from repression to liberation in *Orlando* coincides with Orlando's move from man to woman? Neither Marder, nor Daiches, nor Graham have allowed for the possibility of a gendered reading of *Orlando*, for the fact that those in a position to have 'seen the meaning beforehand', or to 'have the same insights', or to understand 'the real meaning' of the masque may be women. Yet feminist scholars, Annette Kolodny, for example, have stressed the crucial importance of the sex of a reader or interpreter engaged in attributing significance to formal signifiers.[47] How does a hypothesised woman reader help us to displace dominant critical readings and produce a feminist reading of *Orlando*? The passage below shows how the hypothesis of a female reader changes our apprehension of the masque in *Orlando* and awakens us to the significance of *Orlando*'s sexual codes:

> "Better is it," she thought, "to be clothed with poverty and ignorance, which are the dark garments of the female sex; better to leave the rule and discipline of the world to others; better be quit of martial ambition, the love of power, and all the other manly desires if so one can more fully enjoy the most exalted raptures known to the human spirit, which are", she said aloud, as her habit was when deeply moved, "contemplation, solitude, love."

> "Praise God that I'm a woman!" she cried . . . (p.146)

There is a strong sense of emotional release at the end of Orlando's self-mutilating identification with masculinity. Indeed, an unmistakable feeling of jubilation and rapture resonates throughout the passage. A 'rare and unexpected delight' is the fact that Orlando is 'a real woman, at last'. (p.228) The weight that the words 'Praise God that I'm a woman!' are meant to carry in the narrative may be tested by an attempt to substitute the opposite ('Praise God that I'm a man') anywhere in the text. The attempt fails because *Orlando* is subtly but consistently informed by

45. Daiches, *Virginia Woolf*, p.105.
46. 'The "Caricature Value" of Parody and Fantasy in *Orlando*', *University of Toronto Quarterly*, vol. 30, 4, July 1961, p.350.
47. 'A Map for Rereading: or, Gender and the Interpretation of Literary Texts', *New Literary History*, 11, 1980, pp.451–67.

Woolf's feminist perspectives and by her resolve to question the ethos of masculinity. It is significant that Orlando *achieves* femininity and *discovers* womanhood, and that masculinity is left behind.

If, as Jane Marcus has argued,[48] the seductive tone of the papers read to women at Newnham and Girton in 1928 was intended to woo Vita Sackville-West and other lesbians with little or no politicised understanding of their sexuality to feminism, to draw heterosexual women and lesbians together within the framework of a feminist politics, then how true is this also of *Orlando*? For *Orlando* is the text in which Vita herself is displayed, the text in which lesbian consciousness is linked to a feminist awareness of women's disabilities. It is the text which may be read, Nigel Nicolson suggests, as a 'unique consolation' to Vita Sackville-West for having been born a girl and thus forfeiting her inheritance of Knole.[49] It is the text which, as Sandra Gilbert has put it, was 'designed to prove to Everywoman that she can be exactly who or what she wants to be, including Everyman'.[50] Woolf's celebration of love for women and between women in *Orlando* reveals a radical and courageous determination to expose patriarchal expectations of women's sexuality. Her textual strategies are chosen to make the connections between lesbian sexuality and the deeply expanded consciousness of woman-identification that is entirely missing in *The Well of Loneliness*.

The Well of Loneliness is the most celebrated lesbian novel in the English language; the first to be written from the writer's open lesbian perspective. Una Troubridge, Radclyffe Hall's partner, tells us that it was her lover's absolute conviction that the book she wanted to write 'could only be written by a sexual invert, who alone could be qualified by personal knowledge and experience to speak on behalf of a misunderstood and misjudged minority'.[51] But is *The Well of Loneliness* really a feminist novel? Can it be argued that a novel which pleads so passionately for the rights of lesbians is anything else? For the purpose of exploring these and related questions I propose to examine closely a sequence of passages in *The Well of Loneliness* from the point in the narrative at which Lady Anna, Stephen's mother, has confronted her daughter with a letter of complaint from the husband of Angela Crosby, a neighbour with whom Stephen had formed a romantic attachment.

The *Well of Loneliness* is not composed about a strategic centre such

---

48. See Marcus, 'Sapphistry: Narrative as Lesbian Seduction in *A Room of One's Own*', loc. cit.

49. *Portrait of a Marriage*, p.206.

50. 'Costumes of the Mind: Transvestism as Metaphor in Modern Literature', *Critical Inquiry*, vol. 7, Winter 1980, p.406.

51. *The Life and Death of Radclyffe Hall* (London: Hammond, 1961), pp.81–2.

as the sex-change which I earlier analysed in *Orlando* and Radclyffe Hall's method of creating a character differs radically from Virginia Woolf's. Hall deploys a single, unified authorial perspective in order to focus attention on her tortured heroine, Stephen Gordon, whom she endows with both a seemingly infinite propensity to love unwisely and a seemingly infinite capacity to expose herself to self-laceration and suffering.

In order to avoid a serious local scandal Stephen has reluctantly agreed to leave her ancestral home of Morton. This sequence begins by evoking the loneliness of the isolated lesbian. 'As though drawn there by some strong natal instinct' (p.205) Stephen goes straight to her father's study. There an 'immense desolation swept down upon her, an immense need to cry out and claim understanding for herself, an immense need to find an answer to the riddle of her unwanted being'. The passage is, in stylistic terms, a perfect example of the 'came the dawn' tradition of English fiction, Hall's triple repetition of 'immense' recalling, as C.H. Rolph so aptly puts it, a time when 'paper was plentiful, blue pencils lay idle, writers drooled on and on, and tautology took the place of construction'.[52]

As the awful realisation of precisely what leaving Morton will mean for her dawns upon Stephen, the diction of the passage changes, spills rapidly into cliché: 'good, sweet-smelling meadows', 'merciful hills' and 'the lanes with their sleepy dog-roses at evening'. The syntax and language of the passage take on a runaway quality that perfectly reflects Stephen's feverish state of mind as she begins to realise that 'the roses would not be her roses, nor the luminous carpet of trees in the autumn, nor the beautiful winter forms of the beech trees'.(p.266) The triple negative and heavy reliance on assonance ('nor', 'roses', 'forms'), and the ritualistic repetition of parallel clauses all help to evoke Stephen's sense of desolation and despair.

In the locked bookcase Stephen discovers a copy of the work of the sexologist, Richard Krafft-Ebing – probably *Psychopathia Sexualis* – with her name written in the margin in her father's scholarly hand. 'Oh Father', exclaims Stephen, linking the name of the capitalised Father, God, to her biological father, conscious for the first time that her own father had been aware of her lesbian feelings but had felt unable to speak to her openly about them. She appeals to the Father on high on behalf of all those 'maimed, hideously maimed and ugly'. Her outburst peters out in bathetic utterance: 'God's cruel; He let us get flawed in the making.'

Stephen finds an old, well-worn Bible, and, demanding nothing less than a sign from heaven, is rewarded when the book falls open upon the words, 'And the Lord set a mark upon Cain.' These words become an incantation, a mantra which she chants hopelessly in intoxicating and

52. Introduction to *Radclyffe Hall: A Case of Obscenity?*, p.19.

overwhelming sorrow. References to scars and wounds are liberally scattered throughout the novel and the mark of Cain serves as an emblem for lesbian identity. Stephen is discovered in this agitated state by her old governess, Miss Puddleston (Puddle, as the old family retainer is affectionately called) who consoles Stephen: 'Where you go, I go, Stephen' (p.207) in a simple affirmation of loyalty reminding us of the promise made by Ruth to Naomi in The Old Testament. In Puddle's eyes, Stephen's artistic talent becomes equally a compensation for the affliction with which she has been born and a weighty responsibility to be shouldered. For the sake of others like Stephen, 'less strong and less gifted perhaps, many of them,' she argues that it is up to Stephen to 'have the courage to make good'.(p.208)

In the most radical and positive statement so far, Puddle asserts the need for a sense of solidarity between the individual lesbian and the rest of her kind. Here Stephen's lesbianism is not presented as a simple defect of personality, for which personal solutions must be found, but as a general condition affecting the lives of women who are in other respects diverse. Merely identifying oneself as lesbian is not enough. Individual lesbians must accept the responsibility of trying to help other women like themselves.

The passages quoted give the flavour of the religious reference, the purple prose, and the cries of protest which are intermingled with anguish and run through the novel. As Stephen tries to understand her own sexual identity better, so the language of the passage ('as drawn by some natal instinct', 'flawed in the making', 'part of nature', 'the mark of Cain') points to the contradictory aspects in the representation of lesbian sexuality in the text. The lesbian condition is presented as 'natural' because it is part of nature and ordained by God and yet it is also presented as intrinsically tragic and doomed. Pervading the entire novel is a sense of life as painful, tragic and wasted – a sense, too, of the need for difficult readjustment, and an insistent appeal to the reader for tolerance and understanding. Today the idea of the lesbian afflicted with the mark of Cain is difficult to take seriously. This was not so in 1928. As Jeffrey Weeks states, 'for another thirty years or so her novel represented the clearest moral stand on lesbianism, and a position beyond which few women were prepared or able to venture'.[53]

With the exception of Havelock Ellis, who wrote the original introduction to *The Well of Loneliness*, Radclyffe Hall deliberately chose to ignore the more benign theorists of 'inversion', including Hirschfield and Freud, and to underpin *The Well of Loneliness* with theories on lesbian

53. *Coming Out: Homosexual Politics in Britain, from the Nineteenth Century to the Present* (London: Quartet, 1977), p.111.

sexuality largely derived from Krafft-Ebing.[54] The theories of sexuality which underpin the novel imprison Stephen in her biology. Stephen's physical attributes speak masculinity: her sexual orientation is suggested by her muscular shoulders, athletic body, and compact hips. Hall implies that Stephen's inversion is congenital by emphasising her physical resemblance to her father. Her women in *The Well of Loneliness* remain trapped in destructive patterns of dominance and submission, always associated with paradigms of gender in which sexual behaviour is seen as 'natural' and not socially produced, therefore irrefutable and inevitable.

This biological determinism could not be more different from the changes of sex from man to woman and woman to man which the Archduke/Duchess in *Orlando* literally accomplishes in a matter of moments. As Gillian Beer suggests: 'Escape is not necessarily a form of retreat or failure. Escape can mean freedom and the trying out of new possibilities after imprisonment.'[55] For Virginia Woolf sexual identity is always fluid, evanescent and subject to change. Indeed, the shifting aspects of sexual identity in *Orlando* are obvious from the first page: 'He – for there could be no doubt of his sex, though the fashion of the time did something to disguise it –'. From Orlando's introduction Woolf carefully audits the historical shifts in sexuality showing how our definitions of masculinity have altered through the centuries. She tells us, for example, that flamboyant costumes were worn by men under the Tudors and that cross-dressing was a convention in Elizabethan comedy.

A portrait of Orlando as a man 'who looks the world full in the face' is compared with one of Orlando as a woman who 'takes a sidelong glance' at the 'world full of subtlety, even of suspicion'. The man 'has his free hand to seize his sword' but the woman must use hers to 'keep the satins from slipping from her shoulders'. The narrator concludes: 'Had they both worn the same clothes, it is possible that their outlook might have been the same'.(p.171) The nineteenth century which forces women into strict marital roles is tellingly the century in which Orlando is least happy: 'But the spirit of the nineteenth century was antipathetic to her in the extreme, and thus it took her and broke her, and she was aware of her defeat at its hands as she had never been before'.(p.220)

Whereas Virginia Woolf continually questions the norms of heterosexual society, Radclyffe Hall no less consistently aligns lesbian relationships against those norms. Stephen's relationship to the sexual and social mores of her time is largely unexamined. There is no attempt to explore new roles, values or behaviour. Stephen subscribes to the prevalent

54. See Michael Baker, *Our Three Selves: A Life of Radclyffe Hall* (London: Hamilton, 1985), p.218.
55. Beer, 'Beyond Determinism: George Eliot and Virginia Woolf', p.90.

view that marriage is the proper destiny of woman. Even in the context of a lovingly self-sufficient adult relationship, a childless woman is a failure. Stephen sees her own relationship with Mary as incomplete. Their love is 'so fruitful of passion yet so bitterly sterile'.(p.431) She is even prepared to lose the woman she loves to Martin Hallam, because he could give her children. The gesture of renunciation is designed to win sympathy for the invert and to show her lot as inexorably tragic.

What could be more different from the way in which Virginia Woolf imagines the birth of a son in *Orlando*, dramatising a delivery that serenely transcends the problems attendant on actual childbirth in finely-ordered prose? It is a birth which is not entirely painless; *pace* Madeline Moore there are threatening references to blood and to membranes breaking.[56] But it is a birth which, nevertheless, neatly avoids a constellation of questions related to the child's parentage and jubilantly overcomes Woolf's own frustration at being unable to conform to the usual sexual expectations of women, by imaginatively re-constituting experience to suit desire.

In her diary Woolf notes how 'extraordinarily unwilled by me but potent in its own right by the way *Orlando* was! as if it shoved everything aside to come into existence'.[57] The tropes of the body with which Woolf describes the birth of Orlando's son, and the reference to the rhythms of birth ('shoved') in the diary illustrate how questions of literary production (of texts) and maternal reproduction (of children) are both perceived to be important and related aspects of women's creativity. As Maggie Humm has observed, Virginia Woolf consistently uses a 'female iconography of the body' and 'trusts and allows the "bodily" language to reveal sexual politics'.[58] Thus the delivery of Orlando's child is metaphorically linked to the delivery of Orlando's poem, 'The Oak Tree' at the end of a very long gestation. Susan Merrill Squier has pointed out that the kingfisher heralding the miraculous birth of Orlando's son is 'an opaque natural inversion of the Fisher King myth' central to T.S. Eliot's *The Waste Land* and that Woolf's celebration of maternal fruitfulness in *Orlando* can be read as a triumphant riposte against Eliot's preoccupation with 'impotence, both personal and national'.[59]

Orlando challenges patriarchy in a number of different modes: form, reader response, textual practices and ideology. In sharp contrast, *The Well of Loneliness* contains no developed critique of patriarchy. Whereas the

---

56. *The Short Season Between Two Silences: The Mystical and the Political in the Novels of Virginia Woolf* (London: Allen and Unwin, 1984), p.111.

57. *The Diary*, vol. 3, p.168.

58. *Feminist Criticism: Women as Contemporary Critics* (Brighton: Harvester, 1986), p.141.

59. *Virginia Woolf and London: The Sexual Politics of the City* (Chapel Hill: University of North Carolina Press, 1985), p.202.

lesbian consciousness it exhibits is certainly different from the mainstream consciousness of heterosexuality, this is only in terms of sexual preference. Although Stephen has a heightened sense of her own oppression and understands that her suffering is not unique, 'there are so many of us – thousands of miserable, unwanted people, who have no right to love, no right to compassion' (p.207) she fails to make the crucial connections between social and sexual oppression. Thus Stephen's view of the world around her is seen through the window of her consciousness of being a lesbian, but this lesbian consciousness functions primarily as a means of self-justification. What she does not do is register the interdependence of sexuality and power. Quite the opposite, *The Well of Loneliness* masks the interconnectedness of the social trajectories of pleasure and pain. The depiction of the central character primarily in terms of her erotic preference is a very different matter from the literary representation of either a woman-identified woman or of a character who is critical of patriarchy or heterosexuality.

The lack of any politicised definition of lesbianism – hardly available to writers of the time – means that there can be no possibility of envisaging a lesbian relationship rooted in a shared and principled commitment to other women. As Jane Rule has outlined the problem of the text's sexual politics, 'though inept and feminine men are criticized, though some are seen to abuse the power they have, their right to that power is never questioned . . . Male domination is intolerable to her only when she can't assert it for herself. Women are inferior. Loving relationships must be between superior and inferior persons.'[60]

In *The Well of Loneliness* lesbian relationships inevitably mimic heterosexual ones. Stephen drives a fast car and Angela acquires a costly handbag from Stephen as a token of affection. Jamie is masculine, lumbering and clumsy, her lover, Barbara, feminine, frail and delicate, Stephen is 'handsome' (p.11) and her 'masterful' arms would enfold the warm softness of Mary's body.(p.432) Radclyffe Hall's picture of a lesbian exhibiting 'masculine' personality traits and having a 'feminine' love object was influenced by her mentor, Havelock Ellis.

Apart from the touching relationship between Jamie and Barbara, which ends in suicide, there are no abiding relationships between women in *The Well of Loneliness* other than Puddle's life-long devotion to her former pupil, Stephen, and Stephen's affection for her former instructress, Mademoiselle Duphont. The relationships between servant and mistress and teacher and taught are predicated on the idea of service and are essentially non-erotic in character. Some relationships in *Orlando* are also based on historic ties and family loyalties: Orlando's housekeeper is a loyal

60. *Lesbian Images* (New York: Davies, 1975), p.60.

and dedicated family retainer. But dissenting voices are also heard, those of Nick Greene and the gypsies singularly unimpressed by the inheritance of centuries to which Orlando attached so much importance.

The Well of Loneliness contains no *lasting* relationships between women as lovers, or between women as friends, or between mothers and daughters. The relationship between Stephen and her mother is particularly destructive and recriminatory, as was the author's relationship to her own mother who deeply resented the fact that her daughter idealised the husband from whom she was estranged. While the ideal of a 'lasting' relationship may be criticised on the grounds that it asks lesbians to imitate heterosexual marriage, Radclyffe Hall and Una Troubridge enjoyed twenty-eight years of happiness together. When her partner died Una, who had nursed her devotedly, lived on for another twenty years. Her greatest comfort in old age was the belief that she would join her 'infinitely beloved companion' in death.[61] *The Well of Loneliness* would have been a different book, richer and more complex but, of course, unrecognisable, had it admitted the possibility of imperishable love.

By some strange irony Hall's impassioned defence of lesbian sexuality in *The Well of Loneliness* became linked to the Roman Catholic religion, which both she and Una Troubridge had come to embrace; a religion which uncompromisingly condemned sexual variance. This link was to open up endless contradictions for her life and her fiction. The reasons for the double blasphemy Hall was accused of committing in *The Well of Loneliness*; daring to write about the love that dare not speak its name and ascribing the origins of that love to God, the Father, are not difficult to understand. The Roman Catholic religion pardons and absolves sinners on earth whereas the Protestant religion leaves judgement to God after death; thus the attraction of the Catholic faith for homosexuals in search of forgiveness and absolution. But Radclyffe Hall's argument to the effect those who can do nothing about their condition cannot be held to account for their actions was one that failed to convince her critics at the time. As James Douglas railed in a famous editorial in *The Sunday Express*, 'these moral derelicts are not cursed from their birth. Their downfall is caused by their own act and their own will. They are damned because they choose to be damned, not because they are doomed from the beginning.'[62]

The problems which arise when trying to connect lesbian and feminist ideas are intimately tied up with the characterisation of Stephen as an aristocrat. Sex has no connection with subservience only for those on whom the social hierarchy has conferred power. While Woolf's discursive writings indicate an intellectual commitment to socialist principles, these

---

61. Troubridge, *The Life and Death of Radclyffe Hall*, p.139.
62. Quoted by Vera Brittain, *Radclyffe Hall: A Case of Obscenity*, p.56.

concerns are not consistently carried through into her fiction. It was only in the late 1930s that she was to elaborate the radical theory of women, class and oppression which I shall discuss in my final chapter. In 1928, as Raymond Williams has argued, the relationship of Woolf and her circle to the working class was not one of 'solidarity, nor in affiliation, but as an extension of what are still felt as personal or small-group obligations, at once against the cruelty and stupidity of the system and towards its otherwise relatively helpless victims'.[63] Class differences *are* written into Woolf's fiction, for example in *Between the Acts*, in the village and in the pageant. However, Orlando is an aristocrat and the healing fantasy (and irony) is that even as a woman she retains, and hands on, her estate.

Radclyffe Hall was also a socialist and told Ethel Mannin that miners and railwaymen were among her most ardent champions.[64] She refused a rich man's offer to pay her expenses of litigation because thousands of miners were starving after the General Strike.[65] There are sympathetic representations of the working class in Hall's fiction, notably in *Adam's Breed*. But in *The Well of Loneliness* she restricts herself to writing about those sections of her class of which she had direct experience. When she does depart from her class and its internal relationships it is to portray the kind of inter-class relationships compatible with conservative paternalism. The *cri-de-coeur* for sexual freedom Hall utters in *The Well of Loneliness* is in essence a cry for tolerance for her kind, and not for freedom from the social expectations and responsibilities which maintain the hegemony of her class. And *Orlando* too, with all its subtle play on the injustices of women, exhibits the same limitations, so that Woolf's cry for freedom, like Hall's, is essentially a cry for freedom within the class to which she was born. As Gillian Beer puts it, 'Orlando is privileged with wealth, beauty, androgyneity, and immortality. In such conditions differences of opportunity between men and women diminish, but they do not vanish.'[66]

Relationships between members of the same sex may mimic or reproduce class inequalities while removing gender-based ones. In *The Well of Loneliness* Radclyffe Hall recreates the social inequalities of heterosexuality, as does Woolf in *Orlando*. In describing the country house of Orlando, Woolf pictures vividly, if with poetic licence, the memorable features of Knole, the country home of Vita Sackville-West. Woolf's class origins, unlike Sackville-West's, were not aristocratic. She was a member

63. 'The Blomsbury Fraction', in *Problems in Materialism and Culture: Selected Essays* (London: Verso, 1980), pp.155–6.
64. Ethel Mannin, *Confession and Impressions* (London: Jarrolds, 1930), p.228.
65. Ibid. See also Kate Flint, 'Virginia Woolf and the General Strike', *Essays in Criticism*, vol. 36, 4, October 1986, pp.319–34.
66. Gillian Beer, 'The Body of the People in Virginia Woolf,' in Sue Rue (ed.), *Women Reading Women's Writing* (Brighton: Harvester, 1987), p.101.

of the literary (and dissident) bourgeoisie, of an intellectual aristocracy, but not of the landed classes. An outsider to the Sackville-West world of patrician *savoir faire*, she, nonetheless, recognised that her adulation of Vita, a 'high aristocrat', who 'descends from Dorset, Buckingham, Sir Philip Sidney, and the whole of English History', might not be shared by everyone.[67] It was not shared by Jacques Raverat, a Frenchman ('you, poor Frog, care nothing for all this'),[68] nor by the gypsies whose lineage stretched back further still.

Radclyffe Hall's ancestry was distinguished: she was thought to be a descendant of Shakespeare, and she was able to live in style on the fortune she inherited at the age of eighteen from her father. In *The Well of Loneliness* the loss of her ancestral home is a punishment for Stephen's sexual licence, but the birth of a son to Orlando entails the family estates to Orlando/Vita. Vita Sackville-West tells us that old houses had a 'Proustian fascination' for Virginia Woolf: 'Not only did she romanticize them – for she was born a romantic – but they satisfied her acute sense of the continuity of history'.[69] Orlando's name is that of the nobleman in *As You Like It*, severed from his father's fortune as Vita was severed from Knole. Hall shared this love of old country houses. The memory of Morton broods benignly over *The Well of Loneliness*, serving as a symbol of Stephen's rightful place and of her origins. The fact that she is her father's daughter gives Stephen a title to the house, but the fact that she has loved it gives her a spiritual title. In exploring the themes of belonging, Hall brushes against the existential meaning of home vividly evoking Stephen's need to find her way back from exile to a world in which she is no longer a stranger.

The symbol of Morton, like the symbol of Knole, is tied up with a complicated network of hierarchical relationships. Hall roots these in traditional notions of honour and noblesse oblige. *The Well of Loneliness* reflects, without rendering problematic, the values of the upper class: – patriotism, self-sacrifice and honour, a point heavily accentuated when Stephen is awarded the Croix de Guerre for her ambulance work in the 1914 war. Hall, like Brittain, and unlike Woolf, considered herself a patriot. The war sequences in *The Well of Loneliness*, intended to illustrate the national context in which lesbian ambulance drivers were of great service to their country, were ironically those which caused most outrage in 1928.

When Stephen is sexually compromised with Angela Crosby, she agrees to leave the country. This flight confirms the family in its moral authority

67. Letter from Virginia Woolf to Jacques Raverat, dated 26 December, 1924. *The Letters*, vol. 3, p.150.
68. Ibid.
69. 'Virginia Woolf and *Orlando*', *Listener*, 27 January, 1955, p.157.

and in its social power, consolidating her mother's social position and her father's reputation. Orlando, on the other hand, not only flouts patriarchal values but manages to retain the family estates. Stephen is cast in the role of *active* defender of aristocratic values, and in particular of property inheritance. But sadly for her in France she is merely a bird of passage. Although the Parisian lesbian ghetto is her fate she retains the solidly respectable country instincts of one who grew up in the English countryside. Again and again in her unwanted exile, Stephen's vivid imagination transports her back to the 'quiet pleasant things that a home will stand for – security, peace, respect and honour, the kindness of parents, the goodwill of neighbours', (p.340) and to happy memories of the very rural squirearchy responsible for her sense of oppression. So far is Stephen from recognising this truth that the reader too may be seduced into sharing her respect for the upper classes.

Stephen returns to Morton to bury a beloved horse and to lament the old feudal relationships disrupted by the war. A later chance to return to England with her young lover, Mary, comes with Lady Massey's invitation to the couple, which is abruptly withdrawn. The blow is bitter and Hall makes women, Lady Anna and Lady Massey, wholly responsible for Stephen's banishment from England and for her outlaw status. In depicting both titled ladies as the custodians of all that is best in England, Hall literally hands over to them the keys of the kingdom. They alone have the powers of patronage to allow Stephen to be repatriated, or else to turn the keys and lock the gates fast against her entry. The reader is therefore left with the impression that English society turns on the whims of a coterie of ageing, intolerant matriarchs. One has no sense of where power does lie, in the hands of the landowners, the judiciary and the press, for example, at whose hands Hall had suffered personally.

I shall conclude by returning to the question of what, if any, connection there may be between the feminist ideas of *Orlando* and the lesbian consciousness of *The Well of Loneliness*? The attempt to assert one's own sexuality, independent of male control, is the hallmark of a lesbian identity. It is also an important aspect of feminist thinking which has been centrally concerned with the whole issue of men's control over women in the public and private spheres. In women's literature and history we can trace how the needs and values of feminists and lesbians have converged and interlocked. Historically, attitudes to the lesbian have always been determined by more general attitudes to women's sexuality. Homophobia has never been a discrete ideological system but always part of a wider sexual ideology which has set the limits of the permissible in the interests of a social order that is massively premised on heterosexuality and dependent on the inequalities which exist between men and women. Society naturalises and legitimates these inequalities through cultural conditioning.

In 1928 *The Well of Loneliness* challenged the norms whereby those who exercised power, generally but not always male and heterosexual, applied the standards derived from their own experience to others who did not share them, and found the latter inadequate and culpable, thus perpetuating the dominant group's ideas of the legitimacy of its domination, and the subject group's ideas of its own inferiority.[70] *The Well of Loneliness* came directly out of a flourishing post-war lesbian literary culture associated with such women as Romaine Brooks, Natalie Barney and Gertrude Stein in Paris, where Hall and Lady Troubridge arrived in 1927.[71] It was in Paris that Hall, encouraged by Barney and her circle, decided to write *The Well of Loneliness*. To write her lesbian novel, Hall (respected and successful after the appearance of *Adam's Breed*) was prepared to make almost any sacrifice including the shipwreck of her literary career – except the sacrifice of Una Troubridge's peace of mind. But Troubridge offered no opposition.[72]

The significance of *The Well of Loneliness*, at the time of publication and subsequently, is due to its having been recognised as a text marking an important departure from previous representations of lesbian experience, because it was written by a self-proclaimed, if guilt-ridden, lesbian. *The Well of Loneliness* is both a justification and apologia for lesbian sexual practice, whereas *Orlando* is free of any manifestation of guilt. Clearly, *The Well of Loneliness* is a text of major importance in lesbian history. Sonja Reuhl has provided an excellent analysis of how it represents the start of 'a reverse discourse' whereby lesbians were able to challenge dominant definitions of their sexuality and begin to define themselves.[73] As Alison Hennegan has reminded us, if the despairing and embattled world of Stephen Gordon seems far removed from our own it is worth remembering that it was *The Well of Loneliness* that helped to bring about that difference.[74]

However, *The Well of Loneliness* is radical only in so far as any text that refuses to construe lesbianism as illegitimate might be radical. While it challenges the heterosexual hegemony and gives cultural support to those whom society perceives as deviant, Hall's patrician system of values, her reliance on reductive religious and psycho-sexual explanations of

70. See Richard Dyer, 'Stereotyping', in Richard Dyer (ed.), *Gays and Film* (London: BFI, 1980), p.30.

71. See Dolores Klaich, *Woman Plus Woman: Attitudes Towards Lesbianism* (New York: New English Library, 1974), p.180.

72. Troubridge, *Life and Death of Radclyffe Hall*, p.82.

73. 'Inverts and Experts: Radclyffe Hall and the Lesbian Identity', in Rosalind Brunt and Caroline Rowan (eds), *Feminism, Culture and Politics* (London: Lawrence and Wishart, 1982), pp.15–36.

74. Introduction to *The Well of Loneliness* (London: Virago, 1982), p.xvii.

lesbianism, her failure to conceptualize new ways of behaving, and her inability to recognise the social sources of lesbian oppression, make *The Well of Loneliness* a very limited revolt indeed. Although the novel's prevailing mood of guilt and self-hatred is not unmitigated, as acts of kindness and tenderness do bring relief from time to time; in the final analysis resistance to oppression must inevitably give way to despair.

Radclyffe Hall's deeply held belief that sexual behaviour was not determined socially, but by nature or God, removed the possibility of lesbianism as a preferred option for women and also removed any necessity for Stephen to make any connection between her own erotic preferences and the commitment to other women that feminism entails. Such convictions act as a straitjacket, severely curtailing the number of choices open to her. The sexual and the textual practices of *The Well of Loneliness* speak eloquently of these constraints. On the other hand, *Orlando*, a 'jeu d'esprit'[75] with its disregard for conventional plot and character, its flights of fancy through time and space, and its use of the magical and the miraculous, gave Woolf an almost limitless opportunity to satirise the kinds of masculinity that she had experienced as overbearing and oppressive in her own life.

75. Leonard Woolf, *Downhill All the Way: An Autobiography of the Years 1919–1939* (London: Hogarth, 1967), p.146.

5

Femininity and Feminism: Three Novels of the 1930s

The Thinking Reed, The Weather in the Streets and *The Death of the Heart*[1] are texts which make incisive, and hitherto largely unrecognised, statements about gender and class in the 1930s. They are also critical texts for re-evaluating the customary dichotomy between femininity and feminism.[2] Janice Winship, for example, has argued that 'femininity is not merely a passive acceptance by women of patriarchal domination but represents an *active subordination*'.[3] A number of feminist critics have taken the distinction between feminism and femininity as absolute. Rosalind Coward has cautioned against an unquestioning acceptance of woman-centred texts as feminist texts, making essentially the same point as Winship: 'Feminism can never be the product of the identity of women's experiences and interests – there is no such unity. Feminism must always be the alignment of women in a political movement with particular political aims and objectives. It is a grouping unified by its *political interests*, not its common experiences.'[4]

The experience of femininity has always been an unavoidable feature of women's lives. But what has differed greatly at different times is the significance that women have attached to their lived experiences. There

1. *The Death of the Heart* (London: Gollancz, 1938); *The Thinking Reed* (London: Hutchinson, 1936); *The Weather in the Streets* (London: Collins, 1936). All quotations are from the first editions and page references are given in the main body of the text.

2. I use the terms feminine and femininity to define the specific social and cultural expectations regulating the behaviour and attitudes of women as individuals and members of a group. The meaning of the word female used as a noun is biological. Female used adjectivally denotes the biological and sexual aspects of woman's existence. Feminist used adjectivally indicates an attitude of mind disposed to question patriarchal attitudes. Feminist used as a noun denotes one who possesses a politicised understanding of womanhood and a commitment to social, cultural and political change in the interests of women.

3. 'A Woman's World: "Woman" – an Ideology of Femininity', in Women's Studies Group (eds), *Women Take Issue* (London: Hutchinson and Birmingham, Centre for Contemporary Cultural Studies, 1978), pp.134–5.

4. 'Are Women's Novels Feminist Novels?', *Feminist Review*, 5, 1980; reprinted in Elaine Showalter (ed.), *The New Feminist Criticism: Essays on Women, Literature and Theory* (London: Virago, 1986), p.238.

have been, very broadly, two options open to women writers, to emphasise or to play down what is most distinctive about women's lives. Wishing to minimise the importance of basic sexual identities, some women have carefully avoided domestic issues in their writing or have chosen to write about pregnancy and motherhood as placing women at a disadvantage to men.

In all its historical variants feminism has claimed that there is one area of human existence on which it has been uniquely competent to speak. The lives of women have constituted its continuous area of concern and enquiry. Without this privileged relationship to women's lived experience feminism would be lost for an object, bereft of credibility, and left without any *raison d'être*. Indeed, Denise Riley has set out as a basic tenet of feminism that 'all definitions of women must be looked at with an eagle eye, wherever they emanate from and whoever is pronouncing them'.[5]

However, there has never been a cultural consensus which has accepted the world of women to be as important as the world of men. Feminist critics themselves partake of the general intellectual climate of the day and, consciously or not, may perpetuate the dominant cultural view of femininity as trivial, marginal, or otherwise unworthy of serious consideration. Rosalind Coward's influential essay, for all its sharp insights on how woman-centred texts transmit patriarchal ideology, in my view, appears too easily dismissive of both the woman reader and the woman-centred text.

Femininity is historically and discursively constructed, in relation to other categories which are themselves subject to change. It is constantly updated and revised in the various genres of writing (popular as well as literary) in which it finds expression, and has its own history, as, for that matter, has the feminist criticism charged with a special responsibility for interpreting, and re-interpreting, that history. The shifting history of femininity requires reconsideration of some woman-centred texts of the 1930s.

Although femininity is now usually understood as conciliatory – reconciling women to subordination, and feminism is understood as assertive – empowering women to break free from the prison house of oppressive relationships, this has not always been the case. In 1978 the Marxist-Feminist Literature Collective adopted Mary Wollstonecraft and Jane Austen as figures epitomising the feminist and feminine impulses in women's writing. They argued that the two women exemplified how women writers in the past had opted to concentrate their energies on access to the public sphere of life or else had chosen instead to annex their

5. 'Does Sex Have a History? "Women" and Feminism', *New Formations*, 1, Spring 1987, p.36.

concerns to the domestic and emotional sphere. Austen's seemingly narrow choice of subject matter, they contended, should not lead feminists to underestimate her importance. 'Austen's refusal to write about anything she didn't know is as undermining to the patriarchal hegemony as Wollstonecraft's demand for a widening of women's choices: the very "narrowness" of her novels gave them a subversive dimension of which she herself was unaware.'[6]

Elizabeth Bowen also drew attention to the discordant, dissonant, and potentially explosive elements not far from the surface of Austen's novels in a critical essay on Jane Austen written in 1936. Although Austen had drawn no rebels and her characters, according to Bowen, derived pleasure from the straight-forward living of life, they sought ideal circumstances, ideal relationships inside the world they knew. Moreover, they located, and never far from themselves, possible darkness, and chaos.[7] It was primarily from Jane Austen that Bowen inherited her social observation and ironies. These comments on Jane Austen's works may be applied to her own fiction as well.

In its different way each of the texts I have chosen to analyse annexes women's writing to the emotional and to the personal. These novels are all largely concerned with states of feeling, subjectivity and desire. They are interiorised, giving primacy of place to emotional turbulence, to intensity, and to the inwardly directed female sensibility. Each sexualises the psychological and each exemplifies feminine subject matter.

Elizabeth Bowen is a writer who has consistently confined herself in her fiction to themes which she feels to be safely within the range of a woman writer. *The Death of the Heart* conforms to her usual pattern: 'one can be fairly certain that Miss Bowen will not be tempted to write (for instance) a novel about coal-miners or the habits of prize-fighters', speculated the critic, Jocelyn Brook, in 1952.[8] Rebecca West, although more far-reaching elsewhere in her fiction, similarly restricts herself to woman-centred subject matter in *The Thinking Reed*. Rosamond Lehmann writes about the experience of romantic love and loss from the perspective of a middle-class woman separated from her husband.

These feminine texts are concerned with rich feminist themes such as the relationship of women to male authority. Whether or not the handling of such themes is always feminist is an open question to which I shall return later in my argument. Of the three writers only Rebecca West consciously

---

6. 'Women's Writing: *Jane Eyre, Shirley, Villette,* "Aurora Leigh"', *Ideology and Consciousness*, 3, Spring 1978, p.31.

7. Derek Verschoyle, 'Jane Austen', in Derek Verschoyle (ed.), *The English Novelists: A Survey of the Novel by Twenty Contemporary Novelists* (London: Chatto and Windus, 1936), pp.99–110.

8. *Elizabeth Bowen* (London: Longmans Green, 1952), p.30.

thought of herself as a feminist: 'I myself have never been able to find out precisely what feminism is: I only know that people call me a feminist whenever I express sentiments that differentiate me from a door mat or a prostitute.'[9] Rosamond Lehmann appears to have been largely indifferent to feminism believing with her mentor Elizabeth Gaskell that a 'woman's principal work in life is hardly left to her own choice, nor can she drop the domestic charges devolving on her as an individual, for the exercise of the most splendid talents ever bestowed.'[10] Elizabeth Bowen was hostile to feminism – or perhaps just hostile to its influence on Virginia Woolf: 'From whence, then, came this obsession of hers that women were being martyred humanly, inhibited creatively, by the stupidities of a man-made world?'[11] To Bowen, Woolf's feminism seemed 'an aggressive streak, which can but irritate, disconcert, the adorer of Virginia Woolf, the artist'.[12] The writers do not all think of themselves as feminists but the ideological position of an author is not necessarily that of her text.

My final chapter offers detailed analysis of the relevant political issues of the 1930s. What matters here is that these novels were written at a time of acute social and political crisis and that they have been frequently criticised for supposedly disregarding the social and political realities of the day. But far from jettisoning social issues all three novels are sharply revealing not only of the relationships of men and women but also of the ramifications of the social hierarchy.

Writing about popular fiction of this period Martin Ceadel complains of critics' expectations that literature should be 'too self-evidently "about" the major social and political issues'.[13] In his view critics have been too narrow and literal in defining social and political concerns and should have looked for 'many indicators of concern about air power, for example, to be found in the literature of the twenties and thirties which is not directly about fear of war'.[14] Judith L. Johnston has shown that revisions in the fiction of Bowen, West and other women are directly related to the growth of Fascism.[15]

---

9. 'Mr. Chesterton in Hysterics: A Study in Prejudice', *The Clarion*, 14 November, 1913; reprinted in Jane Marcus (ed.), *The Young Rebecca* (London: Virago, 1983), p.219.
10. *The Swan in the Evening: Fragments of an Inner Life* (London: Collins, 1967), p.68.
11. 'The Achievement of Virginia Woolf', in *Collected Impressions* (London: Longmans Green, 1950), p.81.
12. Ibid.
13. 'Popular Fiction and the Next War, 1918–1939', in Frank Gloversmith (ed.), *Class, Culture and Social Change: A New View of the 1930s* (Brighton: Harvester, 1980), p.162.
14. Ibid.
15. 'The Remedial Flaw: Revisioning Cultural History in *Between the Acts*,' in Jane Marcus (ed.), *Virginia Woolf and Bloomsbury: A Centenary Celebration* (London: Macmillan, 1987), p.256.

If one extends to *The Death of the Heart* and *The Thinking Reed* the critical approaches suggested by Ceadel and Johnston, it is possible to read these novels as parables in which the fear of war and of Fascism may be obliquely traced. To purloin Elaine Showalter's metaphor, a radical alteration of our vision takes place so it becomes possible to see meaning in what has previously been empty space: 'The orthodox plot recedes, and another plot, hitherto submerged in the anonymity of the background, stands out in bold relief like a thumbprint.'[16]

Clearly, all is not well in the fictional world of Elizabeth Bowen. Her most explicitly political novel is probably *The Heat of the Day* which explores the reasons why a disaffected Englishman is prepared to betray his country to the Nazis. But a sense of anxiety and discomfort permeates much of Bowen's imaginative writing of the 1930s. The feelings of dislocation, to which her cultivated, disoriented characters often give voice, is induced by the general restlessness which would seem to intimate to the reader that the whole bourgeois world is soon to be turned upside down. There is a particularly profound sense of foreboding in *The Death of the Heart*. To paraphrase the words of a character in *To the North*, Lady Walters, though all ages are restless, the age in which the characters live is manifestly more than restless.

The buried political elements in Elizabeth Bowen and Rosamond Lehmann's writings have yet to be satisfactorily unearthed and analysed, perhaps because the emphasis they place on individual subjectivity has always been difficult to reconcile with political and theoretical perspectives which have been sceptical about traditional concepts of subjectivity and individualism. The concentration on the personal, an irritant to those who consider themselves to be politicised at the best of times, was peculiarly so in the 1930s.

Although the reductive strain of Marxism which holds that 'politically correct' texts must deal overtly with political subject matter is now virtually extinct it was virulent among the British intelligentsia in the 1930s, a time when many writers consciously opted to change the direction and subject matter of their writing in order to forward political ends. Consequently, the three novels under discussion could and often did appear ostrich-like in the context of the social and economic troubles of the day – it was as if West, Lehmann and Bowen had deliberately buried their heads in the sands of women's intimate experience in order to avoid engagement with the suffering around them which was preoccupying so many of their contemporaries. To critics of the time the concerns of *The Weather in the Streets* and *The Thinking Reed* seemed insignificant compared to those generated

16. 'Review Essay: Literary Criticism', *Signs: Journal of Women in Culture and Society*, 1, Winter 1975, p.435.

by the Spanish Civil War.

Examining the critical responses to these texts, at the time of publication and later, reveals the inappropriateness of attempts to evaluate them according to a narrowly prescriptive notion of social relevance. Ironically, although all three novels are spiced with nuances of social class refracted through feminine behaviour and feminist analysis, radical critics, themselves often preoccupied with questions of social class, have failed to recognise their subtleties of class analysis. Thus the critic, Peter Wolfe, totally missing the point of West's social ironies, dismisses *The Thinking Reed*, a text which delivers a scathing indictment of the rich (and ends with intimations of the Wall Street crash), as the work of a 'writer committed to public responsibility', who 'draws critical fire by writing a comedy of upperclass [sic] manners during a time of great public hardship'.[17]

Elizabeth Bowen has also suffered badly at the hands of critics who have wrongly discerned a fundamental lack of seriousness about social issues in her work. Sean O' Faolain, for example, argued that Bowen 'fills the vacuum which the general disintegration of belief has created in life by the pursuit of sensibility'.[18] Raymond Williams invented a new category, 'the fiction of special pleading' and cited Elizabeth Bowen as a skilled practitioner of the art. This type of fiction, according to Williams, takes as absolute one person's feelings and needs, creating other persons in these sole terms, and thus the 'personal novel ends by denying the majority of persons. The reality of society is excluded, and this leads, inevitably, in the end, to the exclusion of all but a very few individual people.'[19]

Such attitudes are not confined to men. In *Only Halfway to Paradise*, a survey of women in post-war Britain, Elizabeth Wilson lumps together very different novelists, Iris Murdoch, Elizabeth Bowen, Rosamond Lehmann and Elizabeth Taylor, on the whole dismissively. Elizabeth Bowen is characterised as manifesting 'a "woman's" sensibility taken to excess'; Rosamond Lehmann in *The Echoing Grove* is said to be 'successful in connecting the general atmosphere of retreat to a special sense of women's peculiar situation'.[20] One wonders why women's situation is deemed 'peculiar'? and whether or not a novel that '*successfully*' linked the mood of the times to a sense of man's situation would be damned with faint praise as merely a limited success? Inscribed within the very terms of this evaluation – introspection *or* social

17. *Rebecca West: Artist and Thinker* (Carbondale and Edwardsville: Southern Illinois University Press, 1971), pp.47–8.
18. *The Vanishing Hero* (London: Eyre and Spottiswoode, 1956), p.188.
19. 'Realism and the Contemporary Novel', *Partisan Review*, vol. 26, 2, Spring 1959, p.209.
20. *Only Halfway to Paradise: Women in Postwar Britain, 1945–1968* (London: Tavistock, 1980), pp.149–150.

engagement, sensibility *or* commitment – are often the values which men (and women who see no need to question patriarchal attitudes) consider important. The criteria used exclude much which is important to women.

Classically, a male critic slides from denigration of a text to contempt for the women who read it. Thus Harry Strickhausen refers to the 'frantic, primarily feminine following which values all of Miss Bowen's work equally and for reasons all its own'. While acknowledging that Elizabeth Bowen's fiction does speak to women he imputes irrationality and lack of critical discernment to the woman reader to explain its appeal.[21] Anthony Burgess provides the best example of this kind of sexism. The faults of women writers are the 'faults a man finds in a woman: they chatter, they are deficient in moral values, they are too empirical, they fall in love with the accident and miss the essence, they are distracted by a golden apple'.[22] As Bonnie Kime Scott has astutely observed, whenever male critics have taken an interest in Rebbecca West, it has been in precisely those aspects of her writing – the late rather than the early West – which feminists have seen as the least important.[23]

What importance should we, therefore, attach to the fact that these texts concentrate on women's needs, refuse to be sidetracked into more general issues, and insist on seeing the sexual as the source of *significant* experience? In so doing in the 1930s when the intellectuals were preoccupied with Spain, mass unemployment, and the threat of Fascism, can it be argued that these texts challenge the notion that what is serious, what is important, what is worth writing about is the world of men?

The critical reputations of Rebecca West, Rosamond Lehmann and Elizabeth Bowen as serious writers were firmly established by the mid-1930s.[24] In each case an existing literary reputation guaranteed that their works were read by both the sexes, and that they were not just restricted to the overwhelmingly female readership that usually accrues to popular works centred on women's predicaments written by women without critical acclaim. But the literary quality of Bowen and Lehmann has obscured the fact that the plot and material of our texts of study are often similar to the romantic stories for working-class women which circulated in the popular new women's weeklies *Peg's Paper* (1919), *Secrets* (1932) and *Oracle* (1933). Victoria Glendinning has observed affinities between *The Death of the Heart* and such popular love stories, and stories of failed love: 'who holds whose hand in the cinema: it is the stuff of which teenage-girls'

21. 'Elizabeth Bowen and Reality', *The Sewanee Review*, vol.73, 1, January–March 1965, p.165.
22. 'Treasures and Fetters', *Spectator*, 21 February, 1964, p.254.
23. 'The Strange Necessity of Rebecca West', in Sue Roe (ed.), *Women Reading Women's Writing* (Brighton: Harvester, 1987), pp.268–9.
24. See bibliography for titles and dates of their respective publications.

magazine stories are made. Elizabeth invests it with the incomprehensible world-shattering outrage which for the person concerned such things have.'[25]

The polished interiors and perfumed gardens of *The Death of the Heart* and *The Thinking Reed* also bring to mind the opulent settings of the melodramas and musicals which Hollywood made familiar to cinemagoers in the 1930s, a time when large sections of the population 'went to the pictures' once or twice a week, and the love affairs of the great movie stars, whether watched on the screen or related to their 'fans' in the newly established mass circulation film magazines, were avidly consumed by millions. But although the category of escapist fiction appears to lend itself easily to *The Thinking Reed* (if rather less happily to *The Death of the Heart* and *The Weather in the Streets*) it is one to be avoided if we wish to do justice to the complexities of these texts.

How, then, do these texts negotiate the tensions and contradictions inherent in romantic fiction? Have romantic narratives been chosen because they are particularly suited to convey critical statements about the psychosexual and sociocultural construction of women, as Rachel Blau Duplessis has suggested?[26] If so to what effect? The question of the effects of any text is always a vexed one, and becomes more so if we are speculating about the past. Janice Radway, has suggested that texts with a strong romantic element, which have traditionally been taken to defuse or to contain any demands women make on men in the 'real world', may equally plausibly support and reinforce women's demands for change by enabling women to 'imagine a more perfect state where all the needs they so intensely feel and accept as given would be adequately addressed'.[27]

Two key demands for change that women have often made of men are that male sexuality be tempered so that it become more sensuous and less aggressive and that men's behaviour in general becomes more responsive to women's needs. These demands are expressed in our three chosen texts, in all of which the emotional response of men to women is clearly shown to be inadequate. An early critic, Elizabeth Hardwick, described Elizabeth Bowen as a 'sturdy, determined writer, a romantic feminist who serves up a perennial dish: the tragedy of the Fine Girl and the Impossible Man'.[28] Hardwick also suggested that Bowen's novels gave 'prodigal relief to both

25. *Elizabeth Bowen: Portrait of a Writer* (London: Weidenfeld and Nicolson, 1977), p.124.

26. *Writing Beyond the Ending: Narrative Strategies of Twentieth-Century Women Writers* (Bloomington: Indiana University Press, 1985), p.4.

27. *Reading the Romance: The Politics of Popular Fiction* (Chapel Hill, University of North Carolina Press, 1984), p.212.

28. 'Elizabeth Bowen's Fiction', *Partisan Review*, vol. 16, 11, November 1949, p.1114.

feminine sentiment and womanly outrage'.[29]

Elizabeth Hardwick saw no inherent contradiction between writing of a robust nature and writing which strongly appealed to women. Clearly approving of Bowen as a 'sturdy, determined writer', she also made the point that, 'these are obviously women's books'.[30] Hardwick's unexpected coupling of 'romantic' and 'feminist' and her association of 'feminine sentiment' with 'womanly outrage' lend support to the argument that femininity and feminism are not necessarily irreconcilable.

In attempting to make women's personal experience acceptable in art, these texts underline the opposition between the values associated with love, reflecting an egalitarian value system, and those associated with the pursuit of status and wealth, which reflect a hierarchical one. Usually a man stands for one set of values, a woman for the other. The texts also make precise distinctions between different strata of the English middle class. All their heroines are critically situated in relation to the behaviour of that class and are given credible observation posts within the narrative from which to reflect upon the lives of the rich. Of necessity, all three women inhabit an inner landscape of private dreams. Their capacity to feel deeply is, if anything, an impediment in a world where other people do not appear to share it.

Portia Quayne in *The Death of the Heart* and Olivia Curtis in *The Weather in The Streets*, having developed no defensive strategies to protect themselves from coming to harm, have consequently no way of recognising the defensive strategies adopted by others. Their uncorrupted belief in the holiness of the heart's affection makes them unable to understand the compromises which having to accommodate themselves to the real world necessitates of those on whom they unwisely bestow their love. Their innocence is not only that of youth and the emotions, it is more particularly a social innocence.[31] This impels them to fall in love with men who are not regarded as socially acceptable and to experience the suffering of women who find themselves in such a predicament.

These novels are concerned with physicality and with women's bodily experiences which are a primary source of pain. They depict suffering in a new way and give it a female specificity. Having or losing a child is important in all three novels – miscarriage (Isabelle), abortion (Olivia), infertility (Anna). Lost, wanted and unwanted children figure in these novels with an insistence it is difficult to ignore – as they do in most women's lives.

29. Ibid., p.1120.
30. Ibid., pp.1120, 1114.
31. Hermione Lee, *Elizabeth Bowen: An Estimation* (London: Vision and Barnes and Noble, 1981), pp.104–5.

Elizabeth Bowen, Rosamond Lehmann and Rebecca West were indeed attuned to suffering, but not of the kind that men always recognise. It is suffering not of a public kind but of a sexual nature that overtakes the lives of Portia, Isabelle and Olivia. The theme of sexual happiness found and lost echoes through these novels. We see romantic torment and loss at its most obsessively intense, blocking everything but the love and loss of her aristocratic lover out of Olivia's life. It is there, more obliquely, in Portia's rejection by two successive men and in her unsuccessful quest for love. It is to be found in the emotional dereliction of the sophisticated Isabelle, who suffers at the hands of her profligate husband and undergoes a painful miscarriage as a consequence.

Marx's words on religious suffering also apply to romantic suffering. It is 'at the same time an *expression* of real suffering and a protest against real suffering'.[32] If these women writers appeared to be dancing to a different piper from many of those around them it was because *as women* they were hearing a different tune. Moreover, what is made clear in their writing is that the oppression of girls and women (by boys and men) is experienced on an everyday basis and is not confined to the public sphere. Asked what was her first experience of Fascism, Rebecca West, who had observed Fascism first-hand in Nazi Germany, interestingly responded 'a lot of boys who stopped my sister and myself and took her hockey stick away from her'.[33]

The fact that radical critics whom one might reasonably expect to respond positively to these women have shown negligible interest in them, or disowned them, is of particular concern as neither Bowen, Lehmann nor West were hostile to the left. It is true that Elizabeth Bowen came from a privileged Irish land-owning background and that she did not accept many of the basic political arguments of the left literary intelligentsia. Like Virginia Woolf she had contempt for the writer who had become merely an 'inventor-mechanic'.[34] But she wrote perceptively about 'the movement' represented by Auden and Isherwood, and the younger writers (with the exception of Dylan Thomas) in her 1936 Faber Collection show either political or sociological preoccupations.[35]

She deplored, moreover, the lack of good socially relevant drama in Britain and applauded the radical experiments of Unity Theatre. Reviewing

32. Quoted by Tania Modleski, *Loving With a Vengeance: Mass Produced Fantasies for Women* (London: Methuen, 1982), pp.47–8.
33. Rebecca West, interviewed by Marina Warner, 'The Art of Fiction', *Paris Review*, 79, 1981, p.130.
34. 'Advance in Formation', review of *New Writing in Europe*, *Spectator*, 17 January, 1941, p.65.
35. See William Heath, *Elizabeth Bowen: An Introduction to her Novels* (Madison: University of Wisconsin Press, 1961), p.72.

John Lehmann's *New Writing in Europe* she commented: 'In terms of achievement, the movement's greatest value was in attack: the norm of most writing in England was (and to an extent, sadly, remains) the norm of middle-class sensibility: art condoled with and flattered, but largely condoled with, the well-to-do.'[36]

The Death of the Heart does not 'condole' with the well-to-do, although it is set in the world of the monied classes. So too is *The Weather in the Streets*. Rosamond Lehmann's acquaintances included many on the left and her photograph album from the 1930s contains many leading radicals including Virginia Woolf, whom she remembered tapping her on the shoulder at a party and saying, '"Remember, we won this for you", meaning the freedom to discuss sex without inhibition in masculine society'.[37] Stephen Spender, whom she met shortly after the birth of her son, Hugo, would come from Oxford with Auden and Isherwood to stay in her country house in the Chilterns and remembers Lehmann in his authobiography as 'one of the most beautiful women of her day'.[38] At the time that she published *The Weather in the Streets* she was married to Wogan Phillips, who joined the Communist Party and was wounded in Spain. She was involved in anti-Fascist work and, with Sylvia Townsend Warner, a key organiser of the public meeting which Virginia Woolf described as 'Rosamond's great meeting for writers to protest against Spain'.[39] Rosamond Lehmann also reviewed working-class writing in *The New Statesman*. Her brother, John, who edited the radical *New Writing*, is usually regarded as a key figure in the intellectual life of the 1930s. Many accounts of the 1930s which refer to John inexplicably make no mention of Rosamond.

Rebecca West was the most radical in her personal politics and in her espousal of left causes. Her politics later moved to the right, but her writing in the 1930s is often concerned with the unequal status of men and women and the concentration of wealth in the hands of the few. In *The Thinking Reed* she exposes the habits of the rich who are, almost without exception, idle, parasitic, boorish and vain.

Times which are worrying and taxing for all are more so for those who have the most to lose if things go wrong. In the loveless world of the *The Death of the Heart* life is a balancing act. The skill that is needed is the skill that anticipates, and thereby prevents, the ultimate disaster. The ultimate disaster is a fall. 'My books', wrote Elizabeth Bowen in an exchange of views with Graham Greene and V.S. Pritchett, 'are my relation

---

36. Bowen, 'Advance in Formation', p.65.
37. *Rosamond Lehmann's Album* (London: Chatto and Windus, 1985), p. 53.
38. Ibid, p.35.
39. *The Diary of Virginia Woolf*, vol. 5, p.142.

to society.'[40] However, the polarity between the outside world and the inside world which a first reading of Bowen's work suggests is deceptive. It is true that Elizabeth Bowen usually refrains from explicit social comment and appears, moreover, sometimes deliberately intent on underlining the disparity between the public and the private worlds. But the depiction of the pre-war life-style of the English upper-middle classes (as predominantly sterile, selfish, dangerous and precariously balanced) in this finely-observed novel of sensibility is arguably no less incisive (and no less damning) than in the more polemic works of many of her contemporaries.

The adolescent Portia in *The Death of the Heart* feels less at home in the tastefully decorated interiors of the Quaynes' opulent town house than in the shabby hotels she lived in as a child. In this 'airy vivacious house, all mirrors and polish, there was no place where shadows lodged, no point where feeling could thicken'. The rooms are unwelcomingly set for 'strangers' intimacy' or else for 'exhausted solitary retreat'.(p.57) The necessity for personal survival is a high priority for the adults. 'We've got to live', is a refrain variously on the lips of the characters, Eddie, St. Quentin and Thomas. It is used to cover up moral lapses and to emphasise the need for painful readjustments. The feckless Eddie counterposes his own worldliness to Portia's naïvety: 'What makes you think us wicked is simply our little way of keeping ourselves going. We must live, though you may not see the necessity.(p.351) St. Quentin does the same: 'Oh, we've got to live, but I doubt if we see the necessity.'(p.129) The more experienced Thomas mentions the spectre that haunts them all, the prospect of privilege about to be removed by external forces, 'The most we can hope is to go on getting away with it till the others get it away from us.'(p.129)

Eddie is employed by Thomas Quayne's firm. If, as seems possible, he is sacked for incompetence he is likely to starve: 'Worse things happen to better people.'(p.428) The emotional insecurities of the characters are aggravated by the political and economic circumstances in which they find themselves. The Major is out of work. In a ruthlessly competitive commercial world there is no longer any niche for his talents. His redundancy is imaged in mechanical terms: 'Major Brutt was a 1914–1918 model: there was now no market for that make. In fact, only his steadfast persistence in living made it a pity that he could not be scrapped.'(p.123) At the quiet seaside town where Portia is sent away on holiday bombardment from the sea is used to throw a minor faux pas into proper perspective: 'Only outside disaster is irreparable.'(p.288)

---

40. *Why Do I Write? An Exchange of Views between Elizabeth Bowen, Graham Greene, and V. S. Pritchett* (London: Marshall, 1948), p.23.

The adult characters reveal their own failings with candour. Anna is even able to describe the adults' emotional anaesthesia as it must feel to Portia. 'If I were Portia? Contempt for the pack of us, who muddled our own lives then stopped me from living mine. Boredom, oh such boredom, with a sort of secret society about nothing, keeping on making little signs to each other.'(p.436) The characters live in a state of heightened consciousness, edgy, tense and anxious. Much honest self-criticism occurs in the post-mortem after Portia has absconded. But the lives that the bourgeoisie lead, or are forced into leading, are interrogated consistently throughout the novel; by Anna with frankness, by St. Quentin with arcane wit, and by Thomas with resignation and defensiveness: 'Anna and I live the only way we can, and it quite likely may not stand up to examination.'(p.432)

It is not easy to determine the exact position from which Elizabeth Bowen's subtle studies of upper-middle class society proceed.[41] To assume, as many critics do, that Bowen simplisticly endorses the beliefs of her adult characters or their lifestyles, is wrong. The text is a veritable chinese box of self-absorbed and self-reflexive characters and supplies many images of spying, watching, and seeing. Such images make it clear that things may not always be what they seem. At one point Portia is referred to as 'God's spy'.(p.349) Anna complains tetchily that Portia does not fit into the Quayne household because her values are different. She forms odd attachments and odder habits, for example, wishing to keep things that Anna and Thomas would throw away, 'begging letters, for instance'. (p.12)

The adult characters are constantly under scrutiny from those whose values and points of view differ from theirs. Their habitual defensiveness reveals a reluctance to admit publicly to what they know privately to be true – that the lives they lead are both destructive of self and exploitative of others. Thomas complains that 'everyone else gets their knives into us bourgeoisie on the assumption we're having a good time. They seem to have no idea that we don't much care for ourselves. We weren't nearly so much hated when we gave them more to hate.'(pp.128–9)

The acquisition of grown-up status is a central theme of *The Death of the Heart*. In a preface to *Encounters: Early Short Stories* Bowen revealed the fears that had haunted her own life since her mother had died when she was thirteen: 'All through my youth I lived with a submerged fear that I might fail to establish grown-up status; and that fear had probably reached its peak when I started writing . . . I was anxious at once to approximate

41. See William Tindall, *Forces in Modern British Literature* (New York: Knopf, 1947), pp.314–15.

to the grown-ups and to demolish them.'[42]

Conflict between the generations provides the key to understanding *The Death of the Heart*. It is also significant that class conflict is not addressed directly in the novel but is displaced onto generational conflict: 'For my generation (possibly the last of which this was true) grown-ups were the ruling class', writes Elizabeth Bowen revealingly.[43] Symbolically, grown-up status can only be achieved by Portia through the attainment of womanhood, which publicly accrues to a young woman upon acquiring society's most prized status symbol – a man. The feminist psychoanalyst, Nancy Chodorow, contends that a daughter's relationship with her father carries the burden of needs which were originally and ideally satisfied by her mother.[44] As Chodorow explains, 'Girls cannot and do not "reject" their mother and women in favor of their father and men, but remain in a bisexual triangle thoughout childhood and into puberty'.[45] When a girl's father does become an important primary person it is in the context of a triangular relationship with the mother in which the girl's relationship to him is 'emotionally in reaction to, interwoven and competing for primacy with, her relation to her mother'.[46]

Portia is painfully conscious of the circumstances in which she came into the world. She is the 'child of an aberration, the child of a panic, the child of an old chap's pitiful sexuality.'(p.343) Her parents' irregular union doomed Portia and her mother, Irene to a rootless existence as exiles in cheap hotels. Each relationship that Portia attempts to form with a man is an imaginative replacement for her missing relationship with the mother who died. Her deeply libidinal love for her lost mother is matched only by her idealisation of the absent father with whom she has never experienced the kind of intimacy she still remembers feeling with her mother.

There are, however, substantive differences between Portia's view of her father and other people's. The old family retainer, Matchett, alone is able to provide a view of her father which answers Portia's emotional needs: 'Why shouldn't Portia hear about her father from someone who sees him as *someone*, not just as a poor ignominious old man?' ventures Anna.(p.436) But it is Portia's recollections of her mother which give her a vivid memory of love in the past and emotional sustenance in the present. And in her descriptions of mother and daughter in Switzerland, walking

42. Preface to *Encounters: Early Short Stories* (London: Sidgwick and Jackson, 1949), pp.x–xi.
43. Ibid.
44. *The Reproduction of Mothering* (Berkeley: University of California Press, 1978), pp.194–5.
45. Ibid., p.140.
46. Ibid., p.192.

arm in arm, sharing chocolates and brioches, hanging stockings out to dry together, Bowen intimates the warmth and closeness that is a crucial absence in Portia's London life. According to Chodorow, women may spend their whole lives loving in mendacious or manipulative ways, sustaining ties with the mother while forming a sexualised attachment to the father or his replacement.

In *The Death of the Heart* Elizabeth Bowen sets out the various attention-seeking ploys to which Portia resorts in her quest for love and the exasperated reactions of middle-class adults used to repressing their own emotions. 'The *idea* of her never leaves me quiet . . . She makes me feel like a tap that won't turn on,' exclaims Anna, (p.343) 'You're like any girl at the seaside, always watching and judging, trying to piece me together into something that isn't there', declares Eddie exasperatedly (p.275) 'This evening the pure in heart have simply got us on toast', observes St. Quentin.(p.433) Portia is thwarted in her attempt to transfer her love from her mother to Eddie, and from Eddie to Major Brutt, by the young man's embarrassment and the old man's fundamental sense of decency.

The meeting in the Karachi Hotel, a genteel, shabby establishment of the kind in which Portia once lived, contains powerful echoes of her parents' relationship and strong vestiges of the emotional intensity which haunted the original liaison. The girl's awkward proposal of marriage to the Major is clearly an act of identification with her mother. Since becoming a woman must involve doing the sort of things that mother does, and becoming the sort of woman that mother was, Portia offers to cook for the Major as her mother did for her father long ago in Notting Hill Gate. The disparity between the ages of the two is oddly reminiscent of the earlier misalliance. It is in these passages that Bowen is at her most skilled in delicately portraying the loneliness of the old man: 'The preposterous happy mirage of something one does not even for one moment desire must not be allowed to last.'(p.414) The evocation of mood and character is punctilious: 'Had nothing in Major Brutt responded to it he would have gone on being gentle, purely sorry for her – As it was . . .'(p.414)

The closing episodes of *The Death of the Heart* leave us with a never-to-be breached closing of adult ranks. The Major telephones the Quaynes to tell them where Portia is and Matchett, the girl's confidante of old, is swiftly dispatched to fetch her home. Denied the only legitimate role that would allow her to leave the Quayne household respectably – as someone's wife – Portia is unceremoniously returned to her old state of dependency. After her brief skirmish into the world of adults she is restored to the position of a child: 'You will wait, like a *good girl?*, [my emphasis](p.416) asks the Major, on leaving the room to arrange for Portia to be restored to adult custody. Reviewing *The Death of the Heart*, Graham Greene noted that as Matchett sets out for the drab hotel, disapproving, firm, authoritative – but the one person who loves Portia and links her to her father and mother in the past – we are allowed to feel that the adults 'have at last done the right thing'.[47] As Barbara Seward reflects, one of the tragic facts about life as Bowen sees it is that 'pure and absolute love demands for its existence at least a partial ignorance of the true nature of our world'.[48] Elizabeth Bowen herself wrote, 'it is not only our fate but our business to lose innocence, and once we have lost that it is futile to attempt a picnic in Eden'.[49]

In her autobiographical fragment *The Swan in the Evening*, Rosamond Lehmann reflects on the sexual ideology which was deeply instilled into her in the course of her middle-class upbringing: 'Girls should be pretty, modest, cultivated, home-loving, spirited but also docile; they should chastely await the coming of the right man, and then return his love and marry him and live as faithful, happy wives and mothers ever after.'[50]

But disappointment often lay in store for many of Lehmann's contemporaries who had tried to do what was expected of them and failed. Like her heroine in *The Weather in the Streets* Lehmann experienced an unhappy first marriage, childlessness and separation from her first husband. *The Weather in the Streets* explores the disillusionment of Olivia Curtis, the 'other woman' in an adulterous love affair, whose status effectively excludes her from any prospect of motherhood or domestic happiness. Unlike her sister, Kate, the mother of four healthy children, who had slipped effortlessly into a suitable marriage with a young country doctor, the childless Olivia is living as a paying guest in the flat of her cousin, Etty, and coping with the reproaches of sexual failure and involuntary celibacy as best she can. The contrast between Olivia and the respectably married members of her own family is potent: 'We sex-starved women have cravings you comfortable wives and mothers don't dream of.'(p.36)

Hardly Portia's age when introduced in her earlier novel, *An Invitation to the Waltz*, the Olivia of *The Weather in the Streets* is ten years older and awaiting the promise that life has yet to deliver. Rosamond Lehmann studiously avoids the equation of adolescent innocence and uncorrupted love. Olivia is not the helpless victim of her circumstances, playing childishly with matches and then taken by surprise when the powderkeg of male sexuality ignites. She is, rather, the highly intelligent survivor of

47. 'Two Novels', review of *The Death of the Heart* and *Days of Hope*, *Spectator*, 7 October, 1938, p.578.
48. See Barbara Seward, 'Elizabeth Bowen's World of Impoverished Love', *College English*, vol. 18, 1, October 1956–May 1957, p.32.
49. 'Out of a Book', *Orion*, 3, 1946; reprinted in Bowen, *Collected Impressions*, p.265.
50. *Rosamund Lehmann's Album*, op.cit., p.68.

a luckless marriage who reads her old Oxford copies of the Victorian novelists for consolation and has quietly chosen to assert her independence by reverting to her maiden name. The affair with Rollo Spencer is unashamedly willed and wanted on Olivia's part from the very start. For her it is a tonic which restores lustre to a dull existence, relieving the monotony of days wasted mending stockings and cleaning stained linings in handbags ('the gramophone's idiot companionship, the unyielding arm-chair, the narrow bed', p.88).

The unbridgeable gap with which Lehmann essentially is concerned in this novel is not between the generations but between men and women. The man with whom Olivia falls in love is a wealthy aristocrat who is married to a delicate, ailing wife. Olivia's is a love which involves total commitment, that can hold back on nothing and which means no less than everything. It is a love which can recognise one particular man only as its appropriate object of desire: 'Rollo, I haven't had a lover. There was no-body I fell in love with, I didn't try experiments . . . only because of love – because I believe in it, because I thought I'd wait for it, although they said schoolgirlish, neurotic, unfriendly . . . It was because of you.'(p.160)

As Byron expressed the discrepancy, man's love is 'of man's life a thing apart' and it is 'women's whole existence'.[51] Jane Miller has observed that a powerful convention within 'the narrative of male seduction' is the attributing to women of views which men find it convenient for women to have. Miller points out that the words which Byron puts into the mouth of the wronged Dona Julia console the libertine, Don Juan.[52] The idea that love is woman's whole existence resonates through *The Weather in the Streets*. There is, however, a crucial difference between *The Weather in the Streets* and *Don Juan*. The overpowering belief in romantic love as the validation of being in *The Weather in the Streets* is written from a woman's perspective: 'It looks now as if I was writing specifically about the predicament of women, though I was not conscious of it at the time', Rosamond Lehmann told Janet Watts in 1981.[53]

Many women readers identified strongly with Olivia in the 1930s ('Most of the women who wrote to me – and my readers have mostly been women – said: "Oh, Miss Lehmann, this is my story! – how did you know?"')[54] Fifty years later *The Weather in the Streets* is still a 'benchmark' book for many women. As Janet Watts explains, 'In her books they have found themselves: their own confusions and pleasures, sorrows, passions

---

51. *Don Juan*, c.1. cxxiii.
52. *Seductions: Studies in Reading and Culture* (London: Virago, 1990), p.28.
53. Quoted in Janet Watts, introduction to *The Weather in the Streets* (London: Virago, 1981).
54. Ibid.

and episodes of farce.'[55] If Rosamond Lehmann's readers' descriptions of their own responses to the novel ('this is my story!') are to be trusted, the account of romantic love in *The Weather in the Streets* is the account which women readers might, if asked, have volunteered themselves. *The Weather in the Streets* is addressed to and interpellates the woman reader whose perspective the familiar narrative of seduction has traditionally failed to recognise or has deliberately rejected in favour of that of the seducer. The novel meticulously records the physiological experiences of loving not wisely but too well. The description of sickness during pregnancy, as Nicola Beauman points out, was unique.[56] The account of the abortion, if not unique, was certainly exceptional for its time.[57] The novel affords unusually candid insights into the whispered confidences and exchanges of telephone numbers between women in times of crisis. Disclosing the secret of her unwanted pregnancy, Olivia is admitted into 'the feminine conspiracy . . . tact, sympathy, pills, and hot-water bottles, we're all in the same boat' (p.271) and realises that the experience of abortion is more common than might be supposed among women in her social circle.

Ironically introduced to Olivia by Etty as a 'public *bene*factor' who has saved '*reg*iments of unfortunate *err*ing women from *ru*in', (p.269) Mr. Treadeven, the abortionist in the exclusive private clinic to which Olivia is sent, appears to be more interested in his prized ornaments, a photograph of himself catching a large, oversized salmon and bronze statuettes of the semi-clad female torso, than he is in the woman in his surgery. Lehmann clearly intends the figure of the abortionist to embody the exploitation and subterfuge to which women who were able to pay for illegal, expensive, and often highly dangerous, abortions had no choice but to submit.

To focus, as Lehmann does, on the aspects of love that men do not see or do not experience, such as pregnancy, sickness and abortion, is to supply the missing pieces in the jigsaw of romance. It is also to allow us to see the whole picture completed and to hear the story told in full. All too often women's concealment of the missing pieces, and their reluctance to tell their story in full, has been an important contributory factor in enabling that story to continue in the old way.

Although women may often enjoy and consent to the erotic and emotional elements of intimate relationships with men, they do not usually consent to being treated badly within such relationships. They do not consent to abandonment. Unwanted pregnancy is no part of any unwritten

55. Ibid.
56. *A Very Great Profession: The Woman's Novel 1914–39* (London: Virago, 1983), p. 155.
57. For a rare description of abortion see Naomi Mitchison, *We Have Been Warned* (London: Constable, 1936).

contract between men and women and nor is abortion. While Rosamond Lehmann declines to relieve women of responsibility for their actions she also writes outside the traditions that assume that women are doomed by nature to suffer at the hands of men and that men cannot help themselves in wronging women. As Jane Miller has argued, 'it is necessary to unravel actual women's stories of seduction from the falsetto productions of men, as a first step towards challenging those accounts of sexual relations . . . controlled as practice and as discourse by men, in their own interests.'[58]

The question is whether Lehmann merely evokes the situation of romantic infatuation in *The Weather in the Streets* or whether she problematises it? Does she approve of Olivia's infatuated state of mind or express reservations about its wisdom? Might she, indeed, do both? Significantly, *The Weather in the Streets* lacks a happy ending. It does not give the woman reader what she wants – a heroine whose greatest accomplishment is her unqualified success in establishing herself as the recipient of the hero's loving care and a hero who declares his undying love and intention of cherishing and protecting the heroine forever out of the depths of his own emotional need.[59]

While such a happy ending is *not* a formal characteristic of many popular types of fiction which invariably punish the woman for illicit sexual relationships, it *is* a formal characteristic of the most typical of the woman-centred novels consumed by women, the popular romance. But the whole direction of *The Weather in the Streets* is opposed to the ethos of much romantic fiction in that Rosamond Lehmann, rather like Elizabeth Bowen, emphasises not the joy and permanence of love but those aspects of love which are hopelessly misdirected, sadly unrequited or callously betrayed. The dream of a baby in a wooden cradle and a cottage with hollyhocks in the garden is destroyed by the carefully counted wad of banknotes which the rational part of Olivia is persuaded to part with. But it is replaced with an emotional legacy of great sadness. The deep conflict of needs exposed within the novel is the conflict within the woman torn in opposite directions between emotional dissidence and social conformity. In *The Weather in the Streets* the curtain is drawn back on Olivia's sexual desire which is candidly acknowledged as the unconscious, unpredictable and dangerously volatile force that Lehmann's readers in a post-Freudian age will recognise it to be.

As in *What Maisie Knew*, the Henry James novel which *The Death of the Heart* most closely resembles, the central character in *The Death of the Heart* is an adolescent whose ability to analyse her own situation is restricted by her chronological age. Because Elizabeth Bowen works

58. *Seductions: Studies in Reading and Culture* (London: Virago, 1990), p.28.
59. Radway, *Reading the Romance*, p.84.

within the consciousness of an immature young woman who can see more than she is able to comprehend, extended logical meditations on Portia's part are few. In fact, our attention as readers is often deliberately drawn to things that Portia does not know. The adults' pregnant references to Anna's lover, Pigeon, a close friend of the Major's who never actually appears as a character in the novel, and their disquisitions on how Major Brutt first entered the Quayne household, are good examples of the reader continually being directed beyond Portia's limited understanding and guided towards a more sophisticated interpretation of events. Many of the most telling adult disclosures, moreover, are made in Portia's absence. It is our own lost innocence which we recognise in Portia. But because Portia makes so many mistakes we are forced to question the wisdom of actions based exclusively on feeling rather than on rational considerations.

Rosamond Lehmann is much closer to her heroine, Olivia. *The Weather in the Streets* is written in the third person for two of its four parts, with occasional uses of the first person and of the present continuous tense. The second book, which details the love affair, is written exclusively in the first person. This section explicitly invites the reader's identification through the narrative first person, 'I' and is the most vivid and subjective, allowing us to inspect Olivia's private thoughts and confidences in intimate detail. Here the emotional logic of events is registered so intensely, and so exclusively, from Olivia's point of view that we momentarily lose all sense of how intensity of feeling may be banishing rational judgement. The later sections dealing with the breakdown of the love affair have a sadder detachment. The narrative switches back to the third person as we view the lovers' collision with the outside world with greater distance and objectivity.

The tone of *The Weather in the Streets* is predominantly intimate and confessional. The reader is quickly made to recognise, as is the heroine, that a love as sequestered and intense as hers cannot last. The awareness that the outside world is never far distant from wherever the lovers happen to find themselves, and the reminder that the outside world cannot approve of the illicit liaison, is rarely absent from Olivia's enjoyment of the moment. Olivia experiences love as an awakening that turns its back on existing social categories, but she is only too aware of what those categories are: 'We don't live by lakes and under clipped chestnuts, but in the streets where the eyes, ambushed, come out on stalks as we pass; in the illicit rooms where eyes are glued to keyholes.' (p.370) Olivia recognises her own capacity for self-delusion and has unclouded and accurate insights into the truth of her situation from time-to-time, 'but now I see what an odd duality it gave to life; being in love with Rollo was all-important, the times with him the only reality; yet in another way they had no existence in reality. It must have been the same for him.' (p.182) Olivia's tragedy is that a rational capacity to understand what is happening to her is undermined by an emotional inability to adapt her behaviour accordingly.

Since nothing intervenes between the reader and the character, Olivia's meditations carry greater narrative authority than Portia's utterances. We are not allowed to forget that the romantic interlude must pass, that the hope of permanent happiness with Rollo is an illusion. Olivia desperately needs love, and very much against her better judgement has been unable to prevent herself from dreaming that she and Rollo will be lovers for the rest of their lives. In her fantasy she even manages to unite herself, Rollo, and his wife after death: 'Rollo would die and I'd step forward afterwards and say I loved him too, and Nicola would turn to me for comfort, we'd set up together.'(p.221)

Rollo, while he quite genuinely does care for her, is a good deal more prosaic, much less committed, and generally better at hedging his bets. Rollo is a prime example of a familiar type; the married man who strays, whom unattached women – often to their cost and often too late – have had to recognise has never intended to be anything other than married from the beginning, 'just as husbands are supposed to behave to their wives when they're up to no good on the sly ... Playing a double game both ways', as Olivia herself reflects.(p.388) The mature Olivia in *The Weather in the Streets* is wiser than the young girl of *Invitation to the Waltz*. The index of the distance she has travelled is that she is able to acknowledge as true, albeit with some bitterness, unpleasant facts that she has hitherto not wanted to face.

The portrayal of the aristocratic Rollo in *The Weather in the Streets* has often been criticised as unconvincing: 'the air of unreality that surrounds Rollo even during the illusion-shattering last weekend episode demonstrates that ... he has been glimpsed from the outside by a woman who can not penetrate a man's mind,' Diana E. LeStourgeon writes.[60] This 'air of unreality' is, however, better understood as the romantic haze which obscures Olivia's vision and as such it is an integral part of the book's artistic purpose and design. For the whole point of the novel is that Olivia, for much of the time, is incapable of seeing Rollo as he really is. She cannot recognise that he has never thought of their situation from her point-of-view, nor promised her anything of importance, that he has never thought of telling his wife the truth about his sexual relationship with Olivia, nor of telling Olivia the truth when he resumed sexual relations with his wife: 'I'm a weak selfish easy-going character, and all I want is a quiet life,' he tells Olivia.(p.77) But her romantic intoxication prevents her investing these words with the significance they deserve: 'Olivia's awareness of her lover never exceeds the bounds of love or art; she apprehends him rather

60. *Rosamond Lehmann* (Boston: Twayne, 1965), p.87.

than observes him; in thought, in the narrative of her consciousness, the idiom of love is never departed from', Elizabeth Bowen wrote perceptively in 1936.[61]

The characterisation of Rollo is linked to the author's own acute awareness that women's expectations of men are also often unreal. The hope that many women invest in men like Rollo is one which women fabricate and of which men remain, for the most part, happily ignorant. The romantic haze impeding Olivia's rational judgement is finally dispelled by her resentment at the unfairness of a situation which replicates in their intimate lives the disparity between his great wealth and her relative poverty: 'Two women in love with him. Two separate intimacies not overlappping at all, both successful: it was what he needed – what suited best his virility and secretiveness. It was all quite clear.'(p.390)

Rollo Spenser with his cultivated accents and tweed overcoat is in no way a virile hero or a 'manly man'. He is, rather, the quintessential upper-class Englishman, emblematic of an inter-war ideal of masculinity as reticent, undemonstrative and essentially restrained. Rollo disappoints not through any poverty of characterisation, or because, in his own way, he does not love Olivia: 'it was only that the word love was capable of so many different interpretations'.(p.392) He disappoints because he manages to intimate successfully, to Olivia and to the reader, that the experience of passion has not had the transfiguring effect on his life that it has had on hers: 'It *was* fun, wasn't it, darling?'(p.436) The word 'fun' with its overtones of schoolboy escapades is Rollo's ineptly reductive last word upon what was for Olivia 'an experience magnificent enough in itself', which 'should have no sequel'.(p.376)

The question why a gifted, interesting woman should throw herself away upon 'a hairdresser's block'? which perplexed critics of *The Mill on the Floss*, is revived a century later in *The Weather in the Streets*. The answer is essentially the same. Women do not always fall in love with men who are their equals in any objective sense, who feel as deeply as they do, or who see the world in the same way. They fall in love with men who do not embody any of the qualities they have themselves, often with dire consequences for the woman's peace of mind.

Offering surprisingly little resistance to the appeals of Rollo's overbearing mother, Olivia relinquishes her lover at the latter's behest. Married love and romantic love are shown to have very different consequences for the woman. Romantic love results in an abortion for Rollo Spenser's mistress. Married love results in a baby for his wife. The man, we are told, is left with slight scars as a result of a car accident. But the woman, we have good reason to suspect, is more heavily scarred by

61. Review of *The Weather in the Streets*, *New Statesman*, 11 July, 1936, p.54.

the loss of the man she loves. *The Weather in the Streets* constructs woman's romantic desire in such a way that it both eroticises and banishes power differences and these return with a vengeance when the spell of erotic attraction is broken. Rollo goes back to the comfort and safety of his respectable marriage. Olivia is left to mourn alone. In important respects *The Weather in the Streets* runs directly against the grain of many familiar nineteenth-century novels. In *Pride and Prejudice*, the book that Olivia reads on the day of her abortion, the impetus of the narrative is to remove misunderstandings, to reconcile difference, to bring the lovers closer together within a framework of moral equality despite their differences of economic status. This is illustrated by the relative ease with which Elizabeth is able to articulate her own claims as a suitable wife for Darcy and to despatch the meddling Lady de Burgh for whom she proves to be more than a match.

In sharp contrast, it is the *absence* of any framework of moral equality in *The Weather in the Streets*, the *lack* of any correlation between the moral and social worth of the characters, which gives Olivia no option but to capitulate to the blackmail exerted on behalf of her son by the odious Lady Spencer ('his children must be legitimate, they must have the orthodox upbringing and inherit', p.186). At the end of *The Weather in the Streets* the reader is left with a dislocating sense of the social world of the rich, as it is depicted in the novel, as being one in which familiar moral bearings and values are either missing or seriously askew.

Assessed simply by the elements of its narrative *The Weather in the Streets* does not promise to be fertile ground for feminism. Should we, therefore, think of it as a locus of femininity tied to the expectations of the social order, sanctioning woman's expression of her sexual needs only within the institution of marriage (or at least the imminent prospect of marriage) and not as a locus of feminism which aspires to expose the social construction of such ideas? There are other possibilities. Olivia and her husband do not live together. She is her own woman. She cannot be restored to the married woman's corner of the romantic triangle. As Margaret Lawrence pointed out in 1937, the figure of the mistress, represented by Olivia, is not an updated version of the older courtesan, but a contemporary model of a free and independent woman:

> Between Olivia and the great ladies who loved in their own way under a law of their own there is little similarity chiefly on account of her poverty. She is very much a twentieth century portrait, one woman probably out of many, trying to find her own way to live as much as it was possible to live with a man, openly admitting her need of him, refusing to depend upon him and coming out badly under social and economic arrangements.[62]

62. *We Write as Women* (London: Joseph, 1937), p.152.

What distinguishes Olivia as a character is her integrity. She will accept only small tokens from her lover – stockings, books, flowers – nothing of any monetary value. She will not be kept by Rollo even though she has great problems in keeping herself. When he presents her with an expensive emerald she is appalled: 'it said nothing about us, just brilliant, unimpeachable, a public ring, saying only with what degree of luxury he could afford to stamp a woman'.(p.179) Olivia's attitude is, given the circumstances, a brave attempt to hold on to some semblance of control over the terms on which their relationship is based. It is a bid for equality within the private world of love which contrasts pointedly with the unequal status of Olivia and Rollo in the world outside it.

In *Black Lamb and Grey Falcon* Rebecca West describes her reasons for writing *The Thinking Reed*, a novel about the rich, 'to find out why they seemed to me as dangerous as wild boars and pythons'.[63] She is disarmingly straightforward about where men's power over women comes from: it comes from money. As Alexandra Pringle points out, all Rebecca West's good people; Margaret in *The Return of the Soldier*, Ellen and her mother in *The Judge*, Harriet in *Harriet Hume*, are all poor: 'Poverty and goodness are one.'[64] In *The Thinking Reed* the rich are able to patronise others because they are economically privileged. The conundrum of why they are as they are is explained not through subtleties of characterisation or plotting but tautologically. It is, West suggests, because they have money: 'I tell you, money is a poison,' said Isabelle. 'Only wealth or some toxic condition like alcoholism could degenerate the brain to that degree'.(p.423)

The setting of much of *The Thinking Reed* is the fashionable, cosmopolitan world of the French riviera in the 1930s. The heroine, Isabelle Sallafranque, has come to detest the brittle, smart, international social set to which her husband, Marc belongs. 'They are complete parasites, who can't earn their keep',(p.427) acidly remarks the one creative person in the novel, the artist Alan Fielding. At a time when the governments of America and Europe must contend with economic crisis and unemployment at home and abroad innumerable, over-indulged, petulant and gorged European and American citizens have opted to become voluntary exiles on the continent living aimless lives adrift among the hotels and fashionable resorts of Europe. Characters such as the Pootses and the Lauristons are lotus eaters; bored, louche and fatuous in their personal tastes and attitudes and seemingly endowed with no redeeming

63. *Black Lamb and Grey Falcon: The Record of a Journey Through Yugoslavia in 1937* (London: Macmillan, 1942; reprinted 1967), p.477.
64. Alexandra Pringle, introduction to Rebecca West, *The Harsh Voice* (London: Virago, 1981), p.ix.

graces. Insufferable although she finds them, they nevertheless, exercise a morbid fascination over Isabelle, largely because they remind her how she too cannot help being morally compromised by her ostentatious display of wealth ('I am a cad because I'm a privileged person, and the two things are bound to be the same', p.439).

Rebecca West believed that there were substantive differences between male and female sensibility but would not be drawn on whether such differences were innate or culturally produced: 'It's awfully hard. You can't imagine what maleness and femaleness would be if you got back to them in pure laboratory state, can you?'[65] The inter-war masculinity West imaged, unlike the gentler, domesticated variety imaged in Lehmann, is irascible, potentially explosive and dangerous for women. The fact that men have unsatiated wants accounts for their attractiveness to women and for their manifold psychological and emotional shortcomings. It strikes Isabelle that 'the difference between men and women is the rock on which civilization will split before it can reach any goal that could justify its expenditure of effort'.(p.464)

Intimate relationships between the sexes in *The Thinking Reed* often have undercurrents of sexual violence. In her relationships with three men close to her; the American whom she first marries, a French aristocrat, and the businessman who becomes her second husband, Isabelle is subjected against her will to various forms of male aggression. She complains bitterly that with none of these men had she been able to chart her own course in life. Instead, she had progressed 'erratically, dizzily, often losing sight of her goal, by repercussion after repercussion with men travelling at violent rates of speed on paths chosen for no other motive than the opportunities they give for violence'. After her husband's reckless plane crash had come 'the violent frivolity' of André, the 'violent coldness' of Laurence, and 'the violent heat' of Marc.(p.451)

As in *The Death of the Heart*, the twin spectres of war and domestic upheaval threaten to bring the monied classes' pursuit of pleasure abruptly to an end. Fearing disaffection among the working class the government of France has forbidden the industrialist, Marc Sallafranque, who has borrowed heavily from the national reparation fund to rebuild his huge car assembly plant, to gamble in public. To save her husband from the disgrace which would inevitably follow were he to be discovered at the gaming tables Isabelle is forced to flaunt her own sexual power and to transform herself into a public spectacle, accosting her husband in a casino and provoking a melodramatic scene in which she accuses him of infidelity. The carefully calculated strategem works. Marc is saved from ruin, but Isabelle miscarries. Her psyche is disturbed and the loss of her baby is the

---

65. Rebecca West, Warner interview, p.125.

consequence of her actions: 'it was entirely necessary that she should let him go on believing that she had been demented and blind instead of cunning and far-sighted'. (p.350) After this traumatic episode Isabelle joins the company of the walking wounded, wandering from sanitorium to sanitorium in search of sedation for her shattered nerves.

Rebecca West consistently opposes the will to live and nurture and the will to create poverty, suffering and war in her writings. In *The Return of the Soldier* a working-class woman's ministrations restore a shell-shocked soldier back to health. In an early article in *The Clarion* Rebecca West wrote sympathetically about the suicide of Emily Davison, a suffragette who threw herself under the king's horse at the Derby. She argued that this suicide, generally construed as an irrational and violent act, was both rational and premeditated, and that its dreadful logic called for great personal courage on Davison's part.[66] Rebecca West's point is that the will-to-death, which seems to be characteristically male, sometimes forces otherwise sane women to mirror the behaviour of men.

Rebecca West said that the two themes of her book were 'the effect of riches on people, and the effect of men on women, both forms of slavery'.[67] Analysing the women's movement she wrote: 'The relations between the rich and the poor are often paralleled by the relations between men and women.'[68] In *Black Lamb and Grey Falcon* she invents a phrase to describe the difference between male and female sensibility: 'Idiots and lunatics. It's a perfectly good division.'[69]

According to Rebecca West, women refract and mimic the behaviour of men because they have no choice but to throw in their lot with them in a symbiotic relationship of mutual dependency. There is little prospect of bliss in such shabby compromises but only the likelihood of extended misery and humiliation on both sides. In her review of Wells's *Marriage* she rails against a handsomely subsidised, parasitic wife, Marjorie Trafford, whose extravagance eventually ruins her husband: 'What would have happened to Marjorie if she had to fend for herself?'[70]

The influence of Henry James, which we have observed on *The Death of the Heart* is also present in *The Thinking Reed*. In an early monograph on James, Rebecca West had criticised Isabel Archer for marrying without

66. 'The Life of Emily Davison', *The Clarion*, 20 June, 1913; reprinted in Jane Marcus (ed.), *The Young Rebecca: Writings of Rebecca West 1911–1917*, (London: Virago, 1983), pp.178–83.

67. Ms. synopsis *The Thinking Reed*, quoted by Victoria Glendinning, *Rebecca West: A Life* (London: Weidenfeld and Nicolson, 1987), p.150.

68. '"A New Woman's Movement": The Need for Riotous Living', *The Clarion*, 20 December, 1912; reprinted in Marcus, *The Young Rebecca*, p.132.

69. Quoted Marina Walker, p.125.

70. Review of *Marriage*, 'The Freewoman', 19 September, 1912; reprinted in Marcus, *The Young Rebecca*, pp.64–9.

love.[71] Her namesake in *The Thinking Reed* is also clearly at fault in this respect. The marital bond is more binding in *The Thinking Reed* than it is in West's short story 'Indissoluble Matrimony' (1914) or her article 'Divorce is a Necessity' (1932). But marriage is at a heavy price and carries dire penalties for Isabelle Sallafranque including enforced separation from her women friends, 'sentenced to a privacy of fate . . . Nobody knows the whole truth about one except one's friends.'(p.152)

However, Isabelle fails to accept even partial responsibility for the system being what it is: 'always she sees her own problem as a personal thing, though she persists in reading other people's problems as social, as illustrative of a larger malaise created by the historical process'.[72] As the upper-class woman already possesses wealth, Rebecca West cannot in *The Thinking Reed* propose economic liberation as a means of ending sexual subservience. Arguing against the employers' exploitation of working women during war time '(presumably on account of the different balance of her ductless glands)', she concludes: 'we will be as different as Mr. Ellis likes, but we are not going to lose money over it.'[73]

The problem Isabelle faces is that within the social and sexual economy of the time, to forfeit her sexual position as Marc's wife is to forfeit her social position as a respectable woman because the one depends on the other. Wealthy though she might be she has no status other than that obtained through a man, no defined role other than 'hanger on'. She does not have the option of work to give her a measure of personal autonomy, nor the privileged relationship to the economic productive base which belongs to her husband as a wealthy manufacturer of automobiles. Even her considerable monetary investments must be managed not by herself but by her Uncle Honoré. Within the prevailing sexual and social ethos a woman, even a rich one, is palpably disadvantaged in the stakes of material existence. Since marriage is the career for which she has been trained she opts to re-enter it after contemplating interruption.

The language of sexuality in *The Thinking Reed* is the language of war and the best that women can do is to seek a truce to their advantage. 'All men are my enemies, what am I doing with any of them?' asks Isabelle (p.452) as she is about to seek a voluntary reconciliation with her husband: 'That is why making love is important, it is a reconciliation between all such enemies, and there are degrees in such reconciliations.' According to Rebecca West, even if heterosexuality remorselessly produces inner conflicts within the psyche of the heroine, it is still the only practical option

71. *Henry James* (London: Nisbet, 1916), p.70.

72. Harold Orel, *The Literary Achievement of Rebecca West* (Basingstoke: Macmillan, 1986), p.149.

73. Review of *War and Women: Essays in Wartime* by Havelock Ellis, *The Daily News*, 26 December, 1916; reprinted in Marcus, *The Young Rebecca*, p.335.

open to women and for this reason husband and wife must present a united front to the outside world. Isabelle regrets 'this horrible offence of treating my husband as if what strangers saw counted, which destroys the whole purpose of marriage, which betrays the trust which is the real point of marriage'.(p.439)

The Thinking Reed avoids questioning the institutional base of patriarchal control of women through marriage, although it serves as a powerful locus of protest against some of its emotional consequences. At the end Isabelle frankly acknowledges the contradictions of her position: 'All the same, it is terrible what men do to women. Even if we annihilate the emotions it sets up, we cannot pretend it has no consequences.'(ibid) She decides to soften the harsh lines of the picture her mind has taken of the world: 'Had you not better learn to put up with men, since there is no third sex here on earth?'(p.452)

This discrepancy returns us to the question with which this chapter started. How does feminism cope with femininity? Recognising an overlap between the two do we simply reclaim femininity, albeit with a difference? In the first place, I would suggest that class is of central concern to feminism. Unless one accepts radical feminist arguments that gender antagonisms alone constitute the 'motor' of history, it is clear that the class-basis of society serves to compound the oppression of women. This is not to argue that the capitalist system is responsible for women's oppression which predated capitalism and can still be found in societies not organised on capitalist lines.

However, women's oppression can only be understood properly if we analyse the intersections of class and gender; how sex is potently defined through class difference and vice versa, and the crucial role that social class plays in keeping women (and men) firmly in their place. In each of our texts women suffer as a consequence of their relationships with individual men who are recognisably representatives of a particular social class and whose values reflect the preferred values of that class. Class is a crucial element in all these relationships, because what men cannot give women, or what they cannot risk losing themselves, is determined by a class system in which the men have an objective vested interest.

Whereas the men in these novels have a strong emotional stake in maintaining the system the three women are declassé, and feel themselves to be outsiders, at best indifferent to the subtle ramifications of the social order. Portia, conceived 'among lost hairpins and snapshots of doggies in a Notting Hill Gate flatlet' (p.344), has inherited an indeterminate social status and is a social embarrassment to the respectable arm of the Quayne family. Isabelle is an American. As an only child, early orphaned and early widowed at twenty-six, she finds herself witnessing the social niceties of the European smart set from a position on its peripheries. Olivia exists on the margins of polite society, in an ill-defined artistic subculture of artists and intellectuals that is far removed from the world of liveried retainers inhabited by the Spencers. The feminist implications of these texts are located to some degree, though not of course, exclusively, in their analysis of class-relations.

All three authors are acutely aware of the dangers to themselves and others produced by the inadequacies of the privileged classes which they dissect. In each novel there is some variant on the death of the heart, and it is implied that for life to be lived at all it has to be emptied of meaning. Emotional atrophy allows the middle classes to carry on as they do and to perpetuate their hegemony over others. The habitual self-justification and self-defensiveness which Portia encounters in the Quayne household is not as easy to identify and to name as the adultery in *What Maisie Knew*. But it is more pervasive and exhibited across the entire spectrum of upper-middle class characters.

Is the romantic writer, as Rosalind Brunt suggests, perhaps 'an inadvertent feminist'?[74] Do these texts leave the reader dissatisfied as part of a process of questioning and revision? What a feminist reading has brought to the surface is an account of gender relations that alerts us to how material realities undermine the romantic thrust of the narrative by pinpointing the economic, social and political elements that link sexuality not only to 'natural' desire but to economic social and political necessity. For as Nancy Chodorow has put it, 'women's apparent romanticism is an emotional and ideological response to their very real economic dependence'.[75]

The contours and categories of class in these texts strike us at once as absolute and under constant threat of being broken down. For the ways in which class is lived by men and women mirror the ways in which sexual difference is lived. The unconscious structures which produce and reproduce subjective identity are also those through which class is experienced and through which emotional, sexual, political and social rebellion is expressed. In these novels women's behaviour, motivated in Portia's case largely by her unconscious needs, in Olivia's by more conscious ones, and in Isabelle's by mainly rational considerations, pinpoints the dangerous instabilities of class identity for both sexes. The concentration on women's sexual conduct in *The Weather in the Streets*, *The Death of the Heart* and *The Thinking Reed* brings to the fore questions about the behaviour of social groups. Women's volatile sexuality signals more general anxieties about volatile social behaviour.

74. 'A Career in Love: The Romantic World of Barbara Cartland', Christopher Pawling (ed.), in *Popular Fiction and Social Change* (Basingstoke: Macmillan, 1984), p.155.
75. Chodorow, *The Reproduction of Mothering*, p.197.

In *The Weather in the Streets*, as in many romantic novels, intimate closeness to a man of a higher social class kindles within the heroine the hope that the power of love will one day prove strong enough to break down the social barriers preventing her happiness. Such ideas and hopes may belong to a radical and egalitarian value system, and, as the original readers of our texts were aware, are potentially disruptive and can sometimes have devastating material effects. The abdication of Edward VIII in 1936 may serve as a salutory reminder of the dangers of underestimating the power of romantic love or of dismissing romantic love as merely the preserve of romantic novelists and their women readers.

• In these novels it is women who naturalise discrepancies between hope, promise and reality. In the end, Olivia voluntarily relinquishes all claims on Rollo, Isabelle opts for reconciliation with Marc, and Portia is returned to the circle of her adoptive family. The attitudes to the upper-middle classes in these texts are complex. At times Olivia's admiration for the Spencers stops just short of adulation. The Quaynes, Thomas and Anna, are limited people and there are important and unresolved differences between husband and wife in their attitudes to life. But both Thomas and Anna appear to be geninely concerned about Portia. They worry about her incessantly. They do the best for her they can. The ambivalences in these texts reflect the contradictory hopes and fears that women have developed in relation to the patriarchal order of domination and submission. Women desire the rewards of feminine conformity and yet such conformity denies important areas of emotional existence. The texts express this double ambiguity, at once expressing and denying illicit desires.

The relationship of women to society in these texts is therefore ambivalent: one which resists while it acquiesces.[76] In the past these novels have usually been read as conciliatory. But it is my contention that they also contain elements which serve to reproduce and reinforce women's sense of resentment. They are neither unambivalently subversive nor straightforwardly conciliatory. Much depends on the importance one attaches to the endings and whether or not one believes that the ending of a narrative has the power to efface what went before from the reader's mind. But women's personal dramas are related to the outside world with precision. Lines like 'injustice matters and unemployment, and the power and hypocrisy of rulers, and revolutions' (p.206), spoken by the resolutely anti-Fascist Jocelyn, one of a new breed of idealistic young men striding around Europe with a purpose in *The Weather in the Streets*, challenge us to read the novels of sensibility of the 1930s in new ways. And the significance of such lines should not be missed simply because we do not

76. I am arguing along similar lines to Terry Lovell's *Consuming Fiction* (London: Verso, 1987), p.71.

usually expect to find them in woman-centred texts.

Feminism must embrace aspects of femininity as central sites of political struggle and its specificity has, to some extent, always been attributable to the way in which it has recognised and drawn upon aspects of women's oppression and transformed these through such active struggle into aspects of feminist strength. Patricia Stubbs lucidly makes this point and draws out its wider implications for literary representations: 'A genuinely feminist novel must surely credit women with more forms of experience than their personal or sexual entanglements . . . Women do not live off their relationships. Like other people they work, and even when they do not work outside the home, they still have contact with the material world, with people and things outside their own more intimate feelings.'[77]

The chosen texts all vividly illuminate the unhappiness of women but, with the possible exception of *The Thinking Reed*, there is no hint of a feminist politics based on gender, and no acknowledgement of the necessity for that struggle on the part of women which I have argued is the prerequisite for the transformation of feminine oppression into feminist strength. The women characters all want to be married, and this desire is attributed to basic human needs, or, if not to basic human needs, to women's needs which are taken to be different from men's. Where there is an erotic element in these novels, for example, in the relationship between Rollo and Olivia, they eroticise power differences and not mutuality and equality. There can be no possibility of a new kind of love between men and women here, for the rock on which a woman's aspiration to change founders is the familiar and closely-observed intractability of the male who refuses to change himself.

These texts sometimes question the relative economic status of men and women. They sometimes offer some updated versions of heterosexual behaviour, the independent woman at the centre of *The Weather in The Streets*, and the wife who understands the limitations of marriage in *The Thinking Reed*. However, in the final analysis, like Anita Brookner's novels today, they confirm women in the role of carriers of sentiment, experience and romance – albeit sometimes disillusioned.

The inference to be drawn from *The Thinking Reed* and *The Weather in the Streets* is that reality consists of two sets of experiences and understandings, two separate cultures each with its own values and priorities, to which men and women respectively subscribe, and that men and women inhabit separate psychological and biological spaces. In *The Death of the Heart* it is a little different and the antinomies are those of

77. *Women and Fiction: Feminism and the Novel 1880–1920* (Brighton: Harvester, 1979), p.xiii.

age. The idea that men and women have different experiences because society devalues what is culturally defined as feminine is compelling. It can, however, lead to an over-simplified picture of the world with an emphasis on the personal which disregards both the societal forms of disadvantage women experience and the concrete gains which women have made. Valerie Hay illustrates such a loss of perspective in arguing that a girl's 'right' to romance is legitimated within our culture as being one of the few 'rights' to anything that women have.[78]

Femininity is the point at which every feminist critic started and feminist consciousness is the point to which her intelligence has led her. But the feminist critic, whatever privileges her education and institutional basis may have bestowed upon her, is still a woman. And as it is impossible for any woman to escape completely from all that is expected of women in patriarchal society, the complex relationship between femininity and feminism must inevitably inform the tensions and contradictions in the critic's own life as it does the tensions and contradictions to be found in many woman-centred texts. Femininity is not that which can be analysed as an abstraction but is that in which both the critic and her woman readers are steeped.

If feminism is to touch fruitfully on the lives of women, then what women are, how women see and define themselves, and the images of themselves women produce, are all mutually inder-dependent and must always be appraised with respect. Feminism as a political project has taken upon itself to transform women's existence; to change the world of women. Because it is impossible to change that which one does not understand this must be tackled from within as well as from without. Therefore, woman-centred texts which are still read by women (even if they are not feminist texts) must always be of interest to the feminist critic as the essential building blocks of a politics of feminist change.

78. *The Necessity of Romance* (Canterbury: University of Kent, 1983), p.16.

–6–

Anti-Fascist Writings

(A) There really was a stench. On one side Dachau, on the other the 'distressed areas' with their ashamed workless men and despairing women. Not many English writers had the hardness of heart . . . to hurry past, handkerchief to nose, intoning, 'My concern is with my art, what troubles are troubling the world about me are not my business; let those whose business it is attend to it, I must be about my own . . .'

(B) I saw that two principles were struggling for mastery of the future. On one side the idea of the Absolute State . . . On the other all that was still hidden in the hard green seed of a democracy which allowed me freedom to write and other women freedom to live starved lives on the dole.

In 1933 this explained for me everything in sight.

Storm Jameson, Journey from the North[1]

Feminist criticism creates feminist texts. In my first chapter I discussed the reasons why *Testament of Youth* was read as a feminist text in 1933, and established why its feminist credentials must now be suspect. As well as texts the feminism of which has stood the test of time, there are others the feminism of which has only recently been recognised. Such a text is Murray Constantine (Katharine Burdekin)'s anti-Fascist dystopian fable *Swastika Night*.[2] The moment at which *Swastika Night* was appropriated for feminism may be precisely located: in 1985 the work was re-issued by the publishing house Lawrence and Wishart, with a new introduction by the feminist critic, Daphne Patai disclosing for the first time the true identity of Murray Constantine – unknown in the 1930s. Her exposition established Katharine Burdekin as a feminist writer whose particular achievement was to recognise that the various elements of Nazi policy combined to make one ideological whole. *Swastika Night* expressed this imaginatively in the form of a dystopian society in which women are

---

1. *Autobiography of Storm Jameson: Journey from the North*, 2 vols (London: Collins and Harvill, 1969–1970), vol. 1, 1969, p.293.

2. *Swastika Night* (London: Gollancz, 1937; reprinted London: Lawrence and Wishart, 1985). *Three Guineas* (London: Hogarth, 1938). All quotations are from the first editions and page references are enclosed in the main body of my text.

reduced to their biological function. Patai compares *Swastika Night* with a later work of futurist fiction, George Orwell's *1984*.[3]

I wish to examine Katharine Burdekin's work in the context of women's writing of the 1930s. This includes considering its connection to Virginia Woolf's *Three Guineas*. By bringing to the surface hitherto unnoticed connections, it becomes possible to illuminate the concerns shared but not recognised by these authors and to make clear some of the unusual and alternative patterns created by these two works.

Swastika Night is set seven centuries into a future in which the descendants of Hitler's Nazis have gained ascendancy over the world. The Empire of the German Nazis extends over the whole of Europe and Africa and that of the Japanese over Asia and America. All the arts except music have perished. All creative expression, all privacy, all human decencies have been lost. Hitler's Bible and some technical works are the only books available and only a few technicians are taught to read. Extrapolating from the known present – the rigidly hierarchical organisation of Hitler's Germany – Burdekin elaborates an inflexible, tiered system of social organisation. At the top of the pyramid is God, the Thunderer, and his son, Adolf, the only man not begotten of woman. At the base of the pyramid are two groups held in ubiquitous contempt, Christians and women. The Christians are a throw-back from the past, atavars who are permitted by the authorities to lead a curious, nomadic existence in the present, their strange creed informed by dogma and superstition, their spiritual beliefs universally mocked and ridiculed. Women have been degraded for centuries and are hardly more than child-bearing animals kept in cages separately from men.

The problem facing the dystopia is that women's low self-esteem has led to a falling birth-rate of girls. Here the Nazis are faced with the most intractable of conundrums. Women cannot be told that more girls are needed, for they might thus acquire a sense of self-worth: 'And yet, if women were to stop reproducing themselves, how could Hitlerdom continue to exist?'(p.14) Unlike *Brave New World* (1932), which is preoccupied with the effects of reproductive technology, *Swastika Night* is singularly unconcerned with the consequences of scientific development. Technological progress in the dystopia ended early in the twentieth century, large stretches of the German Empire are still rural, and vehicles and machinery are rudimentary.

Despite the different form in which it is manifested and the new context into which it is transposed, the logic of the dystopia bears a strong resemblance to that of Burdekin's own world. Indeed *Swastika Night*

3. See also Daphne Patai, 'Orwell's Despair, Burdekin's Hope: Gender and Power in Dystopia', *Women's Studies International Forum*, vol. 7, 2, 1984, pp.85–95.

conveys to the reader fifty years later more about the year 1937 than any imaginary long-term future it purports to invoke. Andy Croft has suggested that anti-Fascist writers in the thirties turned to non-realistic forms such as science fiction in order to satirise the latent Fascism in British society and to deal credibly with a subject of which they had little personal experience. Anti-Fascist fiction in realist modes of writing was generally produced by those who had direct experience of Fascism.[4] Burdekin's male-supremacist society is not merely a metaphorical equivalent for the contemporary world of Hitler and Nazi Germany, it is a metonymic extension of it (and of the Fascistic elements in other patriarchal societies). Between the fictional dystopia of *Swastika Night* and Germany under the Third Reich is both a metonymic continuity and the distance of metaphor.

There are no references to Katharine Burdekin in Virginia Woolf's diaries, and no known connections between Woolf and Burdekin, as there were between Virginia Woolf and Radclyffe Hall. We have no evidence that Virginia Woolf had ever read *Swastika Night* or that she had heard of its existence. There are also important differences between the two works. *Swastika Night* contains positive feminist arguments but the representation of women's experience is, somewhat ironically, minimal. Unlike Burdekin's communist-feminist utopia *At The End of this Day's Business*, *Swastika Night* provides no individuated women characters. Burdekin's conviction that the relationship between men and women in Fascist societies is essentially a relationship of property means that the women in *Swastika Night* are shown as effectively being no more than goods and chattels, reduced from woman to object, reminiscent of the *pornea* prostituted slave women kept in pens in Ancient Greece.

Out of the women's suffering arises neither questioning, understanding, nor resistance. 'None of the women found their lives at all extraordinary. They were no more *conscious* of boredom or imprisonment or humiliation than cows in a field.' (p.231) In *Three Guineas* women's shared experience of marginality ultimately provides a strategy for escape, however long-term or utopian, from narrow and immediate social determinations ('we can best help you to prevent war not by repeating your words and following your methods but by finding new words and creating new methods', p.260). But the women in *Swastika Night* remain ineluctably trapped because they lack a language in which to conceive of resistance to their masters.

Swastika Night radically simplifies many elements of patriarchy. Katharine Burdekin is not primarily interested in the various social institutions that produce and reproduce the patriarchal control of women,

---

4. 'Worlds Without End Foisted Upon the Future – Some Antecedents of *Nineteen Eighty-Four*', in Christopher Norris (ed.), *Inside the Myth: Orwell, Views from the Left* (London: Lawrence and Wishart, 1984), p.196.

but in questioning the power-based sexuality of the Fascist male, and in speculating on the possibility of a future Fascism. Burdekin dramatised the danger of certain hazards then foreseeable, and in common with Woolf she feared irrevocable damage if these tendencies were not checked. The trends which she describes in *Swastika Night* were not a present danger but a present likelihood. What the social theorist diagnoses, *Swastika Night* evokes imaginatively. One might say of *Swastika Night*, as Raymond Williams says of *1984*, that the dystopia is *more* effective because it is a version not a theory, reflecting a mood rather than being an analysis susceptible to disproof.[5]

Three Guineas was extensively reviewed in 1938. Even those critics who disagreed with them, in the main, recognised the importance of the feminist ideas in *Three Guineas*. However, these same critics generally laid less emphasis on, or else failed to take seriously, its analysis of Fascism.[6] Very little is known about the reception of *Swastika Night* in 1937. Publications which had previously reviewed Murray Constantine, such as *The Times Literary Supplement*, overlooked *Swastika Night*. It was, however, reviewed by Jane Morgan in *The Daily Worker*, 'a useful book for those who do not take Fascism seriously enough to recognise its dreadful implications'.[7] Tullis Clare in *Time and Tide* warned 'sensitive readers' not to be 'put off by the Hitler Creed with which this clever novel begins, nor dismiss this as just another of those visions of the future which are mere exercises in ingenuity'.[8]

Swastika Night was first published under the pseudonym Murray Constantine. According to Sheila Hodge, who joined the staff of Gollancz in 1936, Victor Gollancz made a point of inspecting personally all manuscripts he published.[9] It would, therefore, seem probable that Gollancz knew, and for his own reasons actively colluded in disguising, the sexual identity of the author. The pen name, Murray, is sexually ambiguous, and, in the absence of any grounds for suspecting otherwise, the novel would certainly have been read as the work of a man. This misleading impression of male authorship is actively fostered again by the use of the third-person singular pronoun in the publisher's note to the 1940 Left Book Club edition. The Left Book Club from its inception had only

5. *Orwell* (London: Fontana, 1971).

6. See, for example, Anon., *The Times Literary Supplement*, 4 June, 1938, p.379; Robert Lynd, *News Chronicle*, 3 June, 1938, p.4; Theodora Bosanquet, *Time and Tide*, 4, June 1938, pp.778–90; Basil De Selincourt, *Observer*, 5 June, 1938, p.5; Katherine John, *New Statesman and Nation*, 11 June, 1938, pp.995–6; Howard Spring, *Evening Standard*, 9 June, 1938, p.11; G.M. Young, *Sunday Times*, 19 June, 1938, p.7; Mary Stocks, *Manchester Guardian*, 10 June, 1938, p.7.

7. 'Swastika and Murder', *Daily Worker*, 11 August, 1937, p.7.

8. *Time and Tide*, 26 June, 1937, p.872.

9. *The Story of a Publishing House: 1928–1978* (London: Gollancz, 1978), p.64.

a scattering of books by or about women. Of the fifty-five titles published in 1937, four appear to be written by women, including Hilary Newitt's influential, *Women Must Choose*, and two were co-authored by women. In the war fewer books were published, and of the twelve titles in 1940, only *Swastika Night* appears to be by a woman.[10]

The 1940 edition of *Swastika Night*, published at the height of anti-German hostilities, was re-issued in response to numerous requests for a novel as the Left Book Club's choice of the month. Victor Gollancz appeared to be somewhat apprehensive at this time, presumably because the warning that the world might be proceeding towards a totalitarian order might, in the absoluteness of fiction, be taken as an imaginative submission to its inevitability: to augur a Nazi victory in the Second World War. The publisher's note to the second edition explains that events in the novel are intended to be symbolic, rather than prophetic, and calls for an intensification of the struggle to defeat Nazi Germany. The British Library catalogue has no further entries for *Swastika Night* until 1985 when it was reprinted by the Communist publishing company Lawrence and Wishart after representations from feminists in the Communist Party.

To indicate the contemporary forces at work in *Swastika Night* and *Three Guineas* I offer here a summary account of political developments in Hitler's Germany. The purpose of this is to demonstrate how fully in touch both texts were with issues of burning interest to feminists in the 1930s, and how thoroughly they entered into urgent contemporary debates.

The Weimar Republic, established after Germany's defeat in the 1914–18 war, was widely respected for its active commitment to the principle of equal rights for women enshrined in its written constitution in 1918. Legalised abortion, contraception, and equal pay were priorities of the feminist movement in its early days. A higher percentage of women sat in each of the Reichstags between 1919 and 1933 in Germany than in the parliamentary assemblies of any other country.[11] During this time large numbers of German women also entered the labour market, often freeing themselves from economic dependency upon a male wage-earner through so doing. According to the German census of 1928, eleven and a half million women were in employment, of whom over three and a half million were married.[12]

But this remarkable growth of opportunities for women was to produce a strong backlash. A survey of the attitudes of working-class Germans

10. See John Lewis, *The Left Book Club: An Historical Record* (London: Gollancz, 1970), pp.139–55. I have assumed that G.N. Serebrennikov, author of *The Position of Women in the USSR*, is female.
11. Winifred Holtby, *Women and a Changing Civilization* (London: Lane, 1934), p.152.
12. Ibid.

conducted by Erich Fromm just before the Depression revealed strong opposition to these changes. Those interviewed not only disapproved of cropped hairstyles, cosmetics, and women entering the labour market; they also often blamed Germany's social problems on these changes. Fromm wrote perceptively, 'here is an opportunity for political propaganda writers ... to use for their purpose'.[13]

Anxiety about changing gender-roles was deep-rooted and widespread in the Weimar Republic and was ruthlessly exploited by Nazis in their rise to power. One aspect of the Fascist reorganisation of German society was the re-instatement of traditional sexual divisions. Women as well as Jews were removed by persuasion, or forcibly should resistance be offered, from all the professions. The process of displacement is graphically described in Phyllis Bottome's *The Mortal Storm*, a novel in which a young medical student, Freya Roth, falls foul of the Nazis by virtue of being both a Jew and a woman who wants to pursue a professional career: 'I thought we had escaped from the world where women were at a man's mercy – considered only as his tools or his toys', exclaims Freya with feeling.[14] According to the 1934 edition of the German magazine, *Die Aërtztin*, cited in Hilary Newitt's *Women Must Choose*, a text with which Woolf was familiar, Nazi plans for women meant, at a minimum, the displacement of some six or seven hundred women doctors serving in rural and thinly populated areas.[15]

In 1934 the anthropologist, Naomi Mitchison, published her *Vienna Diary*[16] and in the *Left Review* she drew attention to the full catastrophe unleashed by the Nazi regime: 'The last two years have accentuated it all. Fascist and Nazi movements have reduced women to a complete state of subjection, in practice a much worse position than women ever held either in the great days of Rome or among the Teutonic tribes.'[17] By 1930 the once radical feminist movement in Germany had become socially and politically conservative, committed to preserving the institutions of the family and motherhood, and virtually indistinguishable from the other liberal groups which had already succumbed to the spell of Nazi ideology.[18]

13. The findings of Fromm's survey inform Claudia Koonz, *Mothers in the Fatherland* (London: Cape, 1987). The use Koonz makes of Fromm's survey is explored in Linda Gordon's 'Review Essay: Nazi Feminists?', *Feminist Review*, 27 September, 1987, p.102.
    14. Phyllis Bottome, *The Mortal Storm* (London: Faber and Faber, 1937), p.199.
    15. *Women Must Choose: The Position of Women in Europe Today* (London: Gollancz, 1937), quoted in Ethel Mannin, *Women and the Revolution* (London: Secker and Warburg, 1938), p.197. Virginia Woolf had read Hilary Newitt, see *Three Guineas*, p.268.
    16. *Naomi Mitchison's Vienna Diary* (London: Gollancz, 1934).
    17. 'The Reluctant Feminists,' *Left Review*, vol. 1, 3, December 1934, p.93.
    18. Ute Gerhard interprets Weimar feminists' failure to resist as a principled decision to avoid becoming contaminated by 'male' politics. See 'A Hidden and Complex Heritage: Reflections in the History of Germany's Women's Movements', *Women's Studies International Quarterly*, vol. 5, 6, 1982, pp.561–7.

As Winifred Holtby observed, it was precisely because the women's movement had advanced so far under the Weimar Republic that its retrogression under Hitler struck observers as peculiarly significant.[19]

Winifred Holtby was deeply concerned about the effects on women were European examples in employment and other fields to be followed in Britain. Complaining about a spate of Fascist-influenced fashion garments ('Shall I order a Black Blouse?') Holtby noted that as a woman she enjoyed the freedom to feel and think as a citizen and as an individual, but 'if the Blackshirts were victorious, I would be expected to think only as a woman'.[20] In her play, *Take Back Your Freedom*, written in 1935, but published posthumously in 1939, a woman journalist who can no longer bear to lead 'a crippled, ineffective' life without interests outside the home, plots to assassinate a proto-Fascist English dictator, Arnold Clayton. In imitation of Hitler, Clayton has dismissed women from paid work claiming to 'have withdrawn women from the soulless routine and inhumanity of offices into the intimate circle of personal relationships'.[21]

Very broadly interpreted, the originality of Fascism in Germany, and in all its European variants in the 1930s lay in its inspired *presentation* of ideas, beliefs and values which had originated elsewhere. Nazi ideology was often less a cogent, seamless unity than a borrowing of ideologies such as the repudiation of the intellect, the adulation of motherhood, and the ideal of physical perfection. Under the specific social and political circumstances which prevailed in different countries these ideologies were converted into crucial supports for the Nazi power base. Linda Gordon argues that it was only the Nazis frenetic hatred of those stepping outside traditional gender roles which distinguished Fascism from previous conservative movements.[22] There were many contradictions in Nazi attitudes to gender and an inherent irony in the fact that the Nazis assiduously mobilised hundreds of conservative women to exhort other women to make domesticity their first priority through a programme of public meetings. Richard J. Evans has also drawn attention to the contradiction between the Nazi's sentimental idealisation of the family and the ruthless pursuit of eugenic success, and their masculinisation of the process of education and socialisation.[23] Variations on the theme of

19. Holtby, *Women and a Changing Civilization*, p.152.
20. Winifred Holtby, 'Shall I Order a Black Blouse?', *The News Chronicle*, 4 May, 1934, p.10.
21. Winifred Holtby and Norman Ginsbury, *Take Back Your Freedom* (London: Cape, 1939), p.92.
22. Gordon, 'Review Essay: Nazi Feminists?', p.104.
23. *Comrades and Sisters: Feminism, Socialism and Pacifism in Europe, 1870–1945* (Brighton: Wheatsheaf, 1987), p.187.

women's place were manifold and before 1933 some Nazis had even supported ideas of female equality and emancipation.

It was symptomatic of such lack of consistency that one of the best known propagandists for the Nazi regime was a woman, Leni Riefenstahl. Riefenstahl has subseqently claimed that she worked as an independent film maker who was not subject to Nazi political controls. But Susan Sontag's researches have made it clear that *The Triumph of the Will*, Riefenstahl's filmed record of the Munich Olympics, was commissioned and entirely financed by the Nazi government, and that, despite Riefenstahl's protestations to the contrary, it was facilitated by Goebbels at every stage of its production.[24] To a viewer today, the heroic imagery of *The Triumph of the Will* reveals only too clearly the extent to which women shared Hitler's nationalism and were inspired by the rhetoric of racial triumph and the vision of military glory. Notwithstanding that exceptional women like Riefenstahl were permitted to occupy a place in public life, the lot of most women in Nazi Germany fell strictly within traditional gender precepts.

The programme of the Nazi women's movement was resolutely focused on the child, an emphasis derived in part from the anxieties about the falling birth rate prevalent in Nazi and non-Nazi circles in the 1920s.[25] Babies were thought of as potential citizens and potential soldiers, and German women were expected to produce as many children as possible to secure the ultimate victory of the state against its enemies. The five K's of the Nazi women's programme, as they widely came to be known, were the Küche, Keller, Kinderstube, Krankenstube, Kirche (kitchen, cellar, nursery, sick room, and church).

Women were among Hitler's most zealous supporters and there is some prima facie evidence for the belief that the women's vote was an important element in the Nazis' electoral success.[26] The problem of women's collaboration with the Nazis troubled both Virginia Woolf and Katharine Burdekin deeply. Among Virginia Woolf's documents there is a press cutting from *The Sunday Times*, dated 13 September, 1936, in which Hitler is quoted, 'without the devoted and steady collaboration of German women the Nazi movement would never have triumphed.'[27] As early as 1929 Woolf had discussed why women enlarge the male ego in *A Room of One's Own*.

24. 'Fascinating Fascism', *New York Review of Books*, 6 February, 1975, p.24.
25. Jill Stephenson, *The Nazi Organisation of Women* (London: Croom Helm, 1981), p.13.
26. See Jill Stephenson, 'National Socialism and Women Before 1933,' in Peter D. Stachura (ed.), *The Nazi Machtergreifung* (London: Allen and Unwin, 1983), p.38.
27. Virginia Woolf's Reading Notebooks, The Monks House Papers, Sussex University, vol. 2, p.22. I refer to the 3 Reading Notebooks relating directly to *Three Guineas* as MHP RNI, MHP RN2 and MHP RN3.

Swastika Night also explores why women collude readily with their own oppression, why they accept the myth of their own inferiority, and why they demur, and then feebly, only when their children are taken away. As the Italian Marxist, Maria-Antonietta Macciocchi (whose ideas were very influential among British feminists in the 1970s) has explained such behaviour, Fascism depended to a large degree on women's voluntary consent to Fascist ideology.[28]

Feminist historians, however, have more recently drawn attention to the implausibility of explanations based on the sexist assumption that women were emotionally swayed while for men Fascism was a rational option.[29] Renate Bridenthal has preferred to reject psycho-historical explanations and to look for rational reasons behind women's choices.[30] The Knight in *Swastika Night* has his own ideas on the subject: 'They thought, those poor little typically feminine idiots, that if they did all men told them to do cheerfully and willingly, that men would somehow, in the face of all logic, love them still more. They could not see that they were helping to kill love.' (p.120)

In 1931, the year in which the German women's movement was disbanded and an official Nazi women's organisation, the Frauenschaft, was put in its place, Virginia Woolf began to paste together notes from her reading related to *Three Guineas*. Cicely Hamilton's *Modern Germanies: As Seen by an Englishwoman* was also published that year and re-issued in 1933 with a supplement on the victimisation of the Jews.[31] But it was to be several years before Woolf was in a position to work without interruption on her anti-Fascist treatise. In the interim *The Waves*, *The Years*, and *Flush* took precedence. A second scrapbook of press clippings and miscellaneous items now in the Monks House collection at Sussex University covers the period from August 1935 to February 1937 and a third the period from June to December 1937, by which time the international situation had worsened dramatically and Virginia Woolf had resolved to make *Three Guineas* her first priority.

Virginia Woolf's reading notebooks are not exclusively on the subject of Fascism. But among items that she kept for reference a number do refer to Hitler's attitudes to women, to his treatment of the Jews, and to the segregation of the sexes in Fascist societies. Their presence shows her to have been acutely aware of the sinister overtones of Fascism at a time when many of her contemporaries were prepared to give Mosley the benefit of

28. 'Female Sexuality in Fascist Ideology', trans. Michèle Barrett et al., *Tel Quel*, 66, Summer 1976, *Feminist Review*, 1, 1979, p.67.

29. Evans, *Comrades and Sisters*, p.166.

30. 'Beyond "Kinder, Küche, Kirche": Weimar Women at Work', *Central European History*, vol. 6, 2, June 1973, pp.148–66.

31. *Modern Germanies, As Seen by an Englishwoman* (London: Dent, 1931).

the doubt, or to invent the doubt in order to give him the benefit of it. Among Woolf's own acquaintances Harold Nicolson had once edited Mosley's news sheet, *Action*, John Strachey had acted as Mosley's P.P.S., and Christopher Isherwood, Raymond Mortimer and Francis Birrell had each written for his paper.[32] In Lettice Cooper's kaleidoscopic novel of English provincial life *National Provincial*, the antics of the local Fascists matter largely in so far as they are a smokescreen for the 'polite' Fascists of Westminster and Whitehall. But after the ugly display of violence at the Olympia demonstration of 1934, vividly dramatised in Irene Rathbone's *They Call it Peace*, the true colours of British Fascism could no longer be denied and Virginia Woolf wrote to *The Daily Worker* that the march of the unemployed from Jarrow and the Olympia demonstration had persuaded her of the need for a 'popular front.[33] At some time in the 1930s the names of Leonard and Virginia Woolf were added to the list of those whom the Nazis wished to arrest.[34]

In the reading notebooks we can trace Virginia Woolf's attempt to understand the links between racist, sexist, Fascist and patriarchal oppression as the basis of *Three Guineas*, or, as Woolf herself put it in *Three Guineas*, to explore 'the whole iniquity of dictatorship' whether it was 'in Oxford or Cambridge, in Whitehall or Downing Street, against Jews or against women, in England or in Germany, in Italy or in Spain'.(p.187) These links were broadly the same as those that interested Burdekin, but they were not generally recognised in the 1930s and are still contentious today. A cyclostyled letter sent to Virginia Woolf from Monica Whately, secretary to the feminist Six Point Group, concerns the plight of German women held in criminal jails and invites her to form part of a deputation of prominent women to the German Ambassador. 'The degrading of women in Germany,' writes Monica Whately, 'lowers the status of women all over the world'.[35] Whately was also quoted in a press cutting from *The Observer* which Woolf retained: 'If Spain comes under Fascist dictatorship the position of Spanish women will be just as terrible as it is to-day in Italy and Germany, where the Fascists even exercise the right of interfering in such things as women's dress, and the use of cosmetics, and where in Italy, at any rate, it is illegal for women to work for equal pay with men.'[36]

Hitler's words, taken from *The Sunday Times* in 1936, are cited almost

32. Julian Symons, *The Thirties: A Dream Revolved* (London: Cresset, 1960), p.7.

33. See Wendy Mulford, *This Narrow Place: Sylvia Townsend Warner and Valentine Ackland: Life, Letters and Politics, 1930–1951* (London: Pandora, 1988), pp.54–5.

34. See Alexander Zwerdling, *Virginia Woolf and the Real World* (Berkeley: University of California Press, 1986), p.289.

35. Letter from Monica Whately to Virginia Woolf, dated 7 June, 1935. MHP RN3, pp.29–30.

36. *Observer*, 13 September, 1936, MHP RN2, p.35.

verbatim in *Three Guineas*: 'There are two worlds in the life of the nation, the world of men and the world of women. Nature has done well to entrust the man with the care of his family and the nation. The woman's world is her family, her husband, her children and her home.'[37] Also in the reading notebooks is a report of a lecture by a German diplomat in London in which he denied 'fantastic ideas' about the position of women in Germany. 'Nothing could be more ridiculous and stupid than the assertion that National Socialism looked on women only as breeding machines.'[38] It appears that Woolf had sought assurances from the organisers of the Anti-Fascist Exhibition of 1935 to the effect that the exhibition would include a section on women under the Nazi regime and that she had received a dusty answer from Elizabeth Bibesco: 'I am afraid that it had not occurred to me that in matters of ultimate importance even feminists could wish to segregate and label the sexes.'[39] In her autobiography, *Journey to the North*, and in her other writings of the time, Storm Jameson has given a flavour of the passions that resistance to Fascism aroused among her contemporaries in the 1930s: 'As strongly as we have ever felt anything we feel that there should be no paltering with evil.'[40]

Margot Heinemann, who was part of the anti-Fascist struggle and has documented it,[41] recollects the tireless efforts of women to raise money, medical supplies and public support for Spain through countless Aid for Spain Committees and remembers the generosity with which British women welcomed four thousand Basque refugee chilcden into their homes after Guernica.[42] In 1939 Virginia Woolf donated the proceeds from the sale of the manuscript of *Three Guineas* to help refugees from Fascist Europe arriving in Britain. The Women's Committee Against War and Fascism, established in 1934, *did* contain some feminists and did much useful work to secure the release of women in German concentration camps. But for Margot Heinemann, and for the many other women whose lives were given over wholly to the defeat of Fascism, the first priority was to defend democracy.[43] For as it seemed to Hilary Newitt and others at the time, 'only under western democracy is it still possible for a feminist

37. *Sunday Times*, 13 September, 1936, MHP RN2, p.22.
38. *The Times*, 16 December, 1937, MHP RN3, p.47
39. Letter from Elizabeth, Princess Bibesco, to Virginia Woolf, dated 1 January, 1935, MHP RN2, p.51.
40. 'To a Labour Party Official', *Left Review*, November 1934, vol. 1, 2, p.28.
41. Margot Heinemann, 'The People's Front and the Intellectuals', in Jim Fyrth (ed.), *Britain, Fascism and the Popular Front* (London: Lawrence and Wishart, 1985), pp. 157–86.
42. See Sue Bruley, 'Women Against War and Fascism: Communism, Feminism and the People's Front', in Jim Fyrth (ed.) *Britain, Fascism and the Popular Front* (London: Lawrence and Wishart, 1985), pp.131–56.
43. Conversation with Margot Heinemann, May 1988.

movement to exist'.[44] Clearly, the pendulum had swung a long way from questions of gender. We find the orthodox Marxist view that gender was a secondary matter that ought properly to be subsumed into class, clearly articulated in the writing of Ethel Mannin: 'Women alone cannot fight Fascism; the need is not for a new feminist movement, but for the co-operation of women in the general struggle for workers' power against capitalism, of which Fascism is only an advanced form.'[45]

The tragedy of the Spanish republic fired the imagination of artists and intellectuals around the world as had, arguably, no other event in the twentieth century, with the possible exception of the First World War. Virginia and Leonard Woolf were two among more than thirty distinguished British intellectuals (including Vaughan Williams, Tawney, Cole, Forster, and Huxley) who wrote to *The Daily Herald* publicly expressing their sympathy with the deposed Spanish government.[46] To designate the Spanish Civil war a masculinist affair is to equate the war simply with combat – it is a little-known fact that the first British person to die in Spain was a woman, Felicia Browne. Those women writers who were deeply moved by the suffering of women and children in Spain, or by the words of Spain's most brilliant orator, Dolores Ibarruri (La Pasionara), did not make this mistake. Sylvia Townsend Warner and Valentine Ackland joined an ambulance unit in Barcelona and attended an international writers' congress in Madrid in July 1937. Carmel Haden Guest attended a meeting of the World Congress of Women Against War in Fascism held in Paris in 1934. But women authors of anti-Fascist texts, although concerned to dramatise various kinds of oppression – experienced by women, jews, liberals, pacifists, Communists, gypsies, homosexuals – and to hold the Nazis responsible, were not, in the main, explicitly concerned with analysing the gendered causes or consequences of Fascist ideas.[47]

An interesting exception was Winifred Holtby. The moral of *Take Back Your Freedom*, originally entitled, *Dictator*, is that women who bring up their sons to revere masculinity must accept responsibility for sowing the seeds of Fascism. The play ends with the dictator's mother killing her son 'because I made him what he has become'.[48] There are, of course, anti-Fascist novels which put women characters at the forefront of the struggle

44. Newitt, *Women Must Choose*, p.33.
45. Mannin, *Women and the Revolution* (London: Secker and Warburg, 1938), p.31.
46. *Daily Herald*, 20 August, 1936, p.8.
47. For example, Naomi Mitchison, *We Have Been Warned* (London: Constable, 1935); Storm Jameson, *In the Second Year* (London: Cassell, 1936); Barbara Wootton, *London's Burning* (London: Allen and Unwin, 1936); Irene Rathbone, *They Call it Peace* (London: Dent, 1936); Amabel Williams-Ellis, *Learn to Love First* (London: Gollancz, 1939).
48. Holtby, *Take Back Your Freedom*, p.127.

against the Nazis and in which we may find a strong awareness of a woman's right to control her own body and her own destiny. Freya Roth in *The Mortal Storm* defies the Fascists by having a child by her murdered lover and then continuing her medical studies abroad.

One or two popular role-reversal utopias like Victoria Cross's *Martha Brown, M.P., a Girl of Tomorrow* and Elise Gresswell's *When Yvonne was Dictator* do emphasise the fruitful role that women may play in preventing war.[49] Carmel Haden Guest's thriller, *Give Us Conflict*, for example, contains a harrowing episode in which a young woman, Grete Walter, is put to death in a Nazi concentration camp after inciting women to refuse to have children to fight in Hitler's wars.[50] But Walter is clearly defined within the narrative as a Communist, not a feminist. Even Sylvia Townsend Warner's novel, *After the Death of Don Juan* (1938), with its rich evocation of the Spanish landscape and traditions, and the deep sympathy it evokes for Spain's suffering peasantry, appears to be less influenced by feminist ideas than either *Lolly Willowes* (1926) or *Summer Will Show* (1936), a feminist historical novel set against the background of revolutionary France in 1848. As the anti-Fascist struggle in Britain gathered momentum Virginia Woolf found herself an increasingly isolated and lonely figure in attempting to promote an independent feminist opposition to Fascism.

Indeed, far from attributing the origins of Fascism to the power structures of the nuclear family as Virginia Woolf does in *Three Guineas*, anti-Fascist novels of the 1930s like Mary Borden's *Passport for a Girl*, Sally Carson's *If She is Wise* and Sarah Campion's *Duet for Female Voices* often mediated the horror of Fascism through its disruptive effects on 'normal' family relationships.[51] But in her reading notebooks under the entry 'dictators' are two quotations copied from *The Daily Herald* which are intended to help her establish the opposite case; that the system which condones the tyrannical treatment of women in the home will also condone the tyranny of humanity in general. The first of these quotations is an appeal to members of the House of Commons to stand up to dictators. The second is taken from the testimony of a downtrodden Bristol woman applying to the courts for a maintenance order against her husband: 'My husband insists that I call him "Sir".'[52] In *Three Guineas* Virginia Woolf insisted

49. *Martha Brown, M.P., A Girl of Tomorrow* (London: Werner Laurie, 1935); *When Yvonne Was Dictator* (London: Heritage, 1935).

50. *Give Us Conflict* (London: Hutchinson, 1936).

51. *Passport for a Girl* (London: Heinemann, 1939); Sarah Campion, *If She is Wise* (London: Davies, 1935); *Duet for Female Voices* (London: Davies, 1936); Sally Carson, *Crooked Cross* (London: Hodder and Stoughton, 1934); *The Prisoner* (London: Hodder and Stoughton, 1936).

52. See Brenda Silver (ed.), *Virginia Woolf: The Reading Notebooks* (Princeton, New Jersey: Princeton University Press, 1983), p.24, and *Three Guineas*, p.318.

that the woman tackling domestic oppression was 'fighting the Fascist or the Nazi as surely as those who fight him with arms in the limelight of publicity.' She asks, 'should we not help her to crush him in our own country before we ask her to help us to crush him abroad?' (p.98)

The analogy drawn in *Three Guineas* between the patriarchal organisation of the family and of the state ('the public and the private worlds are inseparably connected; that the tyrannies and servilities of the one are the tyrannies and servilities of the other', p.258), was too advanced to be generally understood in its day. Even Katharine Burdekin retains potentially subversive remnants of the traditional family among the despised Christian communities. But it is not merely fanciful. Today the importance of the connection that interested Woolf resonates in the feminist slogan, 'the personal is political'.

By the time that Virginia Woolf visited Europe in 1934 one of her reading notebooks had already been completed. In 1934 Selina Cooper, representing the newly formed Women's World Committee against War and Fascism, went to Germany to report on the extermination of women's rights.[53] It was also the year in which Hitler ruthlessly eliminated the labour leader, Roehm, and the left elements in the Gestapo in the brutal 'Night of the Long Knives', an episode imaginatively transposed into Storm Jameson's dystopian novel, *In the Second Year*. Virginia Woolf, who was already familiar with Mussolini's Italy, now witnessed at first hand the Männerbund, the group of men who were trained to be tough, aggressive and ruthless, 'these brutal bullies go about in hoods & masks, like little boys dressed up, acting this idiotic, meaningless, brutal, bloody pandemonium'.[54] Fascist man, 'the quintessence of virility', as he is caricatured in *Three Guineas*, like Katharine Burdekin's warrior males in *Swastika Night*, is strongly reminiscent of the Freikorpsen, the unofficial bands of demobilised soldiers, later to become Hitler's cadres, who were militantly opposed to liberal and progressive elements in German society after the end of the Great War and often took the law into their own hands putting fear into German civilians.

> It is the figure of a man; some say others deny, that he is Man himself, the quintessence of virility, the perfect type of which all the others are imperfect adumbrations. He is a man certainly. His eyes are glazed; his eyes glare. His body, which is braced in an unnatural position is tightly cased in a uniform.

53. Jill Liddington, *The Life and Times of a Respectable Rebel: Selina Cooper 1864–1946* (London: Virago, 1984), pp.412–18.

54. Anne Olivier-Bell and Andrew McNellie (eds), *The Diary of Virginia Woolf*, 5 vols (Harmondsworth: Penguin, 1979–1982), vol.4, p.223. All further references will be to *The Diary* and give the page and volume number.

Upon the breast of that uniform are sewn several medals and other mystic symbols. His hand is upon a sword. He is called in German and Italian Führer or Duce; in our own language Tyrant or Dictator.(pp.257–8)

In a recent study of the Freikorpsen, *Male Fantasies*, Karl Theweleit refuses to draw an absolute line between the fantasies of hardened fighters and those of the supposedly normal man, which also reflect the misogynistic ideas of his culture.[55] Virginia Woolf also leaves open – subtly shifting the responsibility for adjudication from writer to reader – ('some say') and from personal opinion to public debate ('others deny') a crucial question. Is the Fascist Man she lampoons ('the quintessence of virility') the essence of the male ('Man himself'), the archetype, like the universals in Plato's *The Republic*, of which all others are merely shadows ('imperfect adumbrations')?

The references in *Three Guineas* to the existence of an indigenous British Fascism ('in our own language Tyrant or Dictator'), coupled with her insistence that Fascism, far from being some foreign importation, was deeply rooted and embedded in British soil was hardly calculated to endear Woolf to the Bloomsbury intelligentsia. For as Judith L. Johnston has noted, Woolf's analysis directly challenges the liberal ameliorative history of the older Bloomsbury generation and the optimistic vision of culture expressed by Clive Bell in *Civilization*: 'Woolf envisions contemporary violence not as an interval in the progress of civilisation, but as part of a continuous history of repressive personal and political relationships, rooted in a patriarchal culture.'[56] Worse still, at a time when war appeared imminent and patriotic feeling ran high Woolf was clearly no patriot. Her appreciation of the international dimensions of Fascism made loyalty to any sovereign state impossible: 'As a woman my country is the whole world.'(p.197)

Virginia Woolf's attitudes to men were fraught with deep ambivalences. There is clearly a loss of proportion in *Three Guineas* and an inability to discriminate between those aspects of male behaviour that make women smile (wearing ridiculous uniforms) and those that make women weep (murdering children). These ambivalences were never fully resolved, or if they were resolved it was only in terms of some kind of continuum of male behaviour (reminiscent of Adrienne Rich's female continuum)[57] in which the extremities of male behaviour (arrogance, aggression,

55. *Male Fantasies* (Cambridge: Polity, 1987).
56. 'The Remedial Flaw: Revisioning Cultural History in *Between the Acts*', in Jane Marcus (ed.), *Virginia Woolf and Bloomsbury* (London: Macmillan, 1987), p.255.
57. See Adrienne Rich, 'Compulsory Heterosexuality and Lesbian Existence', *Signs: Journal of Women in Culture and Society*, vol. 5, 4, 1980, pp.631–60; re-issued (London: Onlywoman Press, 1981).

intolerance and self-absorption), can be seen to connect to the behaviour of 'ordinary' men. The temptation simply to 'write men off' and to concentrate on women was one to which Virginia Woolf, particularly when analysing male violence, was strongly susceptible. However, she always stepped back because she knew this to be ultimately incompatible with her vision of a future in which men and women would one day cease to be at cross-purposes. The question 'what are men really like?' and its corrollary, 'can men change?' is the unresolved subtext of Woolf's later work and it remained unresolved because man for her always remained a mystery, unknown and probably unknowable.

Three Guineas was written after weeks of comforting her sister, Vanessa, distraught after the death of her son, Julian Bell, while driving an ambulance in the Spanish Civil War. The quest to understand what one is not oneself, the 'other', usually expressed as the mystery of the eternal feminine, has preoccupied generations of male writers. Though it is one to which we have become habituated in literature we are less used to recognising it in the writing of women. It is a quest which Virginia Woolf, for all the tedium and heartache of trying to make sense of, and learning to live with, the consequences of male behaviour, never abandoned. A working title for *Three Guineas*, 'Men are Like That' was jettisoned, probably as much for its overtones of finality as for fear of the hostility it would evoke. To paraphrase Antonio Gramsci, the optimism of the will overcomes the pessimism of the intellect. It is this redolent belief in the possibility of changing the hearts and minds of men – which in Virginia Woolf's case is clearly the triumph of hope over experience – that should make us think of her as a shining icon of modern feminism in general and a beacon of socialist feminism in particular.

In *Three Guineas* Virginia Woolf briefly revisited the concept of patriarchy which she had first identified in *A Room of One's Own*. Her understanding of patriarchy as power circling around 'the mulberry bush', to which she added the words 'of property, of property, of property' (p.120), is more precise than it had been a decade earlier. In *A Room of One's Own* patriarchy is rather nebulously used to describe the masculine values reflected in the pages of a daily newspaper: 'The most transient visitor to this planet, I thought, who picked up this paper could not fail to be aware, even from this scattered testimony, that England is under the rule of a patriarchy.'[58] Virginia Woolf's willingness to think about the relationships between men and women in class terms clearly shows the influence of the Marxist ideas of her time. 'But who are the capitalists? not women. Every

58. *A Room of One's Own* (London: Hogarth, 1929), p.50.

day I'm having that proved to me.'[59] And she has also arrived at a property-based understanding of class which excludes women from membership of the ruling class on the grounds that they do not own substantial capital. One class, men, 'possesses in its own right and not through marriage practically all the capital, all the land, all the valuables, and all the patronage in England'. The other class 'possesses in its own right and not through marriage practically none of the capital, none of the land, none of the valuables, and none of the patronage in England'.(p.33)

As early as 1929 Virginia Woolf had warned that women's propensity to bolster the male ego was dangerous precisely because it encouraged men to abuse their power: 'Napoleon and Mussolini', she had written sharply, 'both insist emphatically upon the inferiority of women,' for if women were not made to think themselves inferior they 'would cease to enlarge' men.[60] But in the interval between *A Room of One's Own* and *Three Guineas* Mussolini, to whom she refers in passing in *A Room of One's Own* and Hitler, who is not mentioned at all, had between them desecrated Europe. By the year 1938 English intellectuals had divided into warring factions taking different sides in the acrimonious debates on contemporary history.[61] Books had been publicly burned, Jewish and progressive intellectuals imprisoned, 'decadent' avant-garde culture destroyed, the rights of small nations had been trampled over, and there appeared to be no hope of remission in sight.[62] Virginia Woolf was struggling to contain her anger in 'beautiful clear reasonable ironical prose'.[63]

As Judith L. Johnston suggests, the changes that Woolf made in her writing after 1936 were similar to those made by other women writers, including Rebecca West and Elizabeth Bowen, and reflect the writer's consciousness of the approach of war and the rise of Fascism.[64] The difference in tone between *Three Guineas* ('cantankerous') and *A Room of One's Own* ('charming and persuasive')[65] reflects both the impact upon Woolf's writing of a new cultural climate, in which authorial detachment

59. Letter from Virginia Woolf to Shena, Lady Simon, dated 21 November, 1938. Nigel Nicolson and Joanne Trautmann (eds), *The Letters of Virginia Woolf*, 6 vols (London: Hogarth, 1976–1980), vol. 6, p.303. All further references are to *The Letters* and give the volume and page number.

60. *A Room of One's Own*, p.54.

61. See Samuel Hynes, *The Auden Generation: Literature and Politics in England in the 1930s* (London: Faber and Faber, 1976), p.301.

62. See Margot Heinemann, 'Left Review, New Writing and the Broad Alliance Against Fascism', in Edward Timms and Peter Collier (eds), *Visions and Blueprints: Avant-Garde Culture and Radical Politics in Early Twentieth-Century Europe* (Manchester: Manchester University Press, 1987), pp.113–36.

63. *The Diary*, vol. 4, p.298.

64. Johnston, 'The Remedial Flaw', p.256.

65. E.M. Forster, *Virginia Woolf: The Rede Lecture* (Cambridge: Cambridge University Press, 1942), pp.22, 23.

had been widely jettisoned in favour of engagement with the crucial political concerns of the day, and her own personal feelings of outrage at the victory of Fascism in Europe. Preparing to write *Three Guineas*, Woolf noted that she had 'collected enough powder to blow up St. Paul's'.[66]

Three Guineas argues that women are uniquely placed to prevent war because they are less susceptible than are most men to the feelings of aggression and egotism that lead to war, 'to fight has always been the man's habit, not the woman's. Law and practice have developed that difference, whether innate or accidental. Scarcely a human being in the course of history has fallen to a woman's rifle.' (p.13) In 1938 it was a view to which women peace activists, making efforts to prevent war through organisations like the Women's International League for Peace and Freedom, often subscribed. As an example, the veteran pacifist, Helena Swanwick, who like Virginia Woolf took her own life during the course of the war, wrote in her classic work, *The Roots of Peace*, published within weeks of *Three Guineas*: 'Women do, I believe, hate war more fervently than men . . . because war hits them much harder and has very little to offer them in return.'[67] The Co-operative Women's Guild, an organisation of working-class women which met in Virginia Woolf's house, the conferences of which she had attended in 1913 and 1935, was also wedded to pacifist ideals.

Three Guineas, for all its notes and references, its facts and statistics, its anger and energy is a utopian meditation and not a practical manifesto.[68] Its author's is the voice of the long-term visionary and not the short-term pragmatist. The emphasis in *Three Guineas* on peace as more than the absence of war, as the highest of ideals to which human beings must collectively aspire, and the conviction that the male infatuation with violence must be curbed by the example of non-violent alternatives, stayed with Virginia Woolf to the end of her days: 'Unless we can think peace into existence we – not this one body in this one bed but millions of bodies yet to be born – will lie in the same darkness and hear the same death rattle overhead,' she wrote in the thick of the German bombardment.[69] In *Three Guineas* Virginia Woolf reproached her correspondent for his limited vision, 'you have not asked us to dream. You have not asked us what peace is; you have asked us how to prevent war.' She added, 'let us then leave it to the poets to tell us what the dream is'.(p.260)

The concept of the society of outsiders in *Three Guineas* embodies both

66. *The Diary*, vol. 4, p.77.
67. *The Roots of Peace* (London: Cape, 1938), p.183.
68. See Hermione Lee, introduction to *A Room of One's Own* and *Three Guineas* (London: Chatto and Windus, 1984), p.xx.
69. 'Thoughts on Peace in an Air Raid', in *The Death of the Moth and Other Essays* (London: Hogarth, 1942), p.154.

a critique of patriarchal organisations and elements of that 'recurring dream that has haunted the human mind since the beginning of time; the dream of peace, the dream of freedom'.(p.259) This vision is expressed in the hope that positive social change may come about from women's experience of exclusion and marginality. But for this to happen women must detach themselves from patriarchal institutions. They must from this critical distance create a culture and a movement capable of resisting war. They must actively work to promote peace and freedom.

Woolf proposes that members of her society must vow to 'make no part of any claque or audience that encourages war; to absent herself from military displays . . . and all such ceremonies as encourage the desire to impose 'our' civilization or 'our' dominion upon other people'.(p.198) Yet the outsider is not solitary. A favoured pronoun in *Three Guineas* is not 'I' but 'we', confirming the fragile, yet resolute, sense of gender solidarity among women. As Gillian Beer has perceptively noted, the 'alternation between 'I' and 'we' is the living quarrel of Woolf's art, particularly in her later career.' Woolf consistently attaches a deep value to commonality, 'she was fascinated by communities including the family, groups of friends, the nation and history'. As she points out, the self in Woolf's writing is always insufficient and the communal self a more enduring mode.[70] The very last words of *Three Guineas*, taken from the autobiography of George Sand, illustrate the high premium that Woolf consistently placed upon this ideal of communality:

Toutes les existences sont solidaires les unes des autres, et tout être humain qui présenterait la sienne isolément, sans la rattacher à celle de ses semblables, n'offrirait qu'une énigme a débrouiller . . . Cette individualité n'a par elle seule ni signification ni importance aucune.(pp.328–9)

The society of outsiders in *Three Guineas* is not the first example of its kind in Woolf's writing. In an early short story, 'A Society', a group of women who discover that the London Library is full of books, 'for the most part unutterably bad!', form themselves into 'a society for asking questions,' vowing solemnly never to bear a single child between them until they are satisfied with the answers.[71]

However, the society of outsiders in *Three Guineas* is, I believe, the best embodiment of Woolf's ardent desire to move from the self-centred 'I' to the embracing 'we' and to find a creative standpoint which is less

70. 'The Body of the People in Virginia Woolf', in Sue Roe (ed.), *Women Reading Women's Writing* (Brighton: Harvester, 1987), pp.85, 100.
71. 'A Society', in *Monday or Tuesday* (London: Leonard and Virginia Woolf, 1921); reprinted in Susan Dick (ed.), *The Complete Shorter Fiction of Virginia Woolf* (London: Hogarth, 1985; and re-issued London: Triad Grafton, 1987), p.118.

merely personal and spans the bridge between the 'I' of individual consciousness and the 'we' of collective responsibility. Specifically, the outsiders from whom Woolf derives inspiration in *Three Guineas* are, in her own age, Frau Pommer, a German woman who had been imprisoned by the Nazis for protesting against anti-semitism (pp.301–2) and in a previous age, Antigone. Creon's claim to absolute rule over his subjects was 'a far more instructive analysis of tyranny than any our politicians can offer us'.(p.148) As Woolf interpreted it, the crucial ethical question raised in Sophocles's *Antigone* was: to which authority should the citizen owe allegiance? Antigone's distinction between higher and lower authority, between the laws and the Law, is 'a far more profound statement of the duties of the individual to society than any our sociologists can offer us'.(p.148)

Antigone's words translated as "'tis not my nature to join in hating, but in loving'(p.303) are not only the key to understanding *Three Guineas*, but also the key to Woolf's personal philosophy, her pacifism, her discursive writing, her ideals of womanhood, and to much of her later literary output. They are cited in order to establish essential continuities with the past, and to establish her own indomitable resistance to Fascism as part of a long, honourable history of female resistance to totalitarianism. The ultimate risk to which women resisting tyranny and war through non-violent disobedience must be prepared to expose themselves was death. For there could be no mistaking the meaning of Creon's reply to Antigone: 'Pass, then, to the world of the dead, and, if thou must needs love, love them. While I live, no woman shall rule me.'(p.303)

The society of outsiders embraces many contradictions, not least that once an outsider enters into any kind of voluntary association, however loose, she in some measure ceases to be an outsider. However, the principal value of the idea is to intimate that Woolf's own sense of alienation as a woman from the masculine ethos around her was not merely solipsistic. Much of the copious correspondence generated by *Three Guineas* was from women interested in the society of outsiders and struggling with problems of self-definition: 'But of course you're an outsider', she wrote to Shena, Lady Simon: 'Much more effectively than I am.'[72] Many women disagreed and compared their own involvement in society to Virginia Woolf's supposed disengagement. Naomi Mitchison, for example, wrote: 'I think you demand an impossible ability to be and remain au-dessus de la melee, [sic] which only very long-term minded people of either sex can

---

72. Letter from Virginia Woolf to Shena, Lady Simon, dated 15 June, 1938, *The Letters*, vol. 6, p.239.

achieve.'[73] Vita Sackville-West did not accept the claim that women were the non-aggressive sex: 'is it not true that many women are extremely bellicose and urge their men to fight? . . . they ought not to be like that, but the fact remains that they frequently are.'[74]

There was nothing passive about the society of outsiders or in Virginia Woolf's attitude to the prevention of war, although her vision was clearly too utopian to be of practical relevance in 1938. But Woolf found it impossible to scale down her hopes, to forsake her feminist dreams, and to acquiesce in war merely because resistance appeared to be futile. *Three Guineas* is shot through with sardonic anger but it also expresses a vision of humanity that is truly remarkable: 'as a woman, I have no country. As a woman I want no country. As a woman my country is the whole world.'(p.197) If *Three Guineas* offered no practical solution to the problems Europe faced, then we would do well to remember that neither did the militarists.

Katherine Burdekin also offers a powerful critique of patriarchal institutions and attitudes. The experience of marginality and exclusion in her writing is often that of the male outsider. In *Quiet Ways* Burdekin had commented on the English upper-class practice of sending boys away to school and had noted the anxiety of unhappy, isolated boys growing into men. In several of her novels she creates an exemplary man of honour, a man with a strong sense of self and not afraid to speak his mind. Such a figure is the Major in *Quiet Ways*,[75] an old soldier, who denounces the 1914 war, and Giraldus, the free-thinking monk of Glastonbury in *The Rebel Passion*,[76] also the noble scholar, von Hess in *Swastika Night*. Less influentially placed rebels include Billy Trenoweth in *The Reasonable Hope*[77] and Alan Campbell in *Quiet Ways*. Each of these men is fundamentally at odds with his culture. Each is deeply suspicious of any kind of *esprit de corps*, regarding this as the apotheosis of the herd instinct. Each is estranged from the psychic structures of patriarchy, from his own sex. For Katharine Burdekin alienation is the result of a powerful drive in her male characters towards realisation of their alternative potentials. Their quest for wholeness brings them into collision with the masculinist values of society. Yet they escape their estrangement with dignity because they

73. Letter from Naomi Mitchison to Virginia Woolf, dated 21 June, 1938. Quoted in Brenda R. Silver, '*Three Guineas* Before and After: Further Answers to Correspondents', in Jane Marcus (ed.), *Virginia Woolf: a Feminist Slant* (London: Macmillan, 1983), p.264.

74. Letter from Vita Sackville-West to Virginia Woolf, dated 23 July, 1938. Louise DeSalvo and Mitchell A. Leaska (eds), *The Letters of Vita Sackville-West to Virginia Woolf* (London: Hutchinson, 1984), p.442.

75. *Quiet Ways* (London: Butterworth, 1930).

76. *The Rebel Passion* (London: Butterworth, 1929).

77. *The Reasonable Hope* (London: The Bodley Head, 1924).

persevere in an attempt to grasp the truth inside and outside themselves and to align themselves with what is good. Communication and love are opposed to alienation and lovelessness, and because love is the ultimate communication they break their estrangement by learning how to love and by learning how to communicate.

In her pacifist novel, *Quiet Ways*, Katharine Burdekin had criticised the idea of manliness as dependent on violence. In *Swastika Night* she continues this attack through the character of the Knight, von Hess, who contests the Fascist ideals of masculinity. Von Hess has risked disgrace and ostracism to compile his chronicle of the dystopia which reveals the true history as opposed to the fictive history of the State and the 'reduction' of women. To be a man in von Hess's view requires both a soul, and liberation from Hitler. Turning away from the Nazi view of what it means to be a man, he has come also to reject the Nazi view of woman.

In *Swastika Night*, because the female characters have been reduced to total passivity it is the men (the aristocratic von Hess, the Nazi soldier, Hermann, and the English mechanic, Alfred) who between them form the circle of outsiders who learn to question received notions of masculine supremacy. These men begin to dream of what woman might be like were she ever to be liberated from male surveillance and control. Through his friend, Hermann, who did his military service in England, Alfred comes into contact with the local provincial administrator, the Knight. To Alfred, von Hess entrusts his history of the dystopia and the task of establishing an English Truth Society.

In a terse little episode in *Swastika Night* the Nazi soldier, Hermann, finds himself unexpectedly in the role of conscientious objector to the Fascist state. According to Nazi codes of conduct which have been drilled into Hermann since he was a boy, *'nothing is dishonourable, nothing is forbidden, nothing is evil, if it is done for Germany and for Hitler's sake'*.(p.46) Thus Hermann, a loyal Nazi, clearly understands it is his duty to kill his English friend, Alfred, a self-confessed traitor. But even as he draws out his knife he knows that his resolution will fail. Personal loyalty, as Hermann has been forced to acknowledge, does matter, and the sight of Alfred, even sleeping, exercises a stranglehold upon his will. As Hermann hesitates one is reminded of E.M. Forster, 'if I had to choose between betraying my country and betraying my friend, I hope I should have the guts to betray my country'(1939).[78]

By temperament, Hermann is a doer and not a thinker, not a self-reflective or complex character, but prepaied to accept outsider status, even exile from Germany, for Alfred's sake. According to Antigone there are two laws, the written and the unwritten, and it is necessary to improve the

78. 'What I Believe', in *Two Cheers for Democracy* (London: Arnold, 1951), p.78.

written law by breaking it. Just as Virginia Woolf presents the personal courage of Antigone and of Frau Pommer as an inspiration to us, so Katharine Burdekin presents Hermann's rebellion as a personal example that, if repeated, might shake the very foundations on which Fascism is built.

In *Swastika Night* the imagery of the colonised races as a sub-species outside civilisation, upon whom the fears and anxieties of the coloniser are projected, is the familiar currency of the orientalist mentality. The impoverished characterisation of these subjects, as of women, is a weakness of *Swastika Night*, and may even perpetuate the stereotypes to which it is opposed. But there are some senses in which this is endemic in science fiction, the strength of which is often the exploration of ideas rather than their polished literary representation. And perhaps, as Edward Said has argued in *Orientalism*, if the theory of orientalism tells us relatively little of importance about its declared subject, the orient, (just as *Swastika Night* tells us relatively little of importance about women or colonised peoples under the Nazis), it does tell us much about those who have developed the theory for their own aggrandisement.[79]

There is much emphasis in both *Swastika Night* and *Three Guineas* upon the Nazis' rigid segregation and control of women and also upon men's domination and control of members of other racial groups. Both works establish links between power, aggression and sexual pleasure. Man's desire to conquer is responsible for a world ravaged by imperial ambition, violence, competitiveness and greed. But although both Katharine Burdekin and Virginia Woolf clearly believe that the Nazis treat their women with the same contempt with which they also treat the races they have conquered, there is no clear argument in either text as to why the link between racism and sexism should be necessary rather than contingent. Racists are simply assumed to be misogynists and vice versa. In *Swastika Night* personal pleasures are intimately bound up with the intricate exercise of power between men and women and between lighter and dark-skinned groups: rape is a socially approved and conscious method of intimidation used by *all* men to keep *all* women in a state of fear.

Although masculinity in the Fascist male in *Swastika Night* takes an extreme form, it is not so extreme as to be altogether marginal. On the contrary, it has been hegemonic in the past: 'Unshakeable impregnable Empire has always been the dream of virile nations', and jealousy of the British Empire 'one of the motive forces of German imperialism'. In *Swastika Night* the shadows of these 'old ideas and of the vast old Empires' still hang portentously over Germany 'reminding Germans that Empires rise and *fall* reminding them also of their own small beginnings'.(p.114)

79. *Orientalism* (London: Routledge and Kegan Paul, 1978).

In an earlier novel, *Proud Man*, Burdekin had noted the association of the phallus with power and pride.[80]

Freud argued that the phenomenon of 'splitting', the inability to combine love and desire in the same object, is a problem experienced by some men. In *Swastika Night* this is the normal condition of all men. Because women remind men of that which is base, effeminate, or powerless, within their own nature, heterosexual union is a site of revulsion and self-loathing for the Nazi male. Homo-erotic bonds, on the contrary, are potentially liberating in so far as they subvert the ethos of masculinity. Katharine Burdekin, like Virginia Woolf, has an essentially benign view of homosexuality. In *Quiet Ways* she has created an unusually sympathetic view of homosexual desire in an openly lesbian character, Nurse Smith, who asserts, 'we are the only people who can bring understanding and sympathy with our love. And our loves are the only kind that are entirely uncomplicated by sex-antagonism.'[81]

In *Swastika Night* homosexual relationships, or to use Eve Kosofsky Sedgwick's term, 'homo-social' relationships,[82] are detonators of moral responsibility. Such relationships are distinguished both from sexual couplings between men and heterosexual couplings. Raising intimate questions about personal identity, 'homo-social' relationships destabilise the established boundaries of race and class. We have seen that it is not Hermann's sexual impulses but his strongest emotions which are brought into play by a relationship with another man. In *Proud Man*, Katharine Burdekin had created a time traveller, not unlike Orlando, who is able to change sex to make strange the words, concepts and social structures of human existence. The title comes from Isabella's mocking reference to 'proud man, dressed in a little brief authority' in Act 2, scene ii of *Measure for Measure*. Katharine Burdekin wished to alter the readers' perception of what was possible and to show heterosexuality not as a 'natural' state of affairs but as a state into which people are socially conditioned.

In *Proud Man* an adventurous character, Leonora, who is 'always imagining things that have no present existence', is asked what she imagines maleness to be and replies: 'I feel it to be a great warm generous rushing thing like a booming south-west wind in a leafy tree. An admirable thing. Human maleness, I feel, might be very wonderful indeed. Animal maleness is beautiful but unintelligent. Human maleness might be both.'[83]

While the political imagination in the 1930s was creating nightmares,

80. *Proud Man* (London: Boriswood, 1934), p.28.

81. *Quiet Ways*, p.123.

82. *Between Men: English Literature and Male Homosexual Desire* (New York and Guildford: Columbia University Press, 1985).

83. Burdekin, *Proud Man*, p.190.

the literary imagination was at work creating avenues of escape. Towards the end of *Swastika Night* the dull Englishman, Alfred, indulges in a major blasphemy. He decides to test the notion that women are naturally inferior to men by taking notice of his baby daughter, Edith, playing with her as if she were a boy, and, most daringly, resolving to give her a better life than others of her sex. In embracing the feminine side of his nature Alfred breaks out of the prison-cell of the gender order. He sees the once despised little Edith as 'not dirt at all, but the embryo of something unimaginably wonderful'.(p.239)

Speculation on how a dystopian society might be reversed into a fully human one began with Alfred's reflections on the subjugation of women: 'The human values of this world are masculine. There are no feminine values because there are no women. Nobody could tell what we should admire or what we should do, or how we should behave if there were women instead of half-women.'(pp.157–8) His speculation then takes a recognisably feminist turn: 'The highest possible masculine pattern of living should be imposed on women' who should 'now consider themselves superior and bring their daughters up accordingly'.(p.159) In rejecting his conditioning as a man and recognising and developing his potential to change the behaviour of men and women, Alfred has changed himself. And it is in the changed human being who has challenged the gendered authority of society, suggests Burdekin (as does Woolf in *Three Guineas*), that ultimately resides the potential to change the world.

Three Guineas is the best literary example of feminist resistance to Fascism in the 1930s. But it is also ironically the text in which Virginia Woolf chose to set fire to feminism – one inflammatory incident in a book which is ablaze with violent, incendiary images, with rags and petrol and Bryant and May matches. The purpose of Woolf's dramatic gesture is to dispel a narrow definition of feminism as being little more than the advocacy of rights for women. The 'only right,' she wrote provocatively, 'the right to earn a living, has been won'.(p.184) Even so her break with feminism is equivocal.

In *Three Guineas* nineteenth-century pioneering women, Emily Davies, Octavia Hill, and Sophia Jex-Blake are invoked and their priorities, causes and aspirations recast to dovetail with Woolf's own. Their presence provides crucial links with the present and reminds us how deep, large and rich were the causes of 'those queer dead women in their poke bonnets and shawls'. Thus Josephine Butler is cited: 'Our claim was no claim of women's rights only . . . it was a claim for the rights of all – all men and women – to the respect in their persons of the great principles of Justice and Equality and Liberty.'(p.185) These women, Virginia Woolf tells us, were 'fighting the tyranny of the patriarchal state as you are fighting the tyranny of the Fascist state', and 'we [always a significant pronoun – my insertion] are merely carrying on the same fight that our mothers and grandmothers fought'.(p.186)

Feminism, she asserts, is 'a vicious and corrupt word that has done much harm in its day and is now obsolete'. Woolf carefully distinguishes between the dead word feminism – 'a word without a meaning is a dead word, a corrupt word'(p.184) – and a myriad of complex and contradictory impulses in its wake. Woolf jettisoned feminism only in the sense that Winifred Holtby jettisoned it: 'I am a feminist . . . because I dislike everything that feminism implies. I desire an end of the whole business, the demands for equality, the suggestions of sex warfare, the very name of feminist.'[84] Both women saw it as an anachronism so widely misinterpreted that it had outlived any usefulness it might once have had. Virginia Woolf shied away from the term feminist as she shied away from the term 'anti-Fascist' writer which she disliked as 'the fashionable and hideous jargon of the moment'.(p.248) But even so we may see how both designations may legitimately be applied to her work.

Virginia Woolf's reading notebooks do not convey the impression of a woman who has lost interest in feminist issues but quite the opposite; the impression of one who has a sustained an alert interest in many practical and theoretical questions of concern to the feminists of her day. These range from football as a sport for school girls[85] to the performance of Soviet women as air pilots,[86] and from the ordination of women[87] to the need for more women to enter parliament.[88] She collected items of information about how girls performed in school[89] and on why the few women MPs in the house appeared to be so passive.[90] Reminiscences of the early days of the women's suffrage movement[91] attracted her attention as did the domestic division of labour, the statistics about the dishes washed and the floors scrubbed by the average housewife.[92]

Virginia Woolf's wish to see the end of the 'old-style' feminism certainly indicates a revolutionary break with discredited modes of political action and an understandable refusal to temporise. But in this, as in so much

84. Quoted in Vera Brittain, *Testament of Friendship: The Story of Winifred Holtby* (London: Gollancz, 1953; re-issued London: Fontana, 1981), p.134.

85. *Daily Herald*, 15 August, 1936, MHP RN2, p.54.

86. *Daily Telegraph*, 14 August, 1935, MHP RN3, p.28. As Gillian Beer has pointed out, Virginia Woolf had never made a plane journey but was fascinated by flight. See 'The Island and the Aeroplane: The Case of Virginia Woolf', in Homi K. Bhabha (ed.), *Nation and Narration* (London: Routledge, 1990), pp.265–91.

87. MHP RN3, unnamed newspaper cutting, n.d., p.48.

88. Ibid., *Daily Telegraph*, 23 October, 1937, p.43.

89. Ibid., *Evening News*, 29 March, 1937, p.44.

90. Ibid., *Evening Standard*, 20 March, 1936, p.27.

91. Ibid., *Listener*, n.d., p.45.

92. Ibid., unnamed newspaper cutting, n.d., p.21.

else, there is ambivalence, a traditionalist and a revolutionary side-by-side. She was too devoted to women's heritage, had too great a respect for 'those queer dead women in their poke bonnets and shawls'(p.185), for the break ever to be total. And if *Three Guineas* inspires as a vision of women's future, it inspires no less as a homage to the best of women's past.

For Virginia Woolf's actions, as Naomi Black has so perceptively stated, are 'not a disavowal of feminism, but a distinction among its different varieties';[93] and the variety that Woolf opted for was the one with the most radical ambition and the largest goals. If the imagery of *Three Guineas* is the imagery of Greenham Common, the idiom in which those images are expressed is, no less surely, the idiom of Mary Wollstonecraft and Olive Schreiner. The tradition of women's writing for which those women stand is the tradition from which *Three Guineas* derives its authority. It is the tradition to which Virginia Woolf herself belongs.

To recognise that a signifier is a liability is not to reject the worth of all that it signifies. 'The old names', Virginia Woolf writes, 'are futile and false'.(p.248) If Virginia Woolf rejected a specific term it is because she had good reason to distrust its connotations. As the narrative experiments in her novels reveal how well Woolf understood that new uses of language were potentially liberating for women, so her celebratory act of arson in *Three Guineas* clearly reveals how well she understood the extent to which linguistic terms had the power to oppress her sex. If we scrutinise the reading notebooks for signs of where Woolf's thinking might eventually have taken her, we will note how she had begun to play with language, to invent new words, and had tentatively started to redefine the term 'feminist', a reformulation that is disappointedly not carried over in *Three Guineas*.[94] Although Woolf does not again use the word 'feminism' in relation to her own political aspirations, she does refer approvingly to 'the women's movement', a term which is less stigmatised but retains the positive associations she valued. A letter to Shena, Lady Simon, in 1940: 'can one change sex characteristics? How far is the women's movement a remarkable experiment in transformation? Musn't our next task be the emancipation of man?' makes clear that she still felt herself to be part of that movement.[95]

In *Three Guineas* Woolf appears to see no distinction between feminism and humanism: 'in that clearer air what do we see? Men and women working together for the same cause'.(p.185) This is not the abandoning of feminism but its expansion. Viewing it another way, we may well wish

93. 'Virginia Woolf and the Women's Movement,' in Marcus, *Virginia Woolf: a Feminist Slant*, p.181.

94. See Silver, '*Three Guineas* Before and After', p.258.

95. Letter from Virginia Woolf to Shena, Lady Simon, dated 22 January, 1940. *The Letters*, vol. 6, p.379.

to ask why the enlarged definition should threaten any feminist who does not see the tenets of feminism written on tablets of stone? One of the cardinal virtues of feminism has been its ability to adapt, to modernise, and to transform itself according to the needs of the moment. In *Three Guineas* Woolf showed how soundly she had grasped the importance of the need for flexibility and receptiveness to the new. That example, if anything, has helped to ensure the survival of the ideals of feminism as distinct from the (optional) use of feminism's name.

If our study of women's history and literature has taught us anything, it is to respect the immeasurable contribution to that history and literature, and to women's rights and freedoms, that has been made by women who, for one reason or another, have chosen to say that they were not feminists. In the course of studying that history and literature should we find, as we often do, discrepancies that unsettle, it is then incumbent upon us to listen carefully to both the singer *and* the song. As Alexander Zwerdling has noted: 'Woolf's particular contribution to the woman's movement was to restore a sense of the complexity of the issues after the radical simplification that had seemed necessary for political action.'[96] Iconoclasm should never be confused with apostasy.

There is some prima facie evidence for thinking that Virginia Woolf had steeled herself for the rejection of *Three Guineas* by the men in her immediate circle. In 1938 Woolf's principled declaration of independence and solidarity with the disadvantaged, an address delivered to the Workers' Educational Association, later published as 'The Leaning Tower', was still to come.[97] But she had deliberately courted the hostility of her male friends for several years before that. The history of Virginia Woolf's later years is the history of her separation from the literary and political analysis of those around her: 'I sat there splitting off my own position from theirs, testing what they said, convincing myself of my own integrity & justice.'[98]

In her lecture to the WEA, still in 1940 predominantly a working-class organisation, Woolf drew attention to the élitism of the Auden–Isherwood generation and mentioned by name several writers of her own acquaintance. These included Forster and Strachey, 'raised above the mass of people upon a tower of stucco – that is their middle-class birth; and of gold – that is their expensive education.' As a woman belonging to their social class but without their educational advantages, Woolf could not identify with the literary aspirations of a coterie of public-school men. But she did feel affinities with the 'commoners' and 'outsiders' who lacked

96. *Virginia Woolf and the Real World* (Berkeley: University of California Press, 1986), p.217.
97. 'The Leaning Tower,' *The Collected Essays*, vol. 2, pp.167–81.
98. *The Diary*, vol. 5, p.79.

Conclusions

> The suffrage movement had enfranchised women, and from more than their lack of citizenship, it had disproved those theories about their own nature which were – and still are – among their gravest handicaps.
> Winifred Holtby, *Women and a Changing Civilisation*[1]

Writing in 1934 about the effects of the women's suffrage campaign, Winifred Holtby noted that 'an emotional earthquake had shattered the intangible yet suffocating prison of decorum'.[2] For Holtby, the real importance of women's militancy was that it had effectively destroyed most of the old certainties about women's identities. Much writing between the wars is concerned with the expression of cultured and gendered identities in ways appropriate to the new social conditions in which women found themselves. And it is possible to recognise the struggle within the self, so frequently the subject of mid-century realist fictions by women, as being at once substantively the same as our own *and* significantly different by virtue of its enactment in other social, literary and historical contexts.

For writers like Flora Mayor, Rosamond Lehmann and Elizabeth Bowen the criticism of patriarchal values and the expression of gendered identity did not take the form of modernist experimentation. Their debt to the great women writers of the nineteenth century, Elizabeth Gaskell, Jane Austen and George Eliot, is clear in their insistence upon continuities with the past and their use of relatively traditional narratives, albeit informed by a twentieth-century consciousness. To concentrate exclusively on modernism is to do a disservice to these and many other interesting writers whose work tells us much about important traditions of women's writing. It is also to produce a distorted picture of women's literary production in the inter-war period as a whole.

But much remains to be unearthed and re-examined before it becomes possible to read the gendered concerns of women realists in an informed way alongside their modernist sisters. As Janet Todd has put it, 'we should simply do more work of the archival and archaeological type on specific periods, while keeping in mind all the questions and possibilities of

---

1. *Women and a Changing Civilisation* (London: The Bodley Head, 1934), p.52.
2. Ibid., p.53.

feminist criticism in its entirety'.[3] There is, I would argue, a particular need for scholarly analysis of writers – Antonia White and Stevie Smith are obvious candidates but there are many others – which uncovers the mutinous structures of feeling that often lie beneath the deceptively decorous surface of woman-centred texts.

It is clear that the omission of particular writers from literary histories needs to be rectified and existing critical reputations re-assessed. This is an area where feminist argument has been persuasive. The once controversial proposition that Elizabeth Bowen, whose writing until very recently did not appear on 'A' Level literature syllabuses for schools, is as significant a writer as Graham Greene, who frequently did, would today find many defenders. So too would the contention that Sylvia Townsend Warner is a writer of some distinction who deserves the critical acclaim that afficionados of the writing of the 1930s often accord Henry Green.

Turning the spotlight of critical attention away from W.H Auden and the public-school educated poets who have dominated the critical studies of the 1930s and on to women writers would greatly help to redress existing distortions. However, welcome though such a radical change of focus would be, I believe the revisions that are needed to be more fundamental and far-ranging. New feminist understandings of the crucial interstices of gender, race and class must not only throw into question the mainstream critiques of inter-war writing but also many of the masculinist assumptions that have underpinned attempts to create a cultural counter-hegemony on the left. Further feminist research will certainly produce a new topography of the 1930s as it has of modernism.

The 1930s was a unique period in which writing with overtly radical concerns was seen, for the first time, not simply as an honourable *alternative* tradition. Instead, it was, as Andy Croft puts it, a time when 'the Left seems to have genuinely understood how culture works, how impossible it is to legislate for the imagination . . . how the unlikeliest of texts can make the heart beat faster in the unlikeliest of readers'. It was a decade in which the left 'took its concerns, its enthusiasms and its literature into the mainstream of British life, and was welcomed as a valuable, necessary and natural part of that life'.[4]

Faced with the twin evils of Fascism abroad and unemployment and hunger at home women writers did not opt simply to remain absorbed in their personal concerns, 'skating on a pond at the edge of the wood' like children 'who did not specially want it to happen'.[5] On the contrary, women

3. *Feminist Literary History* (Cambridge: Polity, 1986), p.137.

4. *Red Letter Days: British Fiction in the 1930s* (London: Lawrence and Wishart, 1990), pp.9, 11.

5. 'Musée des Beaux Arts', in Edward Mendelson (ed.), *The English Auden: Poems, Essays and Dramatic Writings 1927–1939* (London: Faber, 1977), p.237.

Conclusions

were among the most enthusiastic creators, transmitters and publicists of the vibrant and deeply politicised literary culture of their time. As we have seen, Katharine Burdekin, Virginia Woolf and many others attemped to encompass the plight of those whom the Nazis victimised on the grounds of sex, race, creed or sexual orientation within the sympathetically accommodating orbit of their discursive and imaginative writing.

To claim that Marxist analysis has taken no account of women is an overstatement, although the general case for the neglect of women writers by critics on the left is now widely accepted.[6] However, what is often missing in many otherwise illuminating works on the 1930s is attention to the precise points of contact, agreement, disagreement and friction between feminists and other writers. How and why the concerns and preoccupations of the politically committed woman writer differed from those of her male counterparts are questions that still need to be satisfactorily explored.[7]

The best-known epitaph of the 1930s, Auden's 'low dishonest decade', is also the least helpful. These words in context, in the poem 'September 1, 1939', refer primarily to appeasement and to the allies' share of the responsibility for the rise of Fascism in Germany.[8] However, they have been taken out of context and used – as have Virginia Woolf's pointed criticisms of her contemporaries in 'The Leaning Tower' – to discredit the integrity and motivation of the devotedly political writer in the 1930s and by extension the integrity and motivation of all politically committed writers. But the repudiation of the political in art is not acceptable to the feminist critic. As Terry Eagleton has reminded us, political argument is 'not an alternative to moral preoccupations: it is those preoccupations taken seriously in their full implications'.[9]

Marxism and feminism have shared a common interest in how the

6. Key texts on the 1930s which take little or no account of gender include John Lucas, *The Thirties: A Challenge to Orthodoxy* (Brighton: Harvester, 1978). This contains no reference to women in its chapter headings and says virtually nothing about women elsewhere. Valentine Cunningham, *British Writers of the Thirties* (Oxford: Oxford University Press, 1986) offers an inventory of neglected women writers (p.26) which raises hopes his book largely fails to deliver. Women writers, with the exception of Virginia Woolf, were omitted from Jon Clarke et al. (eds), *Culture and Crisis in Britain in the Thirties* (London: Lawrence and Wishart, 1979) on the grounds that another book was soon to be published which would include them. That study, from the Birmingham Centre for Contemporary Cultural Studies, failed to materialise.
7. American critics have started to answer these questions in relation to American women writers of the 1930s. See Constance Coiner, 'Literature of Resistance: The Intersection of Feminism and the Communist Left in Meridel Le Soeur and Tillie Olsen', in Lennard J. Davis (ed.) *Left Politics and the Literary Profession* (New York: Columbia University Press, 1990), pp.162–85.
8. Mendelson (ed.), *The English Auden*, p.245.
9. *Literary Theory: An Introduction* (Oxford: Blackwell, 1986), p.208.

relationship between politics and aesthetics has come to be articulated in writing. But if feminist criticism is to present a real challenge to orthodoxy – whether of the left or of the right – it is necessary to interrogate the existing socialist and Marxist critiques of the 1930s and to insist that they be properly informed by feminism. The trouble with deconstructing the 'Grand Narratives' of Marxism and socialism in theory is that existing power imbalances do not disappear at the same time. If a case exists for the usefulness of the 'Grand Narratives' of Marxism and socialism, it is not for their retention as the uninhabitable edifices of the past, but for their emancipatory visions of the kind of world which we might wish to help to bring into existence.

The assessment of any claim which Marxists may still wish to make about their own relevance must depend largely upon how Marxism is to be practised. The very survival of Marxism is likely to depend, furthermore, upon the willingness of Marxists to bring to an end the common practice of relegating all other discourses and political and theoretical practices to a subordinate position in relation to Marxism, and upon how receptive it is able to become to other theories and practices including feminism.[10]

Critical approaches employed in relation to women's writing may, of course, be equally fruitful in relation to works by men. But while it is true that women's writing is not autonomous, and that it shares many of its conditions of production with writing by men, it also remains true that the social construction of gender through ideology has historically been constituted in the interests of men, and that literary and other cultural artefacts have historically reflected and perpetuated this major imbalance of power. Although that balance has, to some extent, shifted in favour of women, through the influence of feminist ideas on social, domestic, cultural and political life, patriarchal notions of criticism, aesthetics and representation continue to dominate the English literary critical tradition, and are clearly reflected in the predominance of texts written by men still studied as set texts in most institutions of higher education, and in the predominance of men as teachers in many university English departments.

This study has been concerned with authors who have hitherto been frequently ignored or misunderstood largely because they were women. They were, moreover, not just women, but often women whose writing happened to be concerned with issues other than those accorded centrality within the mainstream tradition of literary criticism, or women whose writing, while being seen to be concerned with these 'central issues',

10. The tiny but influential Communist Party in Britain has accepted feminist critiques of Marxism, voting to transform itself into the Democratic Left and to adopt a constitution that places Marxism on exactly the same footing as feminism.

appeared to respond to them in perplexing and idiosyncratic ways. Unless the balance of critical attention and perspective is redressed, neither the literary history of the 1920s and 1930s nor the political and social history of this time can be properly understood.

The fact that patriarchal society has traditionally discriminated against women solely because they were women is sufficient reason to justify the study of women as women. This book has helped to show that even in what are sometimes mistakenly termed 'post-feminist' times the specialised study of women writers is far from exhausted. We have reached a point where much has been accomplished but much remains to be done.

Bibliography

Abel Elizabeth (ed.), *Writing and Sexual Difference* (Chicago: University of Chicago Press, 1982).

—— Hirsch Marianne, and Langland Elizabeth (eds), *The Voyage In: Fictions of Female Development* (Hanover: University Press of New England, 1983).

Ackland Valentine, *For Sylvia: An Honest Account* (London: Chatto and Windus, 1986).

Alberti Johnna, *Beyond Suffrage: Feminists in War and Peace, 1914–1928* (Basingstoke: Macmillan, 1989).

Albinski Nan Bowman, *Women's Utopias in British and American Fiction* (London: Routledge, 1988).

Alexander Sally, 'Women, Class and Sexual Differences in the 1830's and 1840's: Some Reflections on the Writing of a Feminist History', *History Workshop Journal*, Spring 1984, pp.125–49.

Aiken Conrad, *A Reviewer's ABC: Collected Criticism of Conrad Aiken from 1916 to the Present* (New York: Meridian, 1958).

Allen Walter, *Tradition and Dream* (New York: Phoenix House, 1964).

Alpers Antony, *The Life of Katherine Mansfield* (Oxford: Oxford University Press, 1980).

Angelou Maya, *I Know Why the Caged Bird Sings* (London: Virago, 1984).

Annan Noel, 'The Intellectual Aristocracy', in Plumb J.H. (ed.), *Studies in Social History* (London: Longman, 1955), pp.243–87.

Arlen Michael, *The Green Hat* (London: Collins, 1924).

Armstrong Nancy, *Desire and Domestic Fiction: A Political History of the Novel* (New York: Oxford University Press, 1987).

Bagnold Enid, *A Diary Without Dates* (London: Heinemann, 1918).

—— *The Happy Foreigner* (London: Heinemann, 1920).

Bailey Hilary, *Vera Brittain: The Story of the Woman Who Wrote Testament of Youth* (Harmondsworth: Penguin, 1987).

Baker Michael, *Our Three Selves: A Life of Radclyffe Hall* (London: Hamilton, 1985).

Baldick Chris, *The Social Mission of English Criticism, 1848–1932* (Oxford: Oxford University Press, 1983).

Barnes Djuna, *Nightwood* (London: Faber and Faber, 1936).

Barrett Michèle, 'The Concept of "Difference"', in *Feminist Review*, 26,

Summer 1987, pp.29–41.

—— 'Ideology and the Cultural Production of Gender', in Newton Judith and Rosenfelt Deborah (eds), *Feminist Criticism and Social Change* (London: Methuen, 1985), pp.65–86.

—— *Virginia Woolf: Women and Writing* (London: Women's Press, 1977).

—— *Women's Oppression Today: Problems in Marxist Feminist Analysis* (London: Verso, 1980).

Batsleer Janet, Davies Tony, O' Rourke Rebecca (eds), *Rewriting English: Cultural Politics of Gender and Class* (London: Methuen, 1982).

Baym Nina, *Women's Fiction: A Guide to Novels by and about Women in America, 1820–70* (Ithaca: Cornell University Press, 1978).

Beauman Nicola, *A Very Great Profession: The Woman's Novel 1914–1939* (London: Virago, 1983).

Beauvoir Simone de, *Memoirs of a Dutiful Daughter*, (trans.) James Kirkup (London: Deutsch and Weidenfeld and Nicolson, 1959).

—— *The Prime of Life*, (trans.) Green Peter (London: Deutsch and Weidenfeld and Nicolson, 1962).

Beddoe Deirdre, *Back to Home and Duty: Women Between the Wars 1918–1939* (London: Pandora, 1989).

Beer Gillian, *Arguing With the Past: Essays in Narrative from Woolf to Sydney* (London: Routledge, 1989).

—— 'Beyond Determinism: George Eliot and Virginia Woolf', in Jacobus Mary (ed.), *Women Writing and Writing about Women* (London: Croom Helm, 1979), pp.80–99.

—— 'The Body of the People in Virginia Woolf', in Roe Sue (ed.), *Women Reading Women's Writing* (Brighton: Harvester, 1987), pp.85–113.

—— 'The Island and the Aeroplane: the Case of Virginia Woolf', in Bhabha Homi K. (ed.), *Nation and Narration* (London: Routledge, 1990), pp.265–91.

Bell Julian, (ed.), *We Did Not Fight 1914–1918: Experiences of War Resistors* (London: Cobden Sanderson, 1935).

Bell Quentin, *Virginia Woolf: A Biography*, 2 vols, vol. 1, *Virginia Stephen 1882–1912* (London: Hogarth, June 1972), vol. 2, *Mrs. Woolf 1912–1941* (London: Hogarth, October 1972).

Belsey Catharine, *Critical Practice* (London: Methuen, 1980).

Benewick Robert, *The Fascist Movement in Britain* (London: Allen and Unwin, 1972).

Bennett Tony, *Outside Literature* (London: Routledge, 1990).

Benson Stella, *This is the End* (London: Macmillan, 1917).

Benstock Shari, 'Authorizing the Autobiographical', in Benstock Shari (ed.), *The Private Self: Theory and Practice of Women's Autobiographical Writings* (London: Routledge, 1988), pp.34–62.

—— *Feminist Issues in Literary Scholarship* (Bloomington: University of Indiana Press, 1987).

—— *Women of the Left Bank: Paris 1900–1940* (Austin: University of Texas Press, 1986).

Bergonzi Bernard, *The Myth of Modernism and Twentieth Century Literature* (Brighton: Harvester, 1986).

—— *Reading the Thirties: Texts and Contexts* (London: Macmillan, 1978).

Besant Walter, *All Sorts and Conditions of Men* (London: Chatto and Windus, 1882).

Birrell Olive, *Love in a Mist* (London: Smith and Elder, 1900).

—— *The Seed She Sowed: A Tale of the Great Dock Strike* (London: Methuen, 1891).

Black Naomi, 'Virginia Woolf and the Women's Movement', in Marcus Jane (ed.), *Virginia Woolf, a Feminist Slant* (London and Lincoln: University of Nebraska Press, 1983), pp.180–97.

Blain Virginia, 'Narrative Voice and the Female Perspective in Virginia Woolf's Early Novels', in Clements Patricia and Grundy Isobel (eds), *New Critical Essays on Virginia Woolf* (New York: Vision and Barnes and Noble, 1983), pp.115–36.

Blake Caesar R., *Dorothy Richardson* (Ann Arbor: University of Michigan Press, 1960).

Boone Allen Joseph, *Tradition: Love and the Form of Fiction* (Chicago: University of Chicago Press, 1987).

Booth Wayne, 'Freedom of Interpretation: Bakhtin and the Challenge of Feminist Criticism', in Mitchell W.J.T. (eds), *The Politics of Interpretation* (Chicago: University of Chicago Press, 1982), pp.51–83.

Borden Mary, *The Forbidden Zone* (London: Heinemann, 1929).

—— *Passport for a Girl* (London: Heinemann, 1939).

—— *Sarah Gay* (London: Heinemann, 1931).

Bosanquet Theodora de, 'Men and Books', review of *Three Guineas, Time and Tide*, 14 June, 1938, pp.788–90.

Bottome Phyllis, *The Mortal Storm* (London: Faber and Faber, 1937).

Bowen Elizabeth, 'The Achievement of Virginia Woolf', in *Collected Impressions* (London: Longmans Green, 1950), pp.78–82.

—— 'Advance in Formation', *The Spectator*, 17 January, 1941, p.65.

—— *Collected Impressions* (London: Longmans Green, 1950).

—— *The Death of the Heart* (London: Gollancz, 1938).

—— *Encounters: Early Stories* (London: Sidgwick and Jackson, 1949).

—— 'Jane Austen', in Verschoyle Derek (ed.), *The English Novelists: A Survey of the Novel by Twenty Contemporary Novelists* (London: Chatto and Windus, 1936), pp.99–110.

—— *Friends and Relations* (London: Constable, 1931).

—— *The Hotel* (London: Constable, 1927).

—— *The House in Paris* (London: Gollancz, 1935).

—— 'Out of a Book', *Orion*, 3, 1946; reprinted in *Collected Impressions*, pp.264–9.

—— *To the North* (London: Gollancz, 1932).

—— review of *The Weather in the Streets*, *The New Statesman*, 11 July, 1936.

—— *Why Do I Write? An Exchange of Views between Elizabeth Bowen, Graham Greene, and V.S. Pritchett* (London: Marshall, 1948).

Bowlby Rachel, *Virginia Woolf: Feminist Destinations* (Oxford: Blackwell, 1988).

Brandon Ruth, *The New Woman and the Old Men* (London: Secker and Warburg, 1990).

Branson Noreen, *Britain in the 1920s* (London: Weidenfeld, 1975).

—— *History of the Communist Party of Great Britain 1927–1941* (London: Lawrence and Wishart, 1985).

—— and Margot Heinemann, *Britain in the 1930s* (London: Panther, 1973).

Braybon Gail, *Women Workers in the First World War* (London: Routledge, 1981).

—— and Summerfield Penny, *Out of the Cage: Women's Experiences in Two World Wars* (London: Pandora, 1987).

Brecht Bert, 'Against Georg Lukács', 1967, (trans.) Livingstone Rodney, in Anderson Perry et al. (eds), *Aesthetics and Politics* (London: New Left, 1977), pp.68–86.

Bridenthal Renata, 'Beyond Kinder, Küche, Kirche: "Weimar Women at Work"', *Central European History*, 1973, vol. 6, 2, June 1973, pp.148–66.

—— Grossman Atina and Kaplan Marion (eds), *When Biology Became Destiny: Women in Weimar and Nazi Germany* (New York: New Feminist Library, 1984).

Brierley Walter, *Means Test Man* (London: Methuen, 1935).

—— *Sandwich Man* (London: Methuen, 1937).

Brittain Vera, *Chronicle of Friendship: Vera Brittain's Diary of the Thirties, 1932–1939*, (eds) Bishop Alan with Smart Terry (London: Gollancz, 1986).

—— *Chronicle of Youth: Vera Brittain's War Diary, 1913–1917*, (eds) Bishop Alan with Smart Terry (London: Gollancz, 1981).

—— *The Dark Tide* (London: Richards, 1923).

—— *Honourable Estate: A Novel of Transition* (London: Gollancz, 1936).

—— *Not Without Honour* (London: Richards, 1924).

—— *On Becoming a Writer* (London: Hutchinson, 1947).

—— *On Being an Author* (London: Macmillan, 1948).

—— *Radclyffe Hall: A Case of Obscenity* (London: Femina, 1968).

—— *Testament of Experience* (London: Gollancz, 1957).

—— *Testament of Friendship: The Story of Winifred Holtby* (London: Macmillan, 1940).

—— *Testament of Youth* (London: Gollancz, 1933).

—— *Thrice a Stranger* (London: Gollancz, 1938).

—— *Verses of a V.A.D.* (London: Erskine Macdonald, 1918).

—— 'War Service in Perspective', in Panichas George A. (ed.), *Promise of Greatness*, (London: Cassell, 1968), pp.363–76.

—— and Handley-Taylor Geoffrey (eds), *Selected Letters of Winifred Holtby and Vera Brittain (1920–1935)* (London: Brown, 1960).

—— and Winifred Holtby, Berry Paul and Bishop Alan (eds), *Testament of a Generation: The Journalism of Vera Brittain and Winifred Holtby* (London: Virago, 1985).

Brodzki Bella and Schenck Céleste (eds), *Life/Lines: Theorizing Women's Autobiography* (Ithaca: Cornell University Press, 1988).

Bromley Roger, *Lost Narratives: Popular Fictions, Politics and Recent History* (London: Routledge, 1989).

Brooke Jocelyn, *Elizabeth Bowen* (London: Longmans Green, 1952).

Brownmiller Susan, *Against Our Wills* (Harmondsworth: Penguin, 1975).

Brownstein Rachel M., *Becoming a Heroine: Reading About Women in Novels* (Harmondsworth: Penguin, 1984).

Bruley Sue, 'Women Against War and Fascism: Communism, Feminism and the People's Front and Recent History', in Jim Fyrth (ed.), *Britain, Fascism and the Popular Front* (London: Lawrence and Wishart, 1985), pp.131–56.

Bryher (Ellerman Winifred), *The Heart to Artemis: A Writer's Memoirs* (London: Collins, 1963).

Burdekin Katharine, *Proud Man* (London: Boriswood, 1934).

—— *Quiet Ways* (London: Butterworth, 1930).

—— *The Reasonable Hope* (London: Bodley Head, 1924).

—— *The Rebel Passion* (London: Butterworth, 1929).

—— *Swastika Night* (London: Gollancz, 1937).

Burgess Anthony, 'Treasures and Fetters', *The Spectator*, 21 February, 1964, p.254.

Bussey Gertrude and Timms Margaret, *Pioneers for Peace: The Women's International League for Peace and Freedom* (London: Women's International League for Peace and Freedom, 1980).

Butler Marilyn, new introduction to *Jane Austen and the War of Ideas* (Oxford: Clarenden, 1975; re-issued 1987), pp.ix-xiv.

Butts Mary, *Armed with Madness* (London: Wishart, 1928).

—— *Death of Felicity Taverner* (London: Wishart, 1932).

Caffrey Kate, *'37–'39: The Last Look Round* (London: Gordon and

Cremonesi, 1978).

Caird Mona, *The Morality of Marriage and other Essays in the Status and Destiny of Woman* (London: Redway, 1897).

Cameron Deborah, *Feminism and Linguistic Theory* (London: Macmillan, 1985).

Campion Sarah, *Duet for Female Voices* (London: Davies, 1936).

—— *If She is Wise* (London: Davies, 1935).

Canfield Dorothy, *Home Fires in France* (New York: Holt, 1919).

Cannan May Wedderburn, *Grey Ghosts and Voices* (London: Roundwood, 1976).

—— *The Lonely Generation* (London: Hutchinson, 1928).

Carby Hazel, ' White Woman Listen! Black Feminism and the Boundaries of Sisterhood', in *The Empire Strikes Back: Race and Racism in 70s Britain* (London: Hutchinson and Birmingham: The Centre for Contemporary Cultural Studies, 1982), pp.212–36.

Carnie Ethel, *General Belinda* (London: Jenkins, 1924).

—— *This Slavery* (London: Labour Publishing, 1925).

Sally Carson, *Crooked Cross* (London: Hodder and Stoughton, 1934).

—— *The Prisoner* (London: Hodder and Stoughton, 1936).

Carroll Berenice A., '"To Crush Him in Our Own Country' ': The Political Thought of Virginia Woolf", *Feminist Studies*, 4, 1, February 1978, pp.99–131.

Cartledge Sue and Ryan Joanna, *Sex and Love: New Thoughts on Old Contradictions* (London: Women's Press, 1983).

Castle Terry, 'Sylvia Townsend Warner and the Counterplot of Lesbian Fiction', *Textual Practice*, vol. 4, 2, Summer 1990, pp.213–36.

Catlin George, *For God's Sake Go! An Autobiography* (Gerard's Cross, Smythe, 1972).

Cauldwell Christopher, *The Concept of Freedom* (London: Lawrence and Wishart, 1965).

Cavaliero Glen, 'Sylvia Townsend Warner: An Appreciation', *The Powys Review*, 5, 1, Summer 1979), pp.6–12.

Ceadel Martin, *Pacifism in Britain 1914–1945: The Defining of a Faith* (Oxford: Clarendon, 1980).

—— 'Popular Fiction and the Next War 1918-1939', in Gloversmith Frank(ed.), *Class, Culture and Social Change: A New View of the 1930s* (Brighton: Harvester, 1980), pp.161–85.

Chase Malcolm and Shaw Christopher (eds), *The Imagined Past: History and Nostalgia* (Manchester: Manchester University Press, 1989).

Chisolm Anne, *Nancy Cunard* (London: Sidgwick and Jackson, 1979).

Chitty Susan (ed.), *As Once in May: The Early Autobiography of Antonia White and Other Writings* (London: Virago, 1983).

Chodorow Nancy, 'On the Reproduction of Mothering: A Methodological

Debate', reply to Judith Lorber et al., *Signs: Journal of Women in Culture and Society*, vol. 6, 3, Spring 1981, pp.500–14.

—— *The Reproduction of Mothering* (Berkeley: University of California Press, 1978).

Clare Tullis, review of *Swastika Night, Time and Tide*, 26 June, 1937, p.872.

Clark Jonathan, Heinemann Margot, Margolies David and Snee Carol (eds), *Culture and Crisis in Britain in the Thirties* (London: Lawrence and Wishart, 1979).

Coates Jennifer, *Women, Men and Language: A Sociolinguistic Account of Sex Differences in Language* (London: Longmans, 1986).

Cohn Dorrit, *Transparent Minds: Narrative Modes for Presenting Consciousness in Fiction* (Guildford: Princeton University Press, 1978).

Coiner Constance, 'Literature of Resistance: The Intersection of Feminism and the Communist Left in Meridel Le Sueur and Tillie Olsen', in Davis Lennard J. and Mirabella Bella M. (eds), *Left Politics and the Literary Profession* (New York: Columbia University Press, 1990), pp.162–85.

Compton-Burnett Ivy, *A House and its Head* (London: Gollancz, 1935).

—— *Brothers and Sisters* (London: Gollancz, 1929).

—— *More Women Than Men* (London: Heinemann, 1933).

Cooper Lettice, *The New House* (London: Gollancz, 1936).

—— *National Provincial* (London: Gollancz, 1938).

Coward Rosalind, 'Are Women's Novels Feminist Novels?', *Feminist Review*, 5, 1980, pp.53–78; reprinted in Showalter Elaine (ed.), *The New Feminist Criticism: Essays on Women, Literature and Theory* (London: Virago, 1986), pp.225–39.

—— *Female Desire: Women's Sexuality Today* (London: Paladin, 1984).

—— *Patriarchal Precedents: Sexuality and Social Relations* (London: Routledge and Kegan Paul, 1983).

Craig David and Egan Michael, *Extreme Situations: Literature and Crisis from the Great War to the Atom Bomb* (London: Macmillan, 1979).

Croft Andy, 'The Birmingham Group: Literary Life Between the Wars', *London Magazine*, new series 23, June 1983, pp.13–22.

—— *Red Letter Days: British Fiction in the 1930s* (London: Lawrence and Wishart, 1990).

—— 'Worlds Without End Foisted Upon the Future – Some Antecedents of Nineteen Eighty-Four', in Norris Christopher (ed.), *Inside the Myth: Orwell, Views from the Left* (London: Lawrence and Wishart, 1984), pp.183–217.

Cross Victoria, *Martha Brown, M.P., A Girl of Tomorrow* (London: Werner Laurie, 1935).

Culler Jonathan, *On Deconstruction: Theory and Criticism after Structuralism* (Ithaca: Cornell University Press, 1982), pp.43–64.

Cunard Nancy, *Negro* (London: Lawrence and Wishart, 1934).

Cunningham Gail, *The New Woman and the Victorian Novel* (London: Macmillan, 1978).

Cunningham Valentine, *British Writers of the Thirties* (Oxford: Oxford University Press, 1988).

—— (ed.), *Spanish Front: Writers on the Civil War* (Oxford: Oxford University Press, 1986).

Daiches Davies, *Virginia Woolf* (New York: New Directions, 1942).

Dane Clemence, *Regiment of Women* (London: Heinemann, 1917).

Davies Llewelyn Margaret (ed.), *Life as We Have Known It*, with an introduction by Virginia Woolf (London: Hogarth, 1930).

—— (ed.), *Maternity: Letters from Working Women* (London: Bell, 1915).

Dayus Kathleen, *All My Days* (London: Virago, 1988).

—— *Her People* (London: Virago, 1982).

De la Motte Brunhilde, 'Radicalism – Feminism – Socialism: The Case of the Woman Novelists', in H. Gustav Klaus (ed.), *The Rise of Socialist Fiction 1880–1914* (Brighton: Harvester, 1987), pp.28–49.

Delafield E.M., *Consequences* (London: Hodder and Stoughton, 1919).

—— *The Heel of Achilles* (London: Hutchinson, 1921).

—— *Thank Heaven Fasting* (London: Macmillan, 1932).

—— *Three Marriages* (London: Macmillan, 1939).

Delmar Rosalind, 'What is Feminism?', in Mitchell Juliet and Oakley Ann (eds), *What is Feminism?* (Oxford: Blackwell, 1986), pp.8–33.

De Selincourt Basil, 'A Man's World and War: Plea for the Women', review of *Three Guineas*, *The Observer*, 5 June, 1938, p.5.

DiBattista Maria, *Virginia Woolf's Major Novels: The Fables of Anon* (New Haven: Yale University Press, 1980).

Dickson J.E., 'Women Novelists and War: A Study of the Responses of Seven Women Novelists 1914–1940', unpublished dissertation, Edinburgh University, 1980.

Dinnerstein Dorothy, *The Mermaid and the Minotaur: Sexual Arrangements and Human Malaise* (New York: Harper, 1976).

Dodd Philip and Colls Robert, *Englishness: Politics and Culture 1880–1920* (London: Croom Helm, 1986).

Drabble Margaret, 'Katherine Mansfield: Fifty Years On', *Harpers & Queen*, July 1973, pp.106–7.

Duplessis Rachel Blau, *Writing Beyond the Ending: Narrative Strategies of Twentieth-Century Women Writers* (Bloomington: Indiana University Press, 1975).

Dyer Richard, 'Stereotyping', in Richard Dyer (ed.), *Gays and Film*, (London: British Film Institute, 1980), pp.27–39.

Dyhouse Carol, *Feminism and the Family in England 1880–1939* (Oxford: Blackwell, 1989).

Eagleton Terry, *Literary Theory: An Introduction* (Oxford: Blackwell, 1983).
—— *Marxism and Literary Criticism* (London: Methuen, 1976).
Eakin Paul John, *Fictions in Autobiography: Studies in the Art of Self-Invention* (Princeton: Princeton University Press, 1985).
Leon Edel, *Literary Biography: The Alexander Lectures 1955–1956* (New York: Hart-Davis, 1957).
—— *The Modern Psychological Novel 1900–1950* (New York: Hart-Davis, 1955).
Ellis Havelock, preface to *The Well of Loneliness* (first published London: Cape, 1928; re-issued, London: Hammond Uniform Edition, 1956).
Eliot T.S., *After Strange Gods* (London: Faber and Faber, 1934).
Empson William, *Some Versions of Pastoral* (London: Chatto and Windus, 1935).
Evans J. Richard, *Comrades and Sisters: Feminism, Socialism and Pacifism in Europe, 1870–1945* (Brighton: Wheatsheaf, 1987).
Eyles Leonora, *Captivity* (London: Heinemann, 1922).
—— *Careers for Women* (London: Matthew and Marrot, 1930).
—— *Common Sense About Sex* (London: Gollancz, 1940).
—— *Death of a Dog* (London: Hutchinson, 1936).
—— *Eat Well in War-Time* (London: Gollancz, 1940).
—— *For My Enemy Daughter* (London: Gollancz, 1941).
—— *The Hare of Heaven* (London: Melrose, 1924).
—— *Hidden Lives* (London: Heinemann, 1922).
—— *Margaret Protests* (London: Macdonald, 1919).
—— *The Ram Escapes* (London: Nevill, 1953).
—— *The Shepherd of Israel* (London: Constable, 1929).
—— *Strength of the Spirit* (London: Constable, 1930).
—— *They Wanted Him Dead!* (London: Hutchinson, 1936).
—— *Unmarried but Happy* (London: Gollancz, 1947).
—— *The Woman in the Little House* (London: Richards, 1922).
—— *Women's Problems of To-day* (London: Labour Publishing, 1926).
Flax Jane, 'The Conflict Between Nurturance and Autonomy in Mother-Daughter Relationships and Within Feminism', *Feminist Studies*, vol. 4, 2, June 1978, pp.171–89.
Faderman Lilian, *Surpassing the Love of Men: Romantic Friendships and Love Between Women from the Renaissance to the Present* (London: Women's Press, 1985).
Feldman David and Jones Gareth Stedman (eds), *Metropolis – London: Histories and Representations since 1800* (London: Routledge, 1989).
Fetterley Janet, *The Resisting Reader: A Feminist Approach to American Fiction* (Bloomington: Indiana University Press, 1978).
Field Andrew, *The Formidable Miss Barnes: A Biography of Djuna Barnes*

(London: Secker and Warburg, 1983).

Fleishman Avrom, *Virginia Woolf: A Critical Reading* (Baltimore: Johns Hopkins Press 1975).

Flint Kate, 'Virginia Woolf and the General Strike', *Essays in Criticism*, vol 36, 4, October 1986, pp.319–34.

Flynn Elizabeth and Schweickart Patrocinio (eds), introduction to *Gender and Reading: Essays on Readers, Texts and Contexts* (Baltimore: Johns Hopkins University Press, 1986), pp.ix–xxx.

Ford Isabella, *On the Threshold* (London: Arnold, 1885).

Forster Jeannette, *Sex Variant Women in Literature* (London: Muller, 1958).

Forster E.M., *Two Cheers for Democracy* (London: Arnold, 1951).

—— *Virginia Woolf: The Rede Lecture* (Cambridge: Cambridge University Press, 1942).

Stillman Franks Claudia, *Beyond the Well of Loneliness* (Amersham: Avebury, 1982).

Friedman Susan Stanford, *Penelope's Web: Gender, Modernity, H.D.'s Fiction* (Cambridge: Cambridge University Press, 1991).

—— 'Women's Autobiographical Selves', in Benstock Shari (eds), *The Private Self: Theory and Practice of Women's Autobiographical Writing* (London: Routledge, 1988).

Fromm C. Gloria, *Dorothy Richardson: A Biography* (Urbana: University of Illinois Press, 1978).

Fryer Peter, *The Birth Controllers* (London: Secker and Warburg, 1965).

Fullbrook Kate, *Free Women: Ethics and Aesthetics in Twentieth-Century Women's Fiction* (Hemel Hempstead: Harvester Wheatsheaf, 1990).

—— *Katherine Mansfield* (Brighton: Harvester, 1986).

Fuss A. Diana, *Essentially Speaking: Feminism, Nature and Difference* (London: Routledge, 1989).

Fussell Paul, *The Great War and Modern Memory* (Oxford: Oxford University Press, 1975).

Fyrth Jim (ed.), *Britain, Fascism and the Popular Front* (London: Lawrence and Wishart, 1985).

—— *The Signal Was Spain* (London: Lawrence and Wishart, 1986).

Gallop Jane, *Feminism and Psychoanalysis: The Daughter's Seduction* (London: Macmillan, 1982).

Gardiner Judith Kegan, 'On Female Identity and Writing by Women', *Critical Inquiry*, 8, Winter 1981, pp.347–79.

Gerhard Ute, 'A Hidden and Complex Heritage: Reflections in the History of Germany's Women's Movements', *Women's Studies International Quarterly*, vol.5, 1982, 6, pp.561–7.

Gibbons Stella, *Miss Linsey and Pa* (London: Longmans, 1936).

Gilbert Sandra M. , 'Costumes of the Mind, Transvestism as Metaphor in Modern Literature', *Critical Inquiry*, vol. 7, Winter 1980, pp.391–417.

—— 'Soldier's Heart: Literary Men, Literary Women, and the Great War', *Signs: Journal of Women in Culture and Society*, 8, 1983, pp.422–50.

—— and Susan Gubar, *The Madwoman in the Attic: The Woman Writer and the Nineteenth-Century Literary Imagination* (New Haven and London: Yale University Press, 1979).

—— and Susan Gubar, *No Man's Land: The Place of the Woman Writer in the Twentieth Century*, 2 vols, vol. 1, *The War of the Words* (New Haven: Yale University Press, 1988).

Gillespie Diane Filby, 'Political Aesthetics: Virginia Woolf and Dorothy Richardson', in Marcus Jane (ed.), *Virginia Woolf: a Feminist Slant*, (Lincoln and London: University of Nebraska Press, 1983), pp.133–51.

Gilligan Carol, *In a Different Voice: Psychological Theory and Women's Development* (Cambridge: Harvard University Press, 1982).

Gilman Perkins Charlotte, *The Yellow Wallpaper* (Boston: Small, Maynard, 1892).

Gissing George, *The Nether World* (London: Smith and Elder, 1889).

—— *Thyrza* (London: Smith and Elder, 1887).

Gittings Diane, *Fair Sex: Family Size and Structure 1910–1939* (London: Hutchinson, 1982).

Glendinning Victoria, *Elizabeth Bowen: Portrait of a Writer* (London: Weidenfeld and Nicolson, 1977).

—— *Rebecca West: A Life* (London: Weidenfeld and Nicolson, 1987).

—— *Vita: The Life of Sackville-West* (London: Weidenfeld and Nicolson, 1983).

Goldmann Lucien, *The Hidden God* (London: Routledge, 1964).

Goode John, 'Margaret Harkness and the Socialist Novel', in *The Socialist Novel*, in Klaus Gustav H. (ed.), *Britain: Towards the Recovery of a Tradition* (Brighton: Harvester, 1982), pp.45–67.

Gordon Linda, *Woman's Body, Woman's Right: A Social History of Birth Control in America* (Harmondsworth: Penguin, 1977).

—— 'Review Essay: Nazi Feminists?', *Feminist Review*, 27, Autumn 1978, pp.97–107.

Graham John, 'The Caricature Value of Parody and Fantasy in *Orlando*', *The University of Toronto Quarterly*, vol. 30, 4, July 1961, pp.346–66.

Gramsci Antonio, *Selections from Cultural Writings*, in Forgacs David and Nowell-Smith Geoffrey (eds), (trans.) Boelhower William (London: Lawrence and Wishart, 1985).

Grand Sarah, *The Heavenly Twins* (London: Cassell, 1893).

Greene Gayle and Coppélia Kahn, 'Feminist Scholarship and the Social Construction of Woman', in Greene Gayle and Kahn Coppélia (eds), *Making a Difference: Feminist Literary Criticism* (London: Methuen, 1985), pp.1–36.

Greene Graham, review of 'Two Novels', *The Spectator*, 7 October, 1938, p.578.

Greenwood James, *The Little Ragamuffins* (London: Ward Lock, 1884).

—— *A Night in a Workhouse* (London: Pall Mall Gazette, 1866).

Greenwood Walter, *Love on the Dole* (London: Cape, 1933).

Green Henry, *Living* (London: Hogarth, 1929).

—— *Party Going* (London: Hogarth, 1939).

Gregory Horace, *Dorothy Richardson: An Adventure in Self-Discovery* (New York and Chicago: Holt, Rinehart and Winston, 1967).

Gresswell Elise Kay, *When Yvonne Was Dictator* (London: Heritage, 1935).

Griffiths Richard, *Fellow Travellers of the Right: British Enthusiasts for Nazi Germany 1933–39* (London: Constable, 1980).

Guest Carmel Haden, *Give Us Conflict* (London: Hutchinson, 1936).

Gunn Janet Varner, *Autobiography: Towards a Poetics of Experience* (Philadelphia: University of Philadelphia Press, 1982).

Gusdorf George, 'Conditions and Limits of Autobiography', in Olney James (ed.), *Autobiography: Essays Theoretical and Critical* (Princeton, New Jersey: Princeton University Press, 1980).

Hager Philip E. and Taylor Desmond (eds), *The Novels of World War One: An Annotated Bibliography* (New York: Garland, 1981).

Hall Radclyffe, *Adam's Breed* (London: Cassell, 1926).

—— *The Unlit Lamp* (London: Cassell, 1924).

—— *The Well of Loneliness* (London: Cape, 1928).

Haldane Charlotte, *Motherhood and its Enemies* (New York: Doubleday, 1927).

Hall Ruth, *Dear Dr. Stopes: Sex in the 1920s* (Harmondsworth: Penguin, 1981).

Hamilton Alistair, *The Appeal of Fascism: A Study of Intellectuals and Fascism 1919–1945* (London: Blond, 1971).

Hamilton Cicely, *Lament for Democracy* (London: Dent, 1940).

—— *Knight Errant* (London: Dent, 1935).

—— *Marriage as a Trade* (London: Chapman and Hall, 1909).

—— *Modern Germanies, As Seen by an Englishwoman* (London: Dent, 1931; re-issued with a postscript on the Nazi regime, 1933).

—— *William – An Englishman* (London: Skeffington, 1919).

Agnes Hamilton Mary, review of *Captivity*, *Time and Tide*, 12 May, 1922, pp.448–9.

—— *Follow My Leader* (London: Cape, 1922).

—— *Murder in the House of Commons* (London: Hamilton, 1931).

—— *Remembering My Good Friends* (London: Cape, 1944).

Hanscombe Gillian E., *The Art of Life: Dorothy Richardson and the Development of Feminist Consciousness* (London: Owen, 1982).

—— and Smyers Virginia L.S., *Writing for their Lives: The Modernist*

Women 1910–1940 (London: Women's Press, 1987).

Harding Sandra, *The Science Question in Feminism* (Milton Keynes: Open University Press, 1986).

Hardistry Claire, introduction to Winifred Holtby, *The Crowded Street* (London: Virago, 1981).

Harman Claire, *Sylvia Townsend Warner: A Biography* (London: Chatto and Windus, 1989).

Hardwick Elizabeth, 'Elizabeth Bowen's Fiction', *Partisan Review*, 16, 11, November 1949, pp.1114–34.

—— *Seduction and Betrayal: Women and Literature* (London: Weidenfeld and Nicolson, 1974).

Harkness Margaret (John Law), *A City Girl* (London: Vizetelly, 1887).

—— (John Law), *Out of Work* (London: Sonnenschein, 1888).

Harradan Beatrice, *Where Your Treasure Is* (London: Hutchinson, 1918).

Havely Cicely Palser, 'Carson McCullers and Flannery O'Connor', in Martin Graham and Jefferson Douglas (eds), *The Art of Fiction: Essays on the Modern Novel in Honour of Arnold Kettle* (Milton Keynes: Open University Press, 1982), pp.115–25.

Hawthorn Jeremy (ed.), *The British Working Class Novel in the Twentieth Century* (London: Arnold, 1984).

—— *Identity and Relationship: A Contribution to Marxist Theory of Literary Criticism* (London: Lawrence and Wishart, 1973).

—— *Virginia Woolf's Mrs. Dalloway* (Brighton: Sussex University Press, 1975).

Hay Valerie, *The Necessity of Romance*, *Women's Studies Occasional Papers*, 3 (Canterbury: The University of Kent, 1983).

Heath Stephen, 'Difference', *Screen*, vol. 19, Autumn 1978, pp.51–112.

—— 'Male Feminism', in Jardine Alice and Smith Paul (eds), *Men and Feminism* (London: Methuen, 1987), pp.1–32.

—— *The Sexual Fix* (London: Macmillan, 1981).

—— 'Writing for Silence: Dorothy Richardson and the Novel', in Bryson Norman and Kappeller Suzanne (eds), *Teaching the Text* (London: Routledge and Kegan Paul, 1983), pp.126–47.

Heath William, *Elizabeth Bowen: An Introduction to her Novels* (Madison: University of Wisconsin Press, 1961).

Heilbrun Carolyn, *Towards Androgyny* (London: Gollancz, 1973).

Heinemann Margot, '*Left Review*, New Writing and the Broad Alliance Against Fascism', in *Visions and Blueprints: Avant-Garde Culture and Radical Politics*, in Timms Edward and Collier Peter (eds), *Early Twentieth-Century Europe* (Manchester: Manchester University Press, 1987), pp.113–36.

—— 'The People's Front and the Intellectuals', in Fyrth Jim (ed.), *Britain, Fascism and the Popular Front* (London: Lawrence and Wishart, 1985), pp.157–87.

Hennegan Alison, introduction to *The Well of Loneliness* (London: Virago, 1982), pp.vii–xvii.

Higgins Ruth, 'Testament of Youth', unpublished part 2 tripos dissertation, Cambridge University, 1986.

Higgonnet Margaret and Jenson Jane (eds), *Behind the Lines: Gender and the Two World Wars* (New Haven: Yale University Press, 1987).

Hinkson Pamela, 'A Legacy', *Time and Tide*, 2 September, 1938, pp. 1038–9.

Hodges Sheila, *The Story of a Publishing House: 1928–1978* (London: Gollancz, 1978).

Holderness Graham, 'Miners and the Novel: From Bourgeois to Proletarian Fiction', in Hawthorn Jeremy (ed.), *The British Working-Class Novel in the Twentieth Century* (London: Arnold, 1984), pp.19–32.

Holland Ruth, *The Lost Generation* (London: Gollancz, 1932).

Holtby Winifred, *Anderby Wold* (London: Lane, 1923).

—— *The Crowded Street* (London: Lane, 1924).

—— *Letters to a Friend*, Holtby Alice and McWilliam Jean (eds) (London: Collins, 1937).

—— *The Land of Green Ginger* (London: Cape, 1928).

—— 'So Handy for the Funfair', in *Truth is Not Sober* (London: Collins, 1934), pp.151–72.

—— South Riding: An English Landscape (London: Collins, 1936).

—— *Virginia Woolf: A Critical Memoir* (London: Wishart, 1932).

—— *Women and a Changing Civilization* (London: Lane, 1934).

—— and Norman Ginsbury, *Take Back Your Freedom* (London: Cape, 1939).

Howell Constance, *A More Excellent Way* (London: Sonneschein, 1889).

Humm Maggie, *Feminist Criticism: Women as Contemporary Critics* (Brighton: Harvester, 1986).

Hunt Margaret, 'The De-Eroticism of Women's Liberation: Social Purity Movements and the Revolutionary Feminism of Sheila Jeffreys', *Feminist Review*, 34, Spring 1990, pp.18–23.

Hunt Violet, *I Have This To Say: The Story of My Flurried Years* (New York: Boni and Liveright, 1926).

Hyde Lawrence, 'The Work of Dorothy Richardson', *The Adelphi*, 2, November 1924, pp.506–17.

Hynes Samuel, *The Auden Generation: Literature and Coterie Politics in the 1930s* (London: Faber, 1976).

Ingram Angela, '"Unutterable Putrefaction" and "Foul Stuff": Two Obscene Novels of the 1920's', *Women's Studies International Forum*, vol. 9, 4, 1986, pp.341–54.

Iser Wolfgang, *The Act of Reading: A Theory of Aesthetic Response*

(Baltimore: Johns Hopkins University Press, 1978).

Isherwood Christopher, *Christopher and his Kind, 1925–1939* (London: Eyre Methuen, 1977).

Jacobus Mary, 'The Difference of View', in Mary Jacobus (ed.), *Women Writing and Writing about Women* (London: Croom Helm, 1979), pp.10–21.

James Henry, *Henry James: Autobiography* (ed.), Frederick Dupee (London: Criterion, 1956).

Jameson Fredric , *Marxism and Form: Twentieth Century Dialectical Theories of Literature* (Princeton, New Jersey: Princeton University Press, 1971).

—— *The Prison-House of Language* (Princeton, New Jersey: Princeton University Press, 1974).

—— *The Political Unconscious: Narrative as a Socially Symbolic Act* (London: Methuen, 1981).

Jameson Storm, *A Day Off* (London: Nicholson and Watson, 1933).

—— *Journey from the North*, 2 vols (London: Collins and Harvill, 1969–1970, vol. 1, 1969, vol. 2, 1970).

—— *Love in Winter* (London: Cassell, 1935).

—— 'Miss Brittain Speaks For Her Generation: War as Women Saw It', *The Yorkshire Post*, 28 August, 1933, p.6.

—— 'Miss Vera Brittain's Poignant Book', *The Sunday Times*, 3 September, 1933, p.8.

—— *The Pitiful Wife* (London: Constable, 1923).

—— *The Single Heart* (London: Benn, 1932).

—— 'To a Labour Party Official', *Left Review*, November 1934, vol. 1, 2, pp.29–34.

Jardine Alice and Smith Paul (eds), *Men in Feminism* (London: Methuen, 1987).

Jeffreys Sheila, *The Spinster and Her Enemies: Feminism and Sexuality 1890–1930* (London: Pandora, 1985).

Jehlen Myra , 'Archimedes and the Paradox of Feminist Criticism', *Signs: Journal of Women in Culture and Society*, vol. 6, 4, pp.575–601.

Jelinek Estelle E., *Women's Autobiography: Essays in Criticism* (Bloomington and London: Indiana University Press, 1980).

John Katharine, 'The New Lysistrata', review of *Three Guineas*, *The New Statesman and Nation*, 11 June, 1938, pp.995–6.

Johnson Richard et el. (eds), *Making Histories: Studies in History-Writing and Politics* (London: Hutchinson and University of Birmingham Centre for Contemporary Cultural Studies, 1982).

Johnson Roy, 'The Proletarian Novel', *Literature and History*, 2, October 1975, pp.84–95.

Johnston Judith L., 'The Remedial Flaw: Revisioning Cultural History in

Between the Acts', in Marcus Jane (ed.), *Virginia Woolf and Bloomsury: A Centenary Celebration* (London: Macmillan, 1987), pp.253–77.

Johnstone Richard, *The Will to Believe: Novelists of the 1930s* (Oxford: Oxford University Press, 1982).

Johnson Richard Brimley, *Some Contemporary Novelists (Women)* (London: Parsons, 1920).

Jones Lewis, *Cwmardy* (London: Lawrence and Wishart, 1937).

Jordan June, *Lyrical Campaigns: Selected Poems* (London: Virago, 1989).

Jouve Nicole Ward, *White Woman Speaks with Forked Tongue: Criticism as Autobiography* (London: Routledge, 1991).

Kaplan Cora, 'Pandora's Box: Subjectivity, Class and Sexuality in Socialist Feminist Criticism', in Greene Gayle and Kahn Coppélia (eds), *Making a Difference: Feminist Literary Criticism* (London: Methuen, 1985), pp.146–76.

—— *Sea Changes: Essays on Culture and Feminism* (London: Verso, 1986).

Kaplan Sydney Janet, *Feminine Consciousness in the Modern British Novel* (Urbana: University of Illinois Press, 1975).

—— 'Katherine Mansfield's "Passion for Technique"', in Butruff D. and Epstein E. L. (eds), *Women's Language and Style, Studies in Contemporary Language*, 1 (Akron, Ohio: University of Ohio Press, 1978).

Kauffman Linda (ed.), *Gender and Theory: Dialogues on Feminist Criticism* (Oxford: Blackwell, 1989).

Keane Molly, *Devoted Ladies* (London: Collins, 1934).

Keating P. J., *The Working Classes in Victorian Fiction* (London: Routledge and Kegan Paul, 1971).

Kennard Jean E., *Vera Brittain and Winifred Holtby: A Working Partnership* (Hanover: University Press of New England, 1989).

Kenyon Olga, *Women Novelists Today* (Brighton: Harvester, 1985).

Kermode Frank, *The Sense of an Ending: Studies in the Theory of Fiction* (Oxford: Oxford University Press, 1966).

Kettle Arnold, *Communism and the Intellectuals* (London: Lawrence and Wishart, 1965).

—— *An Introduction to the English Novel*, 2 vols (London: Arrow, 1962).

—— 'W. H. Auden: Poetry and Politics in the Thirties', in Clark Jonathan et al. (eds), *Culture and Crisis in Britain in the Thirties* (London: Lawrence and Wishart, 1979), pp.83–103.

Klaich Dolores, *Woman Plus Woman* (New York: New English Library, 1974).

Klaus Gustav H. (ed.), *The Literature of Labour: Two Hundred Years of Working Class Writing* (Brighton: Harvester, 1985).

—— (ed.), *The Rise of Socialist Fiction 1880–1914* (Brighton: Harvester,

1987).

—— (ed.), *The Socialist Novel in Britain: Towards the Recovery of Tradition* (Brighton: Harvester, 1982).

Kolodny Annette, 'Some Notes on Defining a Feminist Literary Criticism', *Critical Inquiry*, vol. 2, 1, pp.75–92.

Koonz Claudia, *Mothers in the Fatherland: Women, The Family and Nazi Politics* (London: Cape, 1987).

Kristeva Julia, *Desire in Language: A Semiotic Approach to Literature*, Roudiez Léon (ed.), translated by Jardine Alice, Gora Thomas and Roudiez Léon (Oxford: Backwell, 1980).

Kuhn Annette, *Women's Pictures: Feminism and Cinema* (London: Routledge and Kegan Paul, 1982).

Lakoff George and Johnson Mark, *Metaphors We Live By* (Chicago: University of Chicago Press, 1980).

Lakoff Robin, *Language and Women's Place* (New York: Octagon, 1976).

Lawrence D.H., 'Daughters of the Vicar', 1914, in *The Tales of D.H. Lawrence* (London: Martin and Secker, 1934), pp.47–93.

Lawrence Margaret, *We Write as Women* (London: Joseph, 1937).

Layton Lynn, 'Vera Brittain's Testament(s)', in *Behind the Lines: Gender and the Two World Wars*, Higgonet Margaret and Jenson Jane (eds) (New Haven: Yale University Press, 1987), pp.70–83.

Leavis Queenie D., review of *Clear Horizons*, *Scrutiny*, December 1935, vol iv, 3, pp.328–30.

—— 'Caterpillars of the Commonwealth Unite!' *Scrutiny*, 7,2, September 1938, pp.212–14.

—— 'Class War Criticism', *Scrutiny*, 5, 4, March 1937, pp.418–22.

—— 'Lady Novelists and the Lower Orders', *Scrutiny*, 4, 2, September 1935, pp.112–32.

Lee Hermione, *Elizabeth Bowen: An Estimation* (New York: Vision and Barnes and Noble, 1981).

—— *The Novels of Virginia Woolf* (London: Methuen, 1978).

—— Introduction to *A Room of One's Own* and *Three Guineas* (London: Chatto and Windus, 1984), pp.vi–xx.

Leeds Eric J., *No Man's Land: Combat and Identity in World War One* (Cambridge: Cambridge University Press, 1979).

Lefanu Sarah, *In the Chinks of the World Machine: Feminism and Science Fiction* (London: Women's Press, 1989).

Lefkowitz Mary R., *Heroines and Hysterics* (London: Duckworth, 1981).

Lehmann John, *Evil was Abroad* (London: Cresset, 1938).

—— *Whispering Gallery* (London, Longmans Green, 1955).

Lehmann Rosamond, *The Ballad and the Source* (London: Collins, 1944).

—— *Dusty Answer* (London: Chatto and Windus, 1927).

—— *The Echoing Grove* (London: Collins, 1953).

—— *Invitation to the Waltz* (London: Chatto and Windus, 1982).

—— *Rosamond Lehmann's Album* (London: Chatto and Windus, 1985).

—— *The Weather in the Streets* (London: Collins, 1936).

—— *The Swan in the Evening: Fragments of an Inner Life* (London: Collins, 1967).

LeStourgeon Diana E., *Rosamond Lehmann* (Boston: Twayne, 1965).

Lewis Jane, 'The English Movement for Family Allowances', *Histoire Sociale*, 11, 1978, pp.441–59.

—— 'In Search of A Real Equality: Women Between the Wars', in Gloversmith Frank (ed), *Class, Culture and Social Change* (Brighton: Harvester, 1985), pp.208–39.

—— *Women in England 1870–1950: Sexual Division and Social Change* (Brighton: Wheatsheaf, 1984).

Lewis John, *The Left Book Club: An Historical Record* (London: Gollancz, 1970), pp.138–55.

Liddington Jill, *The Life and Times of a Respectable Rebel: Selina Cooper 1864–1946* (London: Virago, 1984).

Light Alison, *Forever England: Femininity, Literature and Conservatism Between the Wars* (London: Routledge, 1991).

Lindsay Jack, *After the Thirties: The Novel in Britain and its Future* (London: Lawrence and Wishart, 1956).

Lodge David, *After Bakhtin: Essays on Fiction and Criticism* (London: Routledge, 1990).

London Jack, *The People of the Abyss* (London: Macmillan, 1903).

Lovell Terry, *Consuming Fiction* (London: Verso, 1987).

—— *Pictures of Reality: Aesthetics, Politics, Pleasure* (London: British Film Institute, 1980).

—— 'Writing Like a Woman: A Question of Politics', in *The Politics of the Theory*, in Barker Francis (ed.), proceedings of the Essex Conference on the Sociology of Literature, July 1982 (Colchester: University of Essex Press, 1983), pp.15–26.

Lucas John (ed.), *The Thirties: A Challenge to Orthodoxy* (Brighton: Harvester, 1978).

Ludovici A.M., *The Future of Woman* (London: Kegan Paul, Trench, Trubner, 1936).

—— *Lysistrata: Woman's Future and Future Woman* (London: Kegan Paul, Trench, Trubner, 1925).

—— *Woman: A Vindication* (London: Constable, 1923)

Lukács Georg, *The Theory of the Novel: A Historico-Philosophical Essay on the Forms of Great Epic Literature*, Bostock Anya (trans.) (London: Merlin, 1978).

—— *The Meaning of Contemporary Realism*, John and Necke Mander (trans.) (Merlin: London, 1963).

—— 'Narrate or Describe?', *Writer and Critic* (London: Merlin 1987), pp.110–48.

Lynd Robert, 'Women, War and the Nazis', review of *Three Guineas*, *The News Chronicle*, 3 June, 1938, p.4.

Lynd Syvia, review of *The Rector's Daughter*, *Time and Tide*, 18 July, 1924, pp.691.

—— *The Swallow Dive* (London: Cassell, 1921).

Macaulay Rose, *Crewe Train* (London: Collins, 1926).

—— *Dangerous Ages* (London: Collins, 1926).

—— *Non-Combatants and others* (London: Hodder and Stoughton, 1916).

Macchiocchi Maria-Antonietta, 'Female Sexuality in Fascist Ideology', *Tel Quel*, 66, Summer 1976, Barrett Michele et al. (eds), *Feminist Review* 1, 1979, pp.67–82.

Macherey Pierre, *A Theory of Literary Production*, Geoffrey Wall (trans.) (London: Routledge and Kegan Paul, 1978).

Hugh MacDiarmid: Complete Poems, 1920–1976, 2 vols, vol. 1, Grieve Michael and Aitken W.R. (eds) (London: Martin, Brian and O'Keeffe, 1978).

Macintyre Stuart, *A Proletarian Science: Marxism in Britain 1918–1933* (Cambridge: Cambridge University Press, 1980).

McKenzie Compton, 'Woman Writer's Triumphant Life Story', *The Daily Mail*, 31 August, 1933, p.4.

Nacnaughtan S.M., *My War Experiences in Two Continents* (London: Murray, 1919).

Mandelson Edward (ed.), *The English Auden: Poems, Essays and Dramatic Writings, 1927–1938* (London: Faber, 1977).

Ethel Mannin, *All Experience* (London: Jarrolds, 1932).

—— *Cactus* (London: Jarrolds, 1935).

—— *Confession and Impressions* (London: Jarrolds, 1930).

—— *The Pure Flame* (London: Jarrolds, 1936).

—— *Sounding Brass* (London: Jarrolds, 1925).

—— *Venetian Blinds* (London: Jarrolds, 1933).

—— *Women and the Revolution* (London: Secker and Warburg, 1938).

—— *Women Also Dream* (London: Jarrolds, 1937).

—— *Young in the Twenties* (Hutchinson: London, 1971).

—— *Women and the Revolution* (London: Secker and Warburg, 1937).

Mansfield Katherine, 'The Daughters of the Late Colonel', in *Collected Stories of Katharine Mansfield*, Murry John Middleton (ed.) (London: Constable, 1954), pp.262–85.

—— *Journal of Katherine Mansfield*, Murry John Middleton (ed.) (London: Constable, 1954).

—— *The Letters of Katherine Mansfield*, Murry John Middleton (ed.), 2 vols (London: Constable, 1928).

—— *Katherine Mansfield's Letters to John Middleton Murry 1913–1922*, Murry John Middleton (ed.) (London: Constable, 1951).

—— *The Letters and Journals of Katherine Mansfield: A Selection*, Stead C.K. (ed.) (London: Lane, 1977).

—— 'Miss Brill', in *Collected Stories of Katherine Mansfield*, Murry John Middleton (ed.) (London: Constable, 1954), pp.330–6.

—— *Novels and Novelists* (London: Constable, 1930).

—— *The Stories of Katherine Mansfield* (Oxford: Oxford University Press, 1984).

Marcus Jane, 'Art and Anger', *Feminist Studies*, 4, 1, February 1978, pp.69–98.

—— *Art and Anger: Reading Like a Woman* (Columbus: Ohio State University Press, 1988).

—— (ed.), *New Feminist Essays on Virginia Woolf* (London: Macmillan, 1981).

—— 'Sapphistry: Narration as Lesbian Seduction in *A Room of One's Own*', in Marcus Jane (ed.), *Virginia Woolf and the Language of Patriarchy* (Bloomington: University of Indiana Press, 1987), pp.163–87.

—— 'Thinking Back Through Our Mothers', in Marcus Jane (ed.), *New Feminist Essays on Virginia Woolf* (London: Macmillan, 1981), pp.1–30.

—— (ed.), *Virginia Woolf: A Feminist Slant* (Lincoln and London: University of Nebraska Press, 1983).

—— (ed.), *Virginia Woolf and Bloomsbury: A Centenary Celebration* (Basingstoke: Macmillan, 1987).

—— (ed.), *Virginia Woolf and the Languages of Patriarchy* (Bloomington: University of Indiana Press, 1987).

—— 'A Wilderness of One's Own: Feminist Fantasy in the Novels of the Twenties: Rebecca West and Sylvia Townsend Warner', in Merrill Squier Susan (ed.), *Women Writers and the City: Essays in Feminist Literary Criticism* (Knoxville: University of Tennessee Press, 1984), pp.134–61.

Marder Herbert, *Feminism and Art: A Study of Virginia Woolf* (Chicago: University of Chicago Press, 1968).

Marwick Arthur, *The Deluge: British Society and the First World War* (London: Macmillan, 1965).

—— *Women at War 1914–1918* (London: Fontana, 1977).

The Marxist-Feminist Literature Collective, 'Women's Writing: *Jane Eyre, Shirley, Villette, Aurora Leigh*', *Ideology and Consciousness*, 3, Spring 1978, pp.27–48.

Mason Mary, 'The Other Voice: Autobiographies of Women Writers', in Olney James (ed.), *Autobiography: Essays Theoretical and Critical*

(Princeton, New Jersey: Princeton University Press, 1980), reprinted in Brodzki Bella and Schenck Céleste (eds), *Life/Lines: Theorizing Women's Autobiography* (Ithaca: Cornell University Press, 1988), pp.19–44.

Masson Rosaline, 'Dark Stars (Unpaid) Unmarried', 2, *Time and Tide*, 11 March, 1921, pp.226–7.

Maugham Somerset, *Lisa of Lambeth* (London: Fisher Unwin, 1989).

Maxwell William, *The Letters of Sylvia Townsend Warner* (London: Chatto and Windus, 1982).

Mayor Flora, *The Rector's Daughter* (London: Hogarth, 1929).

—— *The Squire's Daughter* (London: Constable, 1929).

Garland Mears Amelia, *Mercia, The Astronomer Royal: A Romance* (New York: Simkin, Marshall, Hamilton, Kent, 1895).

Meese Elizabeth and Parke Alice (eds), *The Difference Within: Feminism and Critical Theory* (Amsterdam: John Benjamins, 1984).

Muriel Mellown, 'Vera Brittain: Feminist in a New Age 1896–1970', in Spender Dale (ed.), *Feminist Theorists: Three Centuries of Women's Intellectual Traditions* (London: Women's Press, 1983), pp.314–34.

Melman Billie, *Women and the Popular Imagination in the Twenties: Flappers and Nymphs* (Basingstoke: Macmillan, 1988).

Mengham Rod, *The Idiom of the Time: The Writings of Henry Green* (Cambridge: Cambridge University Press, 1982).

Miller Jane, *Seductions: Studies in Reading and Culture* (London: Virago, 1990).

—— *Women Writing about Men* (London: Virago, 1986).

Miller Nancy K., 'Emphasis Added: Plots and Plausibilities in Women's Fiction', *P.M.L.A*, January 1981, vol. 96,1, pp.36–48.

—— *Subject to Change: Reading Feminist Writing* (New York: Columbia University Press, 1988).

Minow-Pinkney Makiko, *Virginia Woolf and the Problem of the Subject: Feminine Writing in the Major Novels* (Brighton: Harvester, 1987).

Mitchell Juliet, *Women the Longest Revolution: Essays in Feminism, Literature and Psychoanalysis* (London: Virago, 1984).

Mitchison Naomi, *Naomi Mitchison's Vienna Diary* (London: Gollancz, 1934).

—— 'The Reluctant Feminists', *The Left Review*, vol. 1, 3, December 1934, pp.93–4.

—— 'This is What Happened', *Week-End Review*, 26 August, 1933, p.212.

—— *We Have Been Warned* (London: Constable, 1935).

—— *You May Well Ask: A Memoir, 1920–1940* (London: Gollancz, 1979).

Modleski Tania, 'Feminism and the Power of Interpretation: Some Critical Readings', in Lauretis Teresa de (ed.), *Feminist Studies Critical Studies* (Bloomington: Indiana University Press, 1986), pp.121–38.

—— *Loving With A Vengeance: Mass Produced Fantasies for Women* (New York and London: Methuen, 1982).

Moers Ellen, *Literary Women* (London: Virago, 1976).

Moi Toril, *Sexual/Textual Politics* (London: Methuen, 1985).

Montague C. E., *Disenchantment* (London: Chatto and Windus, 1922).

Montgomery John, *The Twenties: An Informal Social History* (London: Allen and Unwin, 1957).

Moody A.D., *Virginia Woolf* (London: Oliver and Boyd, 1963).

Moore Madeline, *The Short Season Between Two Silences: The Mystical and Political in the Novels of Virginia Woolf* (London: Allen and Unwin, 1984).

Morgan Jane, 'Swastika and Murder', review of *Swastika Night, The Daily Worker*, 11 August, 1937, p.872.

Morrison Arthur, *A Child of the Jago* (London: Methuen, 1896).

—— *The Hole in the Wall* (London: Methuen, 1902).

Mowatt C.L., *Britain Between the Wars 1918–1940* (London: Methuen, 1955).

Moylan Tom, *Demand the Impossible: Science Fiction and the Utopian Imagination* (London: Methuen, 1986).

Mulford Wendy, *This Narrow Place: Sylvia Townsend Warner and Valentine Ackland: Life, Letters and Politics, 1930–1950* (London: Pandora, 1988).

Mulhern Francis, *The Moment of 'Scrutiny'* (London: Verso, 1981).

Naremore James, *The World Without A Self* (New Haven: Yale University Press, 1973).

Nevinson Henry, *Neighbours of Ours* (London: Arrowsmith, 1895).

Newitt Hilary, *Women Must Choose: The Position of Women in Europe Today* (London: Gollancz, 1937).

Newton Judith Lowder, *Women, Power and Subversion: Social Strategies in British Fiction, 1778–1860* (Athens, Georgia: University of Georgia Press, 1981).

—— Ryan Mary P. and Walkowitz Judith R. (eds), *Sex and Class in Women's History* (London: Routledge and Kegan Paul, 1983).

Nicolson Nigel, *Portrait of a Marriage* (London: Weidenfeld and Nicolson, 1973).

Odets Clifford, *Waiting for Lefty* (London: Left Book Club, 1937).

O' Faolin Sean, *The Vanishing Hero* (London: Eyre and Spottiswoode, 1956).

Oldfield Sibyl, *Spinsters of this Parish: the Life and Times of F.M. Mayor and Mary Sheepshanks* (London: Virago, 1984).

—— *Women and the The Iron Fist* (Oxford: Blackwell, 1989).

Olney James (ed.), *Autobiography: Essays Theoretical and Critical* (Princeton, New Jersey: Princeton University Press, 1980).

Olsen Tillie, *Silences* (London: Virago, 1978).
—— *Yonnondio: From the Thirties* (London: Faber, 1975).
Orel Harold, *The Literary Achievement of Rebecca West* (Basingstoke: Macmillan, 1986).
O'Rourke Rebecca, 'Summer Reading', *Feminist Review*, 2, Summer 1979, pp.1–17.
Orpen Adela, *Perfection City* (London: Hutchinson, 1897).
Parrish Paul A., 'The Loss of Eden: Four Novels of Elizabeth Bowen', *Critique*, vol. 15, 1, 1973, pp.86–101.
Patai Daphne, introduction to Katharine Burdekin, *Swastika Night* (London: Lawrence and Wishart, 1985), pp.iii–xv.
—— 'Orwell's Despair, Burdekin's Hope: Gender and Power in Dystopia', *Women's Studies International Forum*, 1984, vol. 7, 2, pp.85–95.
Pawling Christopher (ed.), *Popular Fiction and Social Change* (London: Macmillan, 1984).
Pickering Jean, 'On the Battlefield: Vera Brittain's *Testament of Youth*', *Women's Studies*, 13, 1986, pp.75–85.
Pippel Roger, 'Testament of a Woman', review of *Testament of Youth*, *The Daily Herald*, 31 August, 1933, p.13.
Pollitt Harry, *Serving My Time: An Autobiography in Politics* (London: Lawrence and Wishart, 1940).
Popular Memory Group, 'Popular Memory: Theory, Politics and Method', in Johnson Richard et al. (eds), *Making Histories: Studies in History-Writing and Politics* (London: Hutchinson and Birmingham University Centre for Contemporary Cultural Studies, 1982), pp.205–52.
Poovey Mary, *The Proper Lady and the Woman Writer: Ideology as Style in the Works of Mary Wollstonecraft, Mary Shelley and Jane Austen* (Chicago: University of Chicago Press, 1984).
Cowper Powys John, *Dorothy M. Richardson* (London: Joiner and Steele, 1931).
Pringle Alexandra, introduction to Rebecca West, *The Harsh Voice*; reprinted (London: Virago, 1981), pp.vii–xiii.
Pugh Edmund, *A Street in Suburbia* (London: Heinemann, 1895).
Radford Jean (ed.), *The Progress of Romance: Patriarchy and Popular Literature* (London: Routledge and Kegan Paul, 1986).
Radway Janice, *Reading the Romance: The Politics of Popular Fiction* (Chapel Hill: University of North Carolina Press, 1984).
Rathbone Eleanor, *The Case for Family Alliances* (Harmondsworth: Penguin, 1940).
—— *The Disinherited Family* (London: Arnold, 1924).
Rathbone Irene, *They Call it Peace* (London: Dent, 1936).
Ray Gordon, *H.G. Wells and Rebecca West* (London: Macmillan, 1974).
Raymond Ernest, *Tell England: A Study in a Generation* (London: Cassell,

1922).

Raymond Janice, *A Passion for Friends: Towards a Philosophy of Female Affection* (London: Women's Press, 1986).

Reeves Pember Maud, *Round About a Pound a Week* (London: Bell, 1913).

Reilly Catharine (ed.), *Scars Upon My Heart: Women's Poetry and Verse of the First World War* (London: Virago, 1981).

Renault Mary, *Purposes of Love* (London: Longmans, 1939).

Rhondda Margaret, Viscountess, *This Was My World* (London: Macmillan, 1937).

Rhys Jean, *After Leaving Mr. Mackenzie* (London: Cape, 1930).

—— *Good Morning Midnight* (London: Constable, 1939).

—— *The Left Bank: Sketches and Studies of Present-Day Bohemian Paris* (London: Cape, 1927).

Rich Adrienne, 'Compulsory Heterosexuality and Lesbian Existence', *Signs: Journal of Women in Culture and Society*, vol. 5, 4, 1980, pp.631–60.

Richardson Dorothy, 'Beginnings; A Brief Sketch', in Gawsworth John (ed.), *Ten Contemporaries: Notes Toward Their Definitive Bibliography*, 2nd series (London: Joiner and Steele, 1933).

—— 'Data for Spanish Publisher', Prescott Joseph (ed.), *London Magazine*, 6 June, 1959, pp. 14–19.

—— 'Leadership in Marriage', *The New Adelphi*, June-August 1929, pp.345–6.

—— *Pilgrimage*, the collected edition, 4 vols (London: Dent and Cressett, 1938).

—— 'The Reality of Feminism', *The Ploughshare*, new series, 2, September 1917, pp.241–6.

—— 'Women and the Future; a Trembling of the Veil Before the Eternal Mystery of 'La Giaconda' [sic], *Vanity Fair*, 22, April 1924, pp.39–40.

Richter Harvena, *Virginia Woolf: The Inward Journey* (Princeton, New Jersey: Princeton University Press, 1970).

Rickword Edgell, *Literature in Society: Essays and Opinions*, Alan Young (ed.), 2 vols (Manchester: Carcanet, 1978).

Rigney Hill Barbara, *Madness and Sexual Politics in the Feminist Novel: Studies in Brontë, Woolf, Lessing and Atwood* (Madison: University of Wisconsin Press, 1978).

Riley Denise, 'Does Sex Have a History?', *New Formations*, 1, Spring 1987, pp.235–45.

Rintala Marvin, 'Chronicler of a Generation: Vera Brittain's Testament', *Journal of Political and Military Sociology*, 12, 1984, pp.23–35.

Roberts Elizabeth, *A Woman's Place: An Oral History of Working Class Women 1890–1940* (Oxford: Blackwell, 1984).

Robertson Eileen Arnot, *Ordinary Families* (London: Cape, 1933).

Robins Elizabeth, *Way Stations* (London: Hodder and Stoughton, 1913).

Robinson Lilian S., *Sex, Class and Culture* (New York: Methuen, 1986).

Rogers Katharine, *The Troublesome Helpmate: A History of Misogyny in Literature* (Seattle: University of Washington Press, 1966).

Rolph C.H., introduction to Vera Brittain, *Radclyffe Hall: A Case of Obscenity* (London: Femina, 1968), pp.12–28.

Rook Clarence, *The Hooligan Nights* (London: Richards, 1899).

Rose Phyllis, *Woman of Letters: A Life of Virginia Woolf* (Oxford: Oxford University Press, 1978).

Rosenberg John, *Dorothy Richardson The Genius They Forgot: A Critical Biography* (London: Duckworth, 1973).

Ruehl Sonja, 'Inverts and Experts Radclyffe Hall and Lesbian Identity', in Brunt Rosalind and Rowan Caroline (eds), *Feminism, Culture and Politics* (London: Lawrence and Wishart, 1982), pp.15–36.

Rule Jane, *Lesbian Images* (London: Davies, 1975).

Russell Dora, *Hypatia or Women and Knowledge* (London: Kegan Paul, Trench, Trubner, 1925).

Ruthven K.K., *Feminist Literary Studies: An Introduction* (Cambridge: Cambridge University Press, 1984).

Ryan Kiernan, 'Socialist Fiction and the Education of Desire: Mervyn Jones, Raymond Williams, John Berger', in Klaus Gustav H. (ed.), *The Socialist Novel in Britain* (Brighton: Harvester, 1982), pp.166–85.

Sackville-West Vita, *All Passion Spent* (London: Hogarth, 1931).

—— *Letters of Vita Sackville-West to Virginia Woolf*, DeSalvo Louise and Leaska Mitchell A. (eds) (London: Hutchinson, 1985).

—— 'Virginia Woolf and *Orlando*', *The Listener*, vol. 53, 27 January, 1955, p. 157.

Said Edward, *Orientalism* (London: Routledge and Kegan Paul, 1978).

Samuel Raphael and Thompson Paul (eds), *The Myths We Live By* (Cambridge: Polity, 1990).

Sargent Tower Lyman, *British and American Utopian Literature: An Anotated Bibliography*, 2nd edition (Boston: G.K.Hall, 1988).

Sayers Dorothy, *Gaudy Night* (London: Gollancz, 1935).

—— *Unnatural Death* (London: Gollancz, 1927).

Schama Simon, 'To and from the Slaughter', *The Times Literary Supplement*, 16 May, 1980, p.559.

Schreiner Olive, *Women and Labour* (London: Fisher and Unwin, 1911).

Schweickart Patrocinio, 'Reading Ourselves: Towards a Feminist Theory of Reading', in Flynn Elizabeth A. and Schweickart Patrocinio (eds), *Gender and Reading: Essays on Readers, Texts and Contexts* (Baltimore: Johns Hopkins University Press, 1986), pp.31–63.

Schwenger Peter, *Phallic Critiques* (London: Routledge and Kegan Paul, 1984).

Scott Joan W., 'Deconstructing Equality-Versus-Difference: Or, the Uses of Postructuralist Theory for Feminism', *Feminist Studies*, vol. 14, 1, Spring 1988, pp.35–50.

Sedgwick Kosofsky Eve, *Between Men: English Literature and Male Homosexual Desire* (New York: Columbia University Press, 1985).

Segal Lynne, *Is the Future Female? Troubled Thoughts on Contemporary Feminism* (London: Virago, 1987).

Seidler Victor, 'Trusting Ourselves: Marxism, Human Needs and Sexual Politics', in Clarke Simon et al. (eds), *One-Dimensional Marxism: Althusser and the Politics of Culture* (London: Allen and Busby, 1980).

Selden Ramon, *Criticism and Objectivity* (London: Allen and Unwin, 1984).

Selincourt Basil de, review of *Three Guineas*, *The Observer*, 5 June, 1938, p.4.

Seward Basil, 'Elizabeth Bowen's World of Impoverished Love', *College English*, 17, 1, October 1956, pp.30–7.

Kean Seymour Beatrice, *The Romantic Tradition* (London: Chapman and Hall, 1929).

Shaw Marion, 'Feminism and Fiction Between the Wars: Winifred Holtby and Virginia Woolf', in Monteith Moira (ed.), *Women's Writing a Challenge to Theory* (Brighton: Harvester, 1986).

Sharp Evelyn , review of *Testament of Youth*, *The Manchester Guardian*, 29 August, 1933, p.5.

—— *Unfinished Adventure: Selected Reminiscences from an English-woman's Life* (London: Bodley Head, 1933).

Shiach Morag, *Discourse on Popular Culture: Class, Gender and History in Cultural Analysis, 1760 to the present* (Cambridge: Polity, 1989).

Showalter Elaine, 'Feminism and Literature', in Collier Peter and Geyer-Ryan Helga (eds), *Literary Theory Today* (Cambridge: Polity, 1990), pp.179–203.

—— *A Literature of their Own: British Women Writers from Brontë to Lessing* (London: Virago, 1978).

—— (ed.), *The New Feminist Criticism: Essays on Women: Literature and Theory* (London: Virago, 1985).

—— 'Introduction: the Rise of Gender', in Showalter Elaine (ed.), *Speaking of Gender* (New York: Routledge, 1989), pp.1–13.

—— 'Review Essay: Literary Criticism', *Signs: Journal of Women in Culture and Society*, vol. 1, 2, pp.435–60.

—— *Sexual Anarchy: Gender and Culture at the Fin de Siècle* (London: Bloomsbury, 1990).

—— 'Towards a Feminist Poetics', in Jacobus Mary (ed.), *Women Writing and Writing About Women* (London: Croom Helm, 1979), pp.22–41.

Silver Brenda R., 'The Authority of Anger: Three Guineas As Case Study',

Signs: Journal of Women in Culture and Society, vol. 16, 2, Winter 1991, pp.340–70.

—— (ed.), *Virginia Woolf: The Reading Notebooks* (Princeton, New Jersey: Princeton University Press, 1981).

Sims George , *How the Poor Live* (London: Chatto and Windus, 1883).

Sinclair May, *Journal of Impressions in Belgium* (London: Hutchinson, 1915).

—— *Life and Death of Harriett Frean* (London: Collins, 1922).

—— *Mary Olivier: A Life* (London: Cassell, 1919).

—— *The Romantic* (London: Collins, 1920).

—— *The Three Sisters* (London: Hutchinson, 1914).

—— *The Tree of Heaven* (London: Cassell, 1917).

Smith David, *Socialist Propaganda in the Twentieth Century Novel* (London: Macmillan, 1978).

Smith Sidonie, *A Poetics of Women's Autobiography: Marginality and the Fictions of Self-Representation* (Bloomington: Indiana University Press, 1987).

Smith Kime Bonnie, 'The Strange Necessity of Rebecca West', in Roe Sue (ed.), *Women Reading Women's Writing* (Brighton: Harvester, 1987), pp.265–86.

Smith Sheila Kaye, *Joanna Godden* (London: Cassell, 1921).

Snitow Ann, Stansell Christine, Thompson Sharon, *Desire: the Politics of Sexuality* (London: Virago, 1984).

—— *Little England* (London: Nisbet, 1918).

Sontag Susan, *Against Interpretation and Other Essays* (London: Eyre and Spottiswoode, 1967).

—— 'Fascinating Fascism', *The New York Review of Books*, 6 February, 1975, pp.23–30.

Spacks Meyer Patricia, *The Female Imagination: A Literary and Psychological Investigation of Women's Writing* (London: Macmillan, 1976).

Spender Dale, *Feminist Theorists: Three Centuries of Women's Intellectual Traditions* (London: Women's Press, 1983).

—— *For the Record: The Making and Meaning of Feminist Knowledge* (London: Women's Press, 1985).

—— 'The Whole Duty of Woman: Vera Brittain, in Spender Dale (ed.), *Women of Ideas and What Men Have Done to Them: From Aphra Behn to Adrienne Rich* (London: Ark, 1982), pp.627–39.

Spender Stephen, *World Within World: The Autobiography of Stephen Spender* (London: Faber, 1951).

Spring Howard, 'And a Woman Pacifist Says: Men Want War', review of *Three Guineas*, *The Evening Standard*, 9 June, 1938, p.11.

Squier Susan Merrill, *Virginia Woolf and London: The Sexual Politics of*

the City (Chapel Hill: University of North Carolina Press, 1985).
—— (ed.), *Women Writers and the City: Essays in Feminist Literary Criticism* (Knoxville: University of Tennessee Press, 1984).

Stanley Liz, 'Moments of Writing: Is There a Feminist Auto/Biography?', *Gender & History*, vol. 2, Spring 1990, pp.58–67.

Stanton Domna C., 'Autogynography: Is the Subject Different?', in Stanton Domna C. (ed.), *The Female Autograph: Theory and Practice of Autobiography from the Tenth to the Twentieth Century* (Chicago: University of Chicago Press, 1984), pp.3–20.

Steedman Kay Carolyn, *Landscape for a Good Woman: A Story of Two Lives* (London: Virago, 1986).

Stephenson Jill, *The Nazi Organisation of Women* (London: Croom Helm, 1981).

—— 'National Socialism and Women Before 1933', in Stachura Peter D. (ed.), *The Nazi Machtergreifung* (London: Allen and Unwin, 1983).

Stephenson Sylvia, *Surplus* (London: Fisher Unwin, 1924).

Stimpson R. Catharine, *Where the Meanings Are: Feminism and Cultural Space* (London: Methuen, 1988).

—— 'Zero Degree Deviancy: The Lesbian Novel in English', in Abel Elizabeth (ed.), *Writing and Sexual Difference* (Brighton: Harvester, 1982), pp.243–59.

Stocks Mary, *Eleanor Rathbone* (London: Gollancz, 1949).

—— review of *Three Guineas*, 'Manchester Guardian', 10 June, 1938, p.7.

Stopes Marie, *Married Love: A New Contribution to the Solution of Sex Differences* (London: Fifield, 1918).

—— *Wise Parenthood* (London: Fifield, 1918).

Strachey Ray, *The Cause: A Short History of the Women's Movement in Great Britain* (London: Bell, 1928; re-issued London: Virago, 1984).

—— *Our Freedom and its Results* (London: Hogarth, 1936).

Strickhausen Harry, 'Elizabeth Bowen and Reality', *The Sewanee Review*, vol. 73, 1, January-March 1965, pp.158–65.

Struther Jan, *Mrs. Miniver* (London: Chatto and Windus, 1939).

Stubbs Patricia, *Women and Fiction: Feminism and the Novel 1880–1920* (Brighton: Harvester, 1979).

Suleiman Susan R. , 'Introduction: Varieties of Audience-Oriented Criticism', in Suleiman Susan R., and Crosman Inge (eds), *The Reader in the Text: Essays on Audience and Interpretation* (Princeton, New Jersey: Princeton University Press, 1980), pp.3–45.

Swanwick Helena, *I Have Been Young* (London: Gollancz, 1935).

—— *The Roots of Peace* (London: Cape, 1938).

Julia Swindells, 'Falling Short with Marx: Some Glimpses of Nineteenth Century Sexual Ideology', *Journal of Literature Teaching Politics*, vol.

3, 1984, pp.56–71.

—— *Victorian Writing and Working Women: The Other Side of Silence* (Cambridge: Polity, 1985).

Symons Julian, *The Thirties: A Dream Revolved* (London: Cressett, 1960).

Taylor Barbara, *Eve and the New Jerusalem: Feminism and Socialism in the Nineteenth Century* (London: Virago, 1983).

Taylor Richard and Young Nigel (eds), *British Peace Movements in the Twentieth Century* (Manchester: Manchester University Press, 1987).

Theweleit Karl, *Male Fantasies*, (trans.) Conway Stephen (Cambridge: Polity, 1987).

Thomas Hugh, *The Spanish Civil War* (London: Eyre and Spottiswoode, 1961).

Tindall Gillian, *Rosamond Lehmann: An Appreciation* (London: Chatto and Windus, 1985).

Tindall William, *Forces in Modern British Literature* (New York: Knopf, 1947).

Todd Janet, *Feminist Literary History* (Cambridge: Polity, 1978).

Tompkins P. Jane, introduction to Tompkins Jane P. (ed.), *Reader-Response Criticism: From Formalism to Post-Structuralism* (Baltimore: Johns Hopkins University Press, 1980), pp.ix–xxvi.

Topping Bazin Nancy, *Virginia Woolf and the Androgynous Vision* (New Brunswick: Rutgers University Press).

Transue J. Pamela, *Virginia Woolf and the Politics of Style* (Albany: State University of New York Press, 1986).

Trautmann Joanne, *The Jessamy Brides: The Friendship of Virginia Woolf and Vita Sackville-West, Pennysylvania State University Studies*, 36 (Philadelphia: Pennysylvania State University Press, 1973).

Troubridge Una, *The Life and Death of Radclyffe Hall* (London: Hammond, 1961).

Tylee Claire M., *The Great War and Women's Consciousness: Images of Militarism and Womanhood in Women's Writing, 1914–1964* (Basingstoke: Macmillan, 1990).

Vallings Gabrielle, *The Forge of Democracy* (London: Hutchinson, 1924).

—— *The Tramp of the Multitude: A Triptych of Labour* (London: Hutchinson, 1936).

Verschoyle Derek, *The English Novelists: A Survey of the Novel by Twenty Contemporary Novelists* (London: Chatto and Windus, 1936).

Veser Aram H. (ed.), *The New Historicism* (New York: Routledge, 1989).

Vicinus Martha, 'Chartist Fiction and the Development of a Class-Based Literature', in Klaus Gustav H. (ed.), *The Socialist Novel in Britain* (Brighton: Harvester, 1982), pp.7–25.

—— *Independent Women: Work and Community for Single Women 1850–1920* (London: Virago, 1985).

Vaughan Hilda, *The Curtain Rises* (London: Gollancz, 1935).

Walker Alice, 'The Black Writer and the Southern Experience', in *In Search of Our Mother's Gardens: Womanist Prose* (London: Woman's Press, 1984), pp.15–21.

Ward Mary Augusta, *Cousin Philip* (London: Collins, 1919).

Warner Marina, interview with Rebecca West, 'The Art of Fiction LXV', *Paris Review*, 79, 1981, pp.125–30.

Warner Rex, *The Wild Goose Chase* (London: Boriswood, 1937).

Warner Townsend Sylvia, *After the Death of Don Juan* (London: Chatto and Windus, 1938).

—— *The Corner That Held Them* (London: Chatto and Windus, 1948).

—— *Lolly Willowes; or the Loving Huntsman* (London: Chatto and Windus, 1926).

—— *Mr. Fortune's Maggot* (London: Chatto and Windus, 1927).

—— *Summer Will Show* (London: Chatto and Windus, 1936).

—— *The True Heart* (London: Chatto and Windus, 1929).

Waters Chris, *British Socialists and the Politics of Popular Culture 1884–1914* (Manchester: Manchester University Press, 1990).

Weeks Jeffrey, *Coming Out: Homosexual Politics in Britain from the Nineteenth Century to the Present* (London: Quartet, 1977).

Wells H.G., *Ann Veronica* (London: Unwin, 1909).

West Alick, *Crisis and Criticism* (London: Lawrence and Wishart, 1937).

West Rebecca, 'The Agony of the Human Soul in War', *The Daily Telegraph*, 15 September, 1933, p.10.

—— *Black Lamb and Grey Falcon*, 2 vols (London: Macmillan, 1941).

—— *The Harsh Voice: Four Short Novels* (London: Cape, 1935; reprinted London: Virago, 1981).

—— *Harriet Hulme: A London Fantasy* (London: Hutchinson, 1929).

—— *Henry James* (London: Nisbet, 1915).

—— *The Judge* (London: Hutchinson, 1922).

—— 'Pictures of Travel Through Many Varied Lands', *The Daily Telegraph*, 4 December, 1931, p.10.

—— *Return of the Soldier* (London: Nisbet, 1917).

—— *The Thinking Reed* (London: Hutchinson, 1936).

Marcus Jane (ed.), *The Young Rebecca: Writings of Rebecca West 1911–1917* (London: Virago, 1983).

'Review: *Essays in Wartime* by Havelock Ellis', *The Daily News*, 20 December, 1916; reprinted, pp.332–5.

'The Gospel According to Granville-Barker', *The Freewoman*, 7 March, 1912; reprinted, pp.18–23.

'The Life of Emily Davison', *The Clarion*, 20 June, 1913; reprinted, pp.178–83.

'Review: *Marriage*', *The Freewoman*, 19 September, 1912; reprinted, pp.64–9.

'Mr Chesterton in Hysterics: A Study of Prejudice', *The Clarion*, 14 November, 1913; reprinted, pp.218–22.

'A New Woman's Movement: The Need for Riotous Living', *The Clarion*, 20 December, 1912; reprinted, pp.130–5.

Wharton Edith, *The Marne: A Tale of the War* (London: Macmillan, 1918).

—— *A Son at the Front* (London: Macmillan, 1923).

White Amber Blanco, *The New Propaganda* (London: Gollancz, 1939).

White Antonia, *Frost in May* (London: Eyre and Spottiswoode, 1933).

White Evelyn, *Winifred Holtby as I Knew Her: A Study of the Author and her Works* (London: Collins, 1938).

Widdowson Peter, 'Between the Acts?: English Fiction and the Thirties', in Jonathan Clarke et al. (eds), *Culture and Crisis in Britain in the Thirties* (London: Lawrence and Wishart, 1979), pp.133–64.

—— (ed.), *Re-Reading English* (London: Methuen, 1982).

Wilkinson Ellen, *Clash* (London: Harrap, 1929).

Williams Kay, *Just Richmal: The Life and Work of Richmal Crompton Lambourn* (Guildford: Genesis, 1986).

Williams Merryn, *Six Women Novelists* (Basingstoke: Macmillan, 1987).

Williams Raymond, *The Country and the City* (London: Chatto and Windus, 1973).

—— *The Long Revolution* (London: Penguin, 1961).

—— *Marxism and Literature* (Oxford: Oxford University Press, 1977).

—— *Orwell* (London: Fontana, 1971).

—— 'The Bloomsbury Fraction', in *Problems in Materialism and Culture: Selected Essays* (London: Verso, 1980), pp.148–69.

—— 'Realism and the Contemporary Novel', *Partisan Review*, 26, Spring 1959, pp. 201–13.

Williams Rhiannon, '"Hit or Miss?": The Middle Class Spinster in Women's Novels 1916–1936', unpublished part 2 tripos dissertation, Cambridge University, 1985.

Williams-Ellis Amabel, *Learn to Love First* (London, Gollancz, 1939).

—— *Volcano* (London: Cape, 1931).

—— *The Wall of Glass* (London: Cape, 1927).

Wilson Edmund, *The Twenties: From Notebooks and Diaries of the Period*, Edel Leon (ed.) (New York: Farrar, Straus and Giroux, 1975).

Wilson Elizabeth, *Mirror Writing: An Autobiography* (London: Virago, 1982).

—— *Only Halfway to Paradise: Women in Postwar Britain, 1945–1986* (London: Tavistock, 1980).

Wilson Edmund, *The Thirties* (London: Macmillan, 1980).

Wilson J.J., 'Why is *Orlando* Difficult?', in Marcus Jane (ed.), *New Feminist Essays on Virginia Woolf*, (London: Macmillan, 1981), pp.141–52.

Winship Janice, 'A Woman's World: Woman – an Ideology of Femininity', in *Women Take Issue*, Women's Studies Group, Centre for Contemporary Cultural Studies (eds) (London: Hutchinson and Birmingham University, The Centre for Contemporary Cultural Studies, 1978), pp.35–155.

Wood Neal, *Communism and British Intellectuals* (London: Gollancz, 1955).

Wohl Robert, *The Generation of 1914* (London: Weidenfeld and Nicolson, 1980).

Wolfe Peter, *Rebecca West: Artist and Thinker* (Carbondale and Edwardsville: Southern Illinois University Press, 1971).

Woodward Kathleen, *Jipping Street* (London: Harper, 1928; reprinted London: Virago, 1981).

Woolf Leonard, *Downhill All the Way: An Autobiogaphy of the Years 1911–1939* (London: Hogarth, 1967).

—— *Sowing: An Autobiography of the Years 1880–1904* (London: Hogarth, 1960).

—— *Growing: An Autobiography of the Years 1904–1911* (London: Hogarth, 1961).

Woolf Virginia, *Between the Acts* (London: Hogarth, 1941).

—— *The Collected Essays of Virginia Woolf*, Woolf Leonard (ed.), 4 vols (London: Hogarth, 1966–1967), vol. 1, 1966, vol. 2, 1966, vol. 3, 1967, vol. 4, 1967.

—— *The Common Reader* (London: Hogarth, 1925).

—— *The Diary of Virginia Woolf*, Olivier-Bell Anne and McNellie Andrew (ed.), 5 vols (Harmondsworth: Penguin, 1979–1985. vol. 1, 1882–1920, 1979, vol. 2, 1920–1924, 1981, vol. 3, 1925–1930, 1982, vol. 4, 1931–1935, 1983, vol. 5, 1936–41, 1985.

—— *Flush: A Biography* (London: Hogarth, 1933).

—— *Jacob's Room* (Leonard and Virginia Woolf: Richmond, 1922).

—— 'The Leaning Tower', in *The Collected Essays*, vol. 2, pp.162–81.

—— *The Letters of Virginia Woolf*, Nicolson Nigel and Trautmann Joanne (eds), 6 vols (London: Hogarth, 1976-1980),vol. 1, *The Flight of the Mind: 1885–1912*, 1976, vol. 2, *The Question of Things Happening 1912–1922*, 1977, vol. 3, *A Change of Perspective: 1923–1928*, 1977, vol. 4, *A Reflection of the Other Person: 1919–1931*, 1978, vol. 5, *The Sickle Side of the Moon: 1932–1935*, 1979, vol. 6, *Leave the Letters Till We're Dead: 1935–1941*, 1980.

—— *Mrs. Dalloway* (London: Hogarth, 1925).

—— *Jacob's Room* (London: Leonard and Virginia Woolf, 1922).

—— 'Mr. Bennett and Mrs Brown', in *The Collected Essays*, vol. 2, pp.319–37.

—— 'The New Biography', in *The Collected Essays*, vol. 4, pp. 229–35.

—— *Orlando* (London: Hogarth, 1928).

—— 'Professions for Women', in *The Collected Essays*, vol. 2, pp. 284–9.

—— *A Room of One's Own* (Hogarth: London, 1929).

—— 'A Society', in *Monday or Tuesday* (London: Leonard and Virginia Woolf, 1921); reprinted in Dick Susan (ed.), *The Complete Shorter Fiction of Virginia Woolf* (London: Hogarth, 1985), pp. 168–85.

—— 'Thoughts on Peace in an Air Raid', in *The Death of the Moth and Other Essays* (London: Hogarth, 1942), pp.154–7.

—— *Three Guineas* (London: Hogarth, 1938).

—— *To the Lighthouse* (London: Hogarth, 1926).

—— *The Waves* (London: Hogarth, 1931).

—— 'Women and Fiction', in *The Collected Essays*, vol. 2, pp.141–52.

—— *A Writer's Diary*, Woolf Leonard (ed.) (London: Hogarth, 1954).

—— *The Years* (London: Hogarth, 1937).

Wootton Barbara, *In a World I Never Made: Autobiographical Reflections* (London: Allen and Unwin, 1967).

—— *London's Burning* (London: Allen and Unwin, 1936).

Worpole Ken, *Dockers and Detectives: Popular Reading: Popular Writing* (London: Verso, 1984).

Wright Patrick, *On Living in an Old Country* (London: Verso, 1985).

Young E.M., *The Bridge Dividing* (London: Cape, 1922).

—— *Miss Mole* (London: Cape, 1930).

—— *The Vicar's Daughter* (London: Cape, 1922).

Young G.M., 'Women in the Modern World', review of *Three Guineas*, *The Sunday Times*, 19 June, 1938, p.7.

Zarestsky Eli, *Capitalism, The Family and Private Life* (London: Pluto, 1976).

Zegger Dimitrakis Hrisey, *May Sinclair* (Boston: Twayne 1976).

Zimmerman Bonnie, 'What Has Never Been: An Overview of Lesbian Feminist Criticism', in Greene Gayle and Kahn Coppélia (eds), *Making a Difference: Feminist Literary Criticism* (London: Methuen, 1985), pp.177–210.

Zwerdling Alexander, *Virginia Woolf and the Real World* (Berkeley: University of California Press, 1986).

Index

abdication (Edward VIII) crisis, 156
Ackland, Valentine, 170
Addison, 111
Aiken, Conrad, 10
Alexander, Sally, 52
Angelou, Maya, 33–34, 47
Anglo-American Criticism, 14
Antigone, 178, 180–1
Astor, Nancy, 79
Auden, W.H., 8, 136–7, 192–3
  'Musée des Beaux Arts', 192n5
Austen, Jane, 11, 15, 128–9, 191
  Pride and Prejudice, 149
Australia, 62–3
Autobiography, 25–53
  formal features, 31–3, 35–6
  graphe, 42
  referentiality, 49

Bagnold, Enid, 51
Bailey, Hilary, 45
Balzac, 68
Barbor, H.R.,
  Against the Red Sky, 55
Barbusse, Henri,
  Under Fire, 42
Barmby, Catherine, 61
Barnardo's, Dr., 66
Barney, Natalie, 125
Barrett, Michèle, 27
B.B.C., 26
Beauman, Nicola, 144
  A Very Great Profession, 7
Beer, Gillian, 107, 118, 122, 177
Belgium, 51
Bell, Clive,
  Civilization, 173
Bell, Julian, 174,
Bell, Quentin, 106, 187
  Virginia Woolf: A Biography, 106n18,
  188
Bennett, Arnold, 4
Bennett, Tony, 3
Benstock, Shari, 5, 42
  Women of the Left Bank, 5n10
Bentley, Phyllis, 50
Bergonzi, Bernard, 8, 187
Besant, Walter, 68
Bibesco, Elizabeth, 169
Birmingham, 69
Biron, Sir Chartres, 104

Birrell, Francis, 168
Birrell, Olive, 69
birth control, 66–7, 81
Black, Naomi, 185
Blake, William, 63, 69, 188
Booth, Wayne, 22
Borden, Mary, 51n85, 52
  Passport for a Girl, 171
Bottome, Phyllis,
  The Mortal Storm, 164
Bowen, Elizabeth, 127–158, 175, 191–2
  Encounters:Early Short Stories, 139
  Death of the Heart, 4, 9, 127–158
  The Heat of the Day, 131
  To the North, 131
Brecht, Bertolt, 7, 7n15
Bridenthal, Renate, 167
Brittain, Vera, 5, 11, 25–53, 76, 80, 102
  attitudes to servants, 39, 49
  Catlin, George, 40, 50
  friendship with Winifred Holtby, 25,
    38, 50
  Honourable Estate, 43
  Leighton, Roland, 34, 43, 46, 48
  Not Without Honour, 43
  relationship with E. Brittain, 47
  Somerville, 34, 41
  Testament of Youth, 9, 18–19, 22, 25–
    54, 159
  The Dark Tide, 41, 43
  Voluntary and Detachment (VAD), 29,
    39, 44
  women mentors, lack of, 38
Brodzki, Bella, 52
Bromley, Roger, 41
Brontë, Charlotte, 15
  Jane Eyre, 93
Brontë, Emily, 11, 15, 113
Brook, Jocelyn, 129
Brooke, Rupert,
  Sonnets, 43
Brookner, Anita, 157
Brooks, Romaine, 125
Browne, Felicia, 170
Browne, Sir Thomas, 113
Brunt, Rosalind, 155
Bryant and May, 183
Burdekin, Katharine, 166, 168, 172, 190,
  193
  At the End of This Day's Business, 161
  Proud Man, 182

– 229 –

Index

Index

Index

Index

Index